Contents

THE
HITLER
OPTIONS

ALTERNATE DECISIONS OF WORLD WAR II

Edited by Kenneth Macksey

Greenhill Books, London
Stackpole Books, Pennsylvania

Greenhill Books

This edition of *The Hitler Options* first published 1998
by Greenhill Books, Lionel Leventhal Limited,
Park House, 1 Russell Gardens, London NW11 9NN
and
Stackpole Books, 5067 Ritter Road, Mechanicsburg,
PA 17055, USA

British Library Cataloguing in Publication Data
The Hitler Options: alternate decisions of World War II. –
1. World War, 1939 – 1945
2. Imaginary histories
I. Macksey, Kenneth, 1923 –
940.5'4

ISBN 1-85367-312-9

Library of Congress Cataloging-in-Publication Data available

Publishing History
The Hitler Options was first published in 1995
by Greenhill Books and is here reproduced, complete and
unabridged, in paperback.

Printed and bound in Great Britain by
Biddles Ltd, Guildford and King's Lynn

List of Illustrations and Maps

Illustrations

Pages 65–72

1. Churchill inspects Channel coast defences
2. Hitler with Rommel and Kesselring
3. German troops among burning British fuel tanks
4. Guderian and the staff of Panzer Group 2
5. Von Kleist's Panzer Group 1
6. Japanese destroyer hit during the Battle of the Arabian Sea
7. Admiral Yamamoto ponders the dilemmas of Operation ORIENT
8. Hitler and Mussolini with Kesselring and Keitel
9. Battleships of the Mediterranean Fleet with a Swordfish torpedo bomber overhead
10. Raeder and Dönitz debate strategy
11. Hitler with Dönitz and Göring
12. Allied convoy in mid-Atlantic

Pages 153–160

13. Allied Chiefs of Staff make plans to attack Europe's 'soft underbelly'
14. British troops pause while fighting their way up Italy
15. Boeing B-17 Flying Fortresses head for vital targets in Germany
16. Messerschmitt 262 jet fighter
17. Operation GOMORRAH: Hamburg after the first daylight raid
18. General Leslie Groves, commander of the Manhattan Project
19. British Chief of the Air Staff, Sir Charles 'Peter' Portal
20. U.S. B-26 Marauders fly for targets in northern France
21. Montgomery, Eisenhower and Tedder in Normandy
22. British specialised armoured vehicles on the Normandy beaches
23. The shambles on OMAHA Beach

Maps

Contributors

JOHN H. GILL holds degrees from Middlebury College and The George Washington University. A lieutenant colonel in the U.S. Army, he is assigned to the Pentagon and lives in Virginia. He is the author of *With Eagles to Glory: Napoleon and His German Allies in the 1809 Campaign*, as well as numerous articles in British and American journals.

STEPHEN HOWARTH is a retired officer of the Royal Naval Reserve and author of several books on naval, maritime and general history. These include *Morning Glory: A History of the Imperial Japanese Navy 1895–1945; August '39: The Last Four Weeks of Peace; To Shining Sea: A History of the United States Navy 1775–1991*; and (as joint editor with Derek Law, and contributor) *The Battle of the Atlantic 1939–1945: The 50th Anniversary International Naval Conference*. With his late father, the historian David Howarth, he co-wrote *Nelson: The Immortal Memory*. He also writes articles, reviews and obituaries for a wide variety of periodicals. He is a Fellow of both the Royal Geographical Society and the Royal Historical Society.

GENERAL SIR WILLIAM JACKSON served the Crown for fifty years. He was commissioned into the Royal Engineers in 1937, and during the War saw action in Norway, North Africa, Sicily, Italy and Malaya. His last appointment in the Army was as Quartermaster-General in four star rank. He then went to Gibraltar as Governor and C-in-C in 1978, and on his return in 1982 he joined the Cabinet Office Historical Section, writing the last three volumes of the British Official History of the Mediterranean Campaigns. The final volume was published in 1987, when he retired. So far he has written nearly twenty books, mainly on military history, including *Overlord: Normandy 1944* in the Imperial War Museum Strategy Series.

MAJOR TIM KILVERT-JONES joined his Regiment (The Royal Welch Fusiliers) in Germany in 1982. He went on to serve in Northern Ireland, Britain and the Middle East, before attending a weapons staff course at the Royal Military College of Science, Shrivenham in 1989 followed by Staff College, Camberley in 1990. He was posted in December 1990 to Headquarters 3rd Armoured Division BAOR, and in November 1992 he returned to the United Kingdom and his Regiment to command a Rifle Company in Northern Ireland, Tidworth and Canada.

JAMES LUCAS fought as an infantryman in the Tunisian and the Italian campaigns of World War Two before going on to serve in Austria in the Army of Occupation. After demobilisation he worked in the Foreign Office and then the University of London, before joining the staff of the Imperial War Museum in 1960. On retiring in 1986 he became a full-time author and has had more than thirty books published. He has also contributed to military journals, and has led several battlefield tours in Western Europe. For many years he was Secretary of the British Section of the Confédération Européene des Anciens Combattants.

KENNETH MACKSEY, the editor of this book, served in the Royal Tank Regiment from 1941 to 1967. He is now known internationally as a military historian, his 40 books including *Invasion: The German Invasion of England, July 1940; Guderian: Panzer General*; and *The Penguin Encyclopedia of Modern Warfare*.

CHARLES MESSENGER served as a Regular Officer in the Royal Tank Regiment for 21 years and subsequently for a further 13 years in the Territorial Army. He is both a military historian and defence analyst, and the author of numerous books on Second World War topics. These include *The Art of Blitzkrieg: Bomber Harris and the Strategic Bombing Offensive, 1939–1945; World War Two Chronological Atlas*; and biographies of Field Marshal Gerd von Rundstedt and SS General Sepp Dietrich. He has recently written a history of the British Infantry, *For Love of Regiment*, and a review of twentieth-century warfare, *The Century of Warfare*, based on an international TV/video series of that name for which he was the scriptwriter and historical adviser.

BRYAN PERRETT served as an officer in the Royal Tank Regiment and is now a military historian. He has contributed to numerous military journals, and was defence correspondent for an English newspaper during the Falklands and Gulf Wars. His books include *Desert Warfare; A History of Blitzkrieg; Knights of the Black Cross: Hitler's Panzerwaffe and its Leaders; Last Stand! – Famous Battles against the odds; At All Costs! – Stories of Impossible Victories*; and *Seize and Hold: Master Strokes of the Battlefield*.

DR ALFRED PRICE served in the Royal Air Force as an aircrew officer, and, in a flying career spanning fifteen years, specialised in electronic warfare and air fighting tactics. In 1974 he left the Service to become a full-time author and has published more than 40 books and over a hundred magazine articles. Several of his books have become standard reference works on their respective subjects including *Instruments of Darkness* on the history of electronic warfare, *Aircraft versus Submarine* on the history of airborne anti-submarine warfare, *The Hardest Day* on the Battle of Britain, and *The Spitfire Story*. With U.S. writer Jeffrey Ethell he co-authored *World War II Fighting Jets, One Day in a Long War* on the air war over North Vietnam, and *Air War South Atlantic* on the Falklands conflict. He is a Fellow of the Royal Historical Society.

PETER G. TSOURAS served on active duty in the U.S. Army in Germany, and is now a lieutenant colonel in the U.S. Army Reserve. An analyst at the U.S. Army Intelligence and Threat Analysis Center, Washington, D.C., he specialises in twentieth-century European history and its interpretation. He is the author of *Disaster at D-Day: The Germans Defeat the Allies, June 1944*; and *The Great Patriotic War: An Illustrated History of Total War – The Soviet Union and Germany 1941–1945*; and editor of *The Anvil of War: German Generalship in Defense on the Eastern Front*.

Prologue

Probably nobody but a megalomaniac would have embarked deliberately upon a potential world war without formulating a clear military strategy. Yet that was what Adolf Hitler, the self-taught strategist, did in September 1939 when he ordered the German Wehrmacht to conquer Poland.

So it is even more remarkable that, nine months later, having overrun Norway, Denmark, Holland, Belgium, Luxembourg and France, he had yet to settle upon a firm and prudent course of future action which might well have led the German–Italian–Japanese Axis to world domination. Indeed, the moment it became clear on 20 May 1940 that France was on the eve of collapse, a number of promising winning options were available to him. It is one of the great enigmas of twentieth-century history that he let slip marvellous opportunities.

In this book historians contemplate ten options which were open to the Führer. They fall into two categories: in the first Germany possesses the initiative and in the second the Allies adopt strategies which, had they been chosen at the time, would have forced new and undesirable options upon Hitler. Each option is written as if none of the other alternates had taken place.

In the first category Kenneth Macksey considers what might have happened if Germany had invaded Britain in July 1940; Bryan Perrett imagines the possible consequences in 1941 of Admiral Raeder's Mediterranean strategy; James Lucas indicates the possible course of events if Hitler had opted in August 1941 to concentrate on the capture of Moscow; Peter Tsouras forecasts the outcome of an immense Axis joint operation aimed at linking the German–Italian and the Japanese spheres in 1942; Stephen Howarth (writing from the post-war German point of view) investigates the outcome of the Battle of the Atlantic if, along with improved collaboration by the Luftwaffe, the projected, fast German U-boats had been introduced into service in 1942; John Gill considers the repercussions of the Allies receiving intelligence of German possession of an atomic bomb; Alfred Price ponders the effect of German jet fighters if, as a result of adjusted priorities, they had entered service in 1943; and Tim Kilvert-Jones analyses what might have happened on 6 June 1944 in Normandy if Rommel had not been on leave and the German panzer divisions had been differently deployed and thrown into battle at once.

In the second category, General Sir William Jackson, an author of the official history of the war in the Middle East and Mediterranean, studies what might have happened if the Allies had adopted Winston Churchill's preferred strategy of attacking the 'soft underbelly of Europe' in 1944; and Charles Messenger suggests what might have been the result if the entire Allied strategic bombing effort had been concentrated, without diversification, upon creating five additional 'Hamburgs'.

Each author was invited to use his imagination while keeping within the bounds of credibility and reality and projecting ideas based on actual situations. People behave normally, in character. The appearance of later technology is avoided. Each chapter is self-contained and takes no account of what happens in other chapters.

The shattering possibilities which emerge are sensational indeed.

Kenneth Macksey 1995

CHAPTER 1

Operation SEA LION
Germany Invades Britain, 1940
KENNETH MACKSEY

The Decision

The expression in Adolf Hitler's penetrating eyes was one of exultation as he regarded his commanders-in-chief and the top staff officers of Oberkommando der Wehrmacht (OKW). The place was the Felsennest in the Eifel; the time 0900hrs 21 May 1940, less than twelve hours since Panzer Group von Kleist's exciting report of its arrival at Abbeville on the English Channel coast, and only eleven days since the Wehrmacht had launched Operation YELLOW against Holland, Belgium, Luxembourg and France. Now, once the exuberant mutual congratulations had subsided, came the moment to decide what next to do.

'Do we swing north towards Dunkirk and envelop the Allied Armies in Belgium and northern France? Or south towards Paris and the heart of France?' asked General Walter von Brauchitsch, the Army Commander-in-Chief.

'And then what about Britain?' inquired Admiral Erich Raeder, the Navy's urbane chief. 'Do we isolate her and await a plea for peace? Or do we invade?'

'Or just bomb her into submission with my Luftwaffe?' offered the glory-seeking Field Marshal Hermann Göring.

As they debated several options Hitler listened intently to a few suggestions from General Wilhelm Keitel, OKW Chief of Staff, and General Alfred Jodl, the Chief of Operations. Then, as Führer and Supreme Commander, he dramatically threw up his hands.

'Enough!' he demanded. 'My mind is made up. We will turn north and wipe out the enemy, including the British Army before it can escape by sea. Then overrun the rest of France. But it is also my irrevocable intention to invade Britain not later than 15 July, before she can recover from this disaster.' A date which, quite by chance, was neatly to fit the necessary tactical conditions of moonlight and high tides.[1]

13

It would be misleading to say that anybody present received this start-lingly unexpected decision with equanimity. But a Führer order was irre-sistible in the aftermath of the latest triumph and the preceding conquests of Poland, Denmark and Norway. The staffs of OKW and the Navy bent to the task of planning what later came to be called Operation SEA LION – leaving the Army and Luftwaffe to concentrate on completing the current campaign, while conserving all possible resources for the great invasion of England.

OKW Plans and Frustrations

The outline OKW plan which emerged was based on the assumption that France and Norway would be subdued with optimum use of force by the end of June. And that, meanwhile, no effort was to be spared in the build-up of sea, land and air forces and the deployment of SEA LION forces adjacent to the North Sea and English Channel, tasked for a three-phase invasion starting on 1 July.

Phase 1: The winning of aerial superiority by the Luftwaffe as an essential prerequisite of a combined air and seaborne assault on southeast England.

Phase II: The seizing of a bridgehead concurrent with securing local naval supremacy in the Straits of Dover.

Phase III: An advance inland with a view to destroying enemy forces and the out-flanking and eventual encirclement of London.

Already in Britain the looming threat of invasion was recognised by the Government under Prime Minister Winston Churchill, and surmised by press and public as news from France worsened. Arrows on the war maps pointed towards the Channel ports of Boulogne and Calais (which fell, respectively, on 23 and 26 May), Dunkirk and Ostend (the latter being given up without a fight). On the 24th the armoured (panzer) divisions of Panzer Group von Kleist were almost within sight of Dunkirk. Convincing the British War Office that the Allied Armies in Belgium and northern France, including their own BEF, were doomed. For at that moment the vital port of Dunkirk and its long beaches was virtually undefended, with the main Allied Armies located in Belgium, fighting the relentlessly advancing German Army Group B.

Then appeared the miracle. The Germans halted, stopped dead by General Gerd von Rundstedt because he dreaded a (non-existent) threat to his extended left flank; and also because he desired time to rest and repair the panzer divisions before attacking to the south. The order was confirmed by Hitler, with SEA LION in mind, and exploited by Göring, who promised to prevent the Allied evacuation from Dunkirk which the Germans could watch in progress.

As is well known, the Luftwaffe was incapable of fulfilling Göring's boastful pledge. And it was 27 May, far too late, before the Army was permitted to attack again. The Dunkirk defences held firm until 4 June when the last of over 330,000 Allied troops were evacuated to England. But the cost to the British Army alone was enormous. It left behind 2472 guns, about 400 tanks, 63,879 vehicles and vast quantities of stores. And the Royal Air Force, in addition to its losses elsewhere, had lost 100 fighters and 85 pilots. Indeed, on 4 June there was an acute shortage of fighter pilots, who were being lost faster than they could be replaced, and only 36 of the vital Spitfire and Hurricane fighters in store. Meanwhile, in addition to its many losses off Norway, the Royal Navy had also lost 243 ships at Dunkirk, of which six were destroyers, plus 19 destroyers and numerous other vessels damaged.

Italy In – France Out

Moreover further wastage and diversions of Britain's forces were inevitable as the Germans renewed their offensive on 5 June and, despite the need (in the interests of SEA LION) to withhold full air support, broke the crust of French resistance and thrust at Paris and the French hinterland. Five days later General Weygand, the French C-in-C, told his Prime Minister that an armistice must be sought – a plea which Paul Reynaud could only temporarily resist. Especially as that same day Benito Mussolini had boldly announced that Italy now stood at the side of her Axis partner and was at war with France and Britain.

On 22 June the French Government agreed to an armistice – one week ahead of the schedule set by Hitler on 21 May. The invasion of England was now a certainty and its chances of success promising if only the Germans could assemble relatively modest forces. For with the British at an all-time nadir in strength and the Germans in fine fettle, except at sea, the Balance of Forces stood significantly in the German favour.

Balance of Forces

The Royal Navy had taken a pounding off Norway (whence the remaining forces were now withdrawn) and during the evacuation from France. Between Iceland, Scapa Flow, East Coast and South Coast ports it had available on 1 July (including ships on convoy escort duties) four battle-ships, two battle-cruisers, 13 cruisers, 80 destroyers, and two aircraft carriers. The remainder of the fleet was in the Mediterranean squaring up to Italy.

Against this formidable fleet the Germans could assemble only two battle-cruisers (*Scharnhorst* and *Gneisenau*), two obsolete World War I battleships, one heavy and three light cruisers and half a dozen destroyers, plus a few fast torpedo boats (E-boats). Raeder now sought to conserve this meagre force, cancelling a projected raid by the battle-cruisers against the evacuation convoys from Norway.

But what the Germans lacked at sea against the Royal Navy they hoped to compensate for with air power. Despite wastage over France, the highly experienced Luftwaffe expected by 30 June to have fit for action some 700 single-engine Me-109 fighters, 250 twin-engine Me-110 fighters, 1100 long-range He-111, Ju-88 and Do-17 medium bombers and reconnaissance aircraft and 300 short-range Ju-87 dive bombers. They would be organised into three Air Fleets of which Air Fleet 2 (General Albert Kesselring) and Air Fleet 3 (General Hugo Sperrle) would bear the brunt of the attack on southern England; while Air Fleet 5 (General R. Stumpff) would attack the north-east from Norway. And to lift the airborne forces in the assault and help maintain the Army once ashore in England, there would be some 700 tri-motor Ju-52s, and a number of the big Ju-90 and Focke-Wulf Kondor four-engine transports, as well as 150 gliders.

Opposing them would be a mere 600 of the RAF's good Spitfire and Hurricane fighters, backed up by a few squadrons of inferior two-seater Defiant fighters and twin-engine Blenheim night fighters. Of these only some 200 Spitfire and Hurricanes and 36 Blenheims would be in No 11 Group (AV Marshal Keith Park) tasked to defend south-east England and the Straits of Dover. True, fighter production was picking up – from 265 in April to 446 in June. But a mere 1200 fighter pilots, against an establishment of 1450, with only six trained replacements expected per day, was the gravest of shortages. Only in one respect, in fact, did Air Chief Marshal Sir Hugh Dowding's Fighter Command possess a clear advantage over the Luftwaffe. It happened to be fighting in its own air space, with the benefit of a sophisticated radio command and control system supplied by up-to-the-minute information of aircraft positions pinpointed by radar. However, even this latter, crucial facility suffered from many technical limitations, such as a 300% factor of inaccuracy and lack of low-level detection sets, which could not be delivered until August.

Worst off of all, however, was the British Army, which had manpower a-plenty but was largely stripped of its weapons and ammunition. Come 1 July it would muster no more than 760 field guns, 160 anti-tank guns, less than 200 modern medium and heavy tanks and nearly 300 light tanks of the type which had been slaughtered in France. Small arms were also in short supply, as indeed was almost every other item of equipment, including suitable motor vehicles. Faced with these deficiencies, General Sir Edmund Ironside, the C-in-C Home Forces, felt able only to adopt a linear defensive strategy in the hope of holding off the enemy until the factories manu-factured more weapons or winter weather intervened. 'The Army,' he told a disappointed Churchill, 'has not been trained to take the offensive. To create an offensive spirit suddenly, with no mobility, no armour and no training, is impossible.'

So Ironside started construction on a succession of stop-lines beginning at the coast and covering the main line of defence (the GHQ Line) which was sited to guard London, Bristol and the Midlands. It would be left to semi-mobile, partially armoured units to counter-attack if the enemy gained a foothold.

British Plans

It was guesswork where the enemy intended to land. For a paucity of information from air photography had to be added to the almost total elimination of the British contacts (including the Secret Service) in Europe. Agents had been captured or neutralised. Enemy air superiority made daylight reconnaissance flights extremely hazardous, except for the handful of high altitude Spitfire machines, which lacked the range to photograph north German ports where the principal seaborne forces were expected to assemble. These deficiencies blinded the Intelligence organisation. Therefore it was unwarranted speculation alone which postulated the notion that the main German effort would be launched across the North Sea into East Anglia early in July, when tides and moonlight were most suitable. A cross-Channel attempt was not overlooked, but rated less likely as long as Fighter Command was undefeated and the Navy dominated the Straits of Dover.

In consequence, Ironside positioned his best armed and trained formations (including the inexperienced 2nd Armoured Division with its 178 light tanks) in East Anglia and in the GHQ Line, though locating the partially battle-experienced 1st Armoured Division (with its mixture of 70 medium and 82 heavy tanks) south of London. Thus he unwittingly played into German hands. For it was upon Kent that the blow would fall, since there alone could adequate fighter cover be provided. And it would fall on that sector which Lt Gen Andrew Thorne's XII Corps defended with the so-called mobile 1st (London) Division, and with a bizarre miscellany of coastal batteries and anti-aircraft guns interspersed with garrison troops holding the coastline of the Isle of Thanet, Deal, Dover and Shorncliffe. 1st (London) Division's mobile title was, of course, as derisory as its artillery arm, which consisted of only 34 field guns of various calibres and 12 assorted pieces with a speculative anti-tank capability. Rightly the division's commander, Maj Gen C.F. Liardet, called his resources 'ludicrous'.

German Plans

General Thorne might well have considered the situation hopeless had he been aware of the plan adopted by the Germans. It was General von

Rundstedt's intention, once a measure of air superiority had been won, to employ the 7th Parachute Division and 22nd Airlanding Division to seize an airhead on the open ground between Dover and Hythe, as a preliminary to amphibious landings by 6th Mountain Division to the west of Dover, and 17th Infantry Division between Folkestone and Hythe. Then, as the air and beachheads were being secured and expanded, 9th Panzer Division would be brought ashore, on S-Day plus 1, directed without delay at Canterbury with a view to disrupting British counterstrokes.

Thus schemed the German Army, whose C-in-C, von Brauchitsch, regarded the Channel assault as little more than an up-scaled river crossing operation. With this optimism, however, Admiral Raeder was in disagreement. To him, even if the essential prerequisite achievement of air superiority was achieved, the operation was fraught with peril. Addressing Hitler, he pointed out, 'The British fleet, despite its recent heavy losses, is by no means diminished. Whereas we have suffered disproportionate losses, including damage to *Scharnhorst* and *Gneisenau*. Of course, by good fortune we might obtain possession of substantial lodgements on the south coast. But sustaining them could be another matter. We might even manage to sweep enemy minefields and lay our own defensive barrages. But we have only 30 U-boats and their torpedoes, I regret to report, are defective. And as for landing craft . . .? Well, it will be a miracle of organisation and training to have enough ready in time!'

On the other hand, there were sailors like Kommodore Friedrich Ruge who contended that, although navigating flotillas of improvised, unequally matched landing craft through sandbanks and minefields in difficult tidal conditions would probably create what he called 'Formation Pigpile', there was no reason why characteristic German determination and flexibility should not overcome the difficulties. And in this belief in the viability of SEA LION, he was strongly backed by Hermann Göring who boasted: 'Leave it to my Luftwaffe! We'll start preliminary operations now. By Eagle Day on 8 July we'll be ready to smash the RAF. All I want then is four or five days of good weather. Then just let my dive-bombers get at the Royal Navy.'

Royal Navy Dilemmas

In the minds of the besieged British populace, who had yet to experience the realities of air attack, the Navy was their true, traditional bulwark against invasion. But admirals had at last come to appreciate the bomber menace in the realisation that the majority of their ships were not armed with high-angle guns. They rightly feared that, in the absence of fighter cover, there was deadly risk from daylight bombing, especially in the Straits of Dover.

For anti-invasion duties on 1 July (but not including one battleship, two aircraft carriers, three cruisers and 30 destroyers on Atlantic convoy escort duties) the Admiralty deployed:

At Scapa Flow:	two battleships, two battle-cruisers, one aircraft carrier, three cruisers and nine destroyers
At Rosyth:	two cruisers
At Liverpool:	one battleship
In the Tyne:	one cruiser and twelve destroyers
In the Humber:	three cruisers and seven destroyers
At Harwich:	nine destroyers
At Sheerness:	one cruiser and three destroyers
At Dover:	five destroyers
At Portsmouth:	five destroyers

Distributed around the east and south coasts as mobile vedettes, 1100 lightly armed trawlers and small craft were tasked as convoy escorts and forewarners of an approaching enemy.

Admiral Sir Charles Forbes, C-in-C Home Fleet, concurred with his opponent, Raeder, that the Germans might come ashore almost unopposed. He and the Admiralty were plagued by uncertainties. They hoped to receive enough early warning from ships and aircraft for their destroyers to intercept and forestall invasion flotillas, which were expected by night. Failing that, a major effort would be postponed until a powerful force of cruisers and destroyers could be assembled, under fighter cover, to annihilate the enemy. Only if the German battle-cruisers put to sea would Forbes send his battleships and battle-cruisers south of the Wash.

The Air Battle: First Phase

General Kesselring began probing the British air defences on 5 June, after the Battle of Dunkirk and as the final drive against France began. From those few airfields then at his disposal he sent over high-level reconnaissance missions by Dornier Do-17Ps and night bombers whose activities gradually accustomed the populace to the throb of unsynchronised engines, the bark of guns and the occasional rushing-whistle and crump of bombs. Tension in the island mounted, partly due to spy-mania and a plethora of (usually unsubstantiated) reports of clandestine behaviour, but also due to trigger-happy soldiers or members of the newly formed Local Defence Volunteers (LDV) who mounted guard on cliff tops and vital points and whose score of innocents shot was sometimes three per night.

Between 5 and 18 June, 13 airfields, 16 factories and 14 ports suffered minor damage. Satisfyingly, 11 bombers were shot down. Thus the German strategy was revealed as evidence accumulated of their possession of an electronic, blind-bombing aid. At the same time the Germans became aware of the extent of British radar coverage and the sophisticated system of radio control of fighters whenever they ventured across the Channel, especially by day.

As more airfields were made operational and the Luftwaffe's logistics improved, Kesselring stepped up pressure. On the 19th he launched the first of many dive-bomber attacks on convoys passing through the Straits of Dover, with the intention of bringing on an advantageous fighter confrontation of attrition. For Kesselring correctly surmised that many RAF squadrons had yet to recover from the fighting in France; and that his opponent, Air Marshal Dowding, was bent on conserving his precious fighters against the day when the Luftwaffe must open a major attempt to win air superiority.

For the next ten days, as General Sperrle's Air Fleet 3 was released from support of the Army and began to join the attacks on convoys and ports, Kesselring's and Air Marshal Park's fighters sparred with ever increasing ferocity. When No 11 Group's losses mounted unacceptably and more ships, including priceless destroyers, were sunk, Dowding asked for the convoys to be stopped. But Churchill vetoed this, on the grounds that it was bending to the enemy will. But he relented on 29 June, when two destroyers were sunk (one in Dover harbour), several ships damaged and 15 RAF fighters lost, against 15 German bombers, a seaplane minelayer and nine fighters. That day the Straits of Dover were closed to shipping in daylight and the destroyers withdrawn from Dover harbour. This was a move of arguably vital significance since it surrendered command of the Straits on the same day as long-range, heavy artillery located at Sangatte near Calais began a sporadic bombardment of Folkestone, Dover and shipping.

General Hans Jeschonnek, the Luftwaffe's Chief-of-Staff, conferred with Sperrle and Kesselring at the latter's command post overlooking a deserted Straits of Dover on 30 June. Both Air Fleet commanders insisted upon the vital necessity of drawing enemy fighters into combat. But Jeschonnek rejected Sperrle's suggested attacks on the British airfields, contending that this would give premature warning of an impending invasion. Instead they agreed to widen the frontage of intense bombing on shipping and ports between Devonport and the Humber, rising to a new peak on the eve of Eagle Day, now fixed for the 9th, when radar installations would receive the full weight of Luftwaffe attention.

The pre-Eagle Day phase was to prove extremely costly to the RAF. Between 5 and 7 July, when Luftwaffe losses were an affordable 95 fighters, the RAF lost 200 aircraft, including 73 fighters, far exceeding replacement rates. In part this was because Dowding attempted to conserve fighters by committing them in pairs of squadrons and thus at a penal inferiority of numbers; but credit is also due to German combat skills.

Eagle Days[2]

Come the night of the 8th, after a full-scale assault on four radar stations and certain forward airfields, Fighter Command was nearly at full stretch. With three radar stations temporarily out of action, its command and control system was deprived of vital information. Thus, when the airfields were attacked on the 9th, interceptions were patchy, with several Germans formations roaming unchecked. Nevertheless, damage was relatively light due to the bombers too frequently bombing only secondary targets and suffering heavy losses. Moreover, because the radar sites were left alone, command and control began to recover when the battle was resumed on the 10th, somewhat surprisingly, by small formations which did only minor damage.

The 11th, however, was to prove climactic and decisive. That day, when No 11 Group was unable to put 200 fighters in the air, neighbouring Groups were also heavily engaged. In the evening a maximum Luftwaffe effort, directed at the key, inland Sector Stations of Middle Wallop, Biggin Hill and Kenley inflicted losses the RAF could not much longer sustain. That day, along with 15 bombers, 47 fighters were lost, with 28 pilots killed or wounded. True, the Luftwaffe lost 54 bombers; but only 36 fighters (of which only 9 were Me-109s) and 12 pilots. Henceforward Fighter Command fell into decline as German confidence, bolstered by grossly exaggerated claims of British losses, improved.

The French Navy Neutralised

Meanwhile the British Government's anxiety about the French Navy had led to a decision on 27 June for pre-emptive action. Even if it had known that captains were expressly forbidden to allow their ships to fall into German hands (and thus fundamentally alter the balance of naval power) this would have been seen as no guarantee. On 3 July three battleships, four cruisers, eleven destroyers and three submarines in British harbours were persuaded to surrender almost bloodlessly. But, in a dolorous action at Oran, where the best units lay and Admiral Gensoul refused to yield, Force H under Admiral Sir James Somerville was forced to open fire, sinking a battleship, crippling a battle-cruiser, seriously damaging several smaller vessels and killing more than 1000 sailors. It brought the French Vichy Government to the verge of declaring war on Britain. But it also meant that Royal Navy squadrons in the Eastern Mediterranean and at Gibraltar were free to cope with the Italian Navy and come to Britain's rescue – as soon they might have to, reasoned the Admiralty, watching evidence of aggressive German intentions accumulating.

On the Brink

As the air battle resounded overhead and Dover and Folkestone were pounded by long-range heavy artillery, motley flotillas of German invasion craft were observed in daylight by the British entering the Straits. Initially these movements were interpreted by Intelligence as normal coastal traffic bound for Spain, but eventually they were evaluated in their true significance. On the 12th, when the RAF lost 26 fighters and 18 pilots and its airfields again were battered (with 70 machines destroyed on the ground), the Chiefs of Staff warned Churchill that invasion was imminent. Nightly bombardments of the invasion ports from sea and air now began.

Also on the 12th, however, the Luftwaffe lost 31 bombers and 29 fighters (with 20 pilots), causing Kesselring to request a 24-hour postponement of S-Day (still scheduled for the 13th) because the RAF was insufficiently subdued. His plea was most favourably received by Raeder, who dreaded SEA LION more than ever even if the Channel was smooth as a mill-pond. And he was backed by Göring, who pointed out that the weather forecast for the 13th was marginal with cloud and winds which might scatter the airborne forces on their way to the Dover Dropping Zones. It was to everybody's relief (except the soldiers and sailors under bombardment in port) when Hitler agreed to a postponement until the 14th, 'subject to a favourable weather report next day'.

In fact, the weather on the 13th was better than expected, allowing the Luftwaffe to launch another maximum effort. In addition to aerial mine-laying on the flanks of the channels to the invasion beaches (which crippled a cruiser *en route* from Sheerness to bombard the assembling landing craft), Kesselring's formations filled coastal air space with a view to cleansing it of hostile fighters. Meanwhile Sperrle's Air Fleet 5 concentrated on Plymouth and Portsmouth with the intention of pinning down the Royal Navy. At the end of a day of ferocious combat, the ever-optimistic Kesselring told Jeschonnek that he reckoned the fighters of his Air Fleet 2 could hold the ring strongly enough to let the airborne and amphibious forces make a landing on the 14th – a conviction that fitted well with next day's forecast of good weather throughout the 14th and 15th.

'Let Tomorrow be S-Day'

At noon, despite his own and Raeder's misgivings, Hitler gave the word. 'Let tomorrow be S-Day.' And then he boarded his special train, bound for Calais where he intended to watch events in person.

Already on 400 airfields and in the ports, last-minute preparations had been made. Anticipating the go-ahead, Kesselring had launched more attacks on coastal airfields and radar stations and succeeded in driving back the weary RAF squadrons to their inner bases. That afternoon, as the German long-range guns began a programmed bombardment of batteries guarding the Straits, the Luftwaffe struck hard at targets hitherto left alone – the railway system and roads of south-east England which, within 40 minutes, were badly disrupted. Caught on the hop, Fighter Command engaged at a disadvantage but raised the day's price for the Luftwaffe to 31 fighters and 30 bombers. But the RAF lost 65 fighters and 34 bombers, a blow from which it never recovered.

At 1720hrs the British Chiefs of Staff agreed that full precautions must be taken 'for immediate action'. Even as enemy shipping from more distant ports was putting to sea, precautionary orders were being issued, followed prematurely at 2007hrs by the code-word CROMWELL, which sent troops to their battle stations and placed all telegraph facilities under Army control. Here and there confusion reigned because some LDV commanders ordered the ringing of church bells to announce parachutists had landed. But inland there was an uneasy anti-climax accompanied by the drone of British and German bombers and, on both sides of the Channel, a rising fury of gunfire.

Already minesweepers were opening channels for the jostling flotillas of prahms and other assorted craft which, in good order but choppy seas which upset many non-sailors, were transporting 6th Mountain Division to the beaches west of Dover; and, in 'Pigpile' formation, 17th Infantry Division to Hythe. Of opposition there was little as they approached an enemy coast lit by the flames of war.

But it was shortly before dawn that the first Germans arrived in DFS-230 gliders, launched from 3000 feet to land on commanding positions at Langdon, the Citadel, Aycliff and Lydden Spout. Each of these objectives, except the Citadel, was taken after brisk scraps. By first light, virtually all coherent opposition to the approaching German flotillas (whose presence was already notified by the firing of signal rockets from startled Auxiliary Patrol vessels five miles out to sea) was eliminated.

Waves of strafing German fighters and bombers now roared across the open ground between the Citadel and Hythe, intimidating opposition to the low-flying stream of lumbering Ju-52s as they dropped their cargoes of parachutists. Within 30 minutes of touchdown, the commander of 19th Parachute Regiment to the east of Folkestone was triumphantly signalling that the ground was clear to receive aircraft of 22nd Air Landing Division with its heavy equipment. 20th Parachute Regiment, meanwhile, to the north of Hythe, temporarily had its hands full with troops of 1st (London) Division.

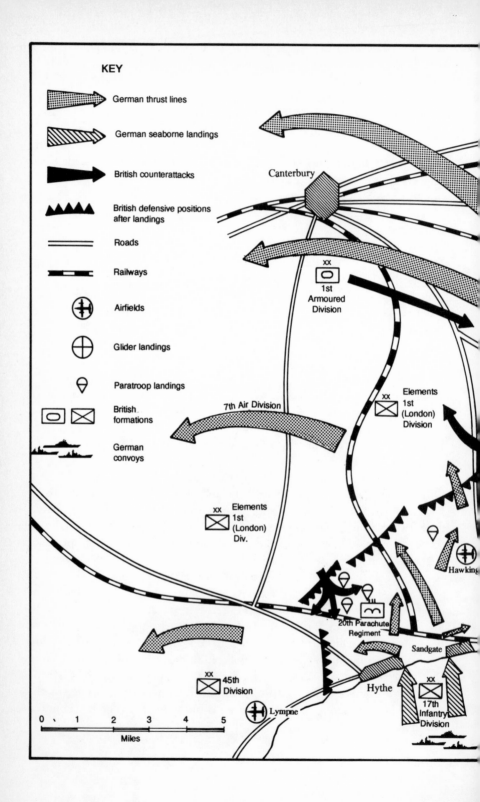

KEY

German thrust lines

German seaborne landings

British counterattacks

British defensive positions after landings

Roads

Railways

Airfields

Glider landings

Paratroop landings

British formations

German convoys

Canterbury

XX
1st Armoured Division

7th Air Division

Elements 1st (London) Division

Elements 1st (London) Div.

20th Parachute Regiment

Hawking

Sandgate

Hythe

XX
17th Infantry Division

45th Division

Lympne

0   1   2   3   4   5
Miles

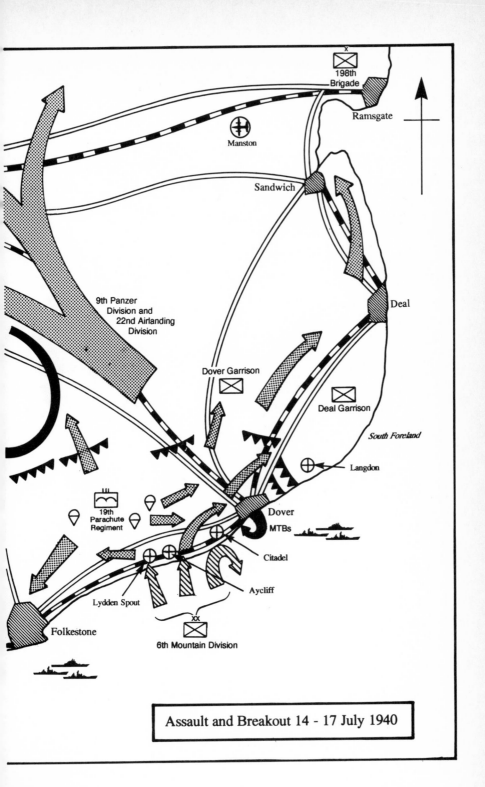

198th Brigade

Ramsgate

Manston

Sandwich

Deal

9th Panzer Division and 22nd Airlanding Division

Dover Garrison

Deal Garrison

South Foreland

Langdon

19th Parachute Regiment

Dover

MTBs

Citadel

Aycliff

Lydden Spout

Folkestone

6th Mountain Division

Assault and Breakout 14 - 17 July 1940

For the leading wave of General Ferdinand Schörner's 6th Mountain Division, coming ashore to the west of Dover, it was far from a walkover, however. Craft carrying 141st Mountain Regiment to the foot of the Shakespeare Cliff came under intense fire from harbour guns and infantry small arms as they disembarked in shambolic order. While the cross-Channel guns continued their pummelling, the old battleships *Schlesien* and *Schleswig Holstein* came off worst against the as yet unsubdued 9.2in guns of the Citadel. Close support was quite inadequate from escorting German destroyers, T-, S- and R-boats because of distractive harassment by five MTBs racing out of the harbour to attack with torpedoes and cannon. A massacre on the beaches followed by Schörner's total abandonment of this attempt was the outcome.

But where 143rd Mountain Regiment landed below Lydden Spout it was another story. Here, where the cliff top and shore line were already dominated by the gliderborne troops, the mountaineers landed and climbed the cliff unopposed. Within three hours the initial foothold was expanded into a defensible bridgehead, in conjunction with 19th Parachute Regiment which seized the Citadel by assault from the rear.

Meanwhile General Herbert Loch's 17th Infantry Division was struggling ashore between Sandgate and Hythe against little initial opposition from an enemy who was subdued by fire from the cross-Channel guns and escort vessels. Once ashore, however, seasick men flopped behind the promenade as small arms fire opened against them. And they did not take heart until they saw the newly developed PzKwIII deep-wading tanks emerging from ramped prahms which had grounded at the water's edge. At 0450hrs ten of these machines began crawling inland on a 4000-metre front with infantry in attendance. Within half an hour a foothold was secured along the old Royal Military Canal. At 0600hrs contact had been made with 20th Parachute Regiment. It was then only a matter of hours before a link-up was completed with 19th Parachute Regiment and the mountaineers on the right.

Struggle for the Beachhead

Now began a classic build-up race as Generals Thorne and Liardet strove to contain the German penetration, in the hope that the Germans might be isolated by warships and bombers; as the Navy and RAF did all in its power to intervene in the face of a pervasive Luftwaffe presence; and as the Germans poured in a flow of troops, heavy weapons, ammunition and supplies by air and sea regardless of losses which, in fact, were by no means exorbitant. Indeed, there was only one short curtailment of shipments when, later in the day, the approach of two cruisers and 16 destroyers from the Nore and eight destroyers from Portsmouth was observed – a threat which attracted heavy daylight bombing by the Luftwaffe and attacks by U-boats and S-boats in mine-infested waters. This culminated in a night action with heavy losses to both sides followed by a temporary withdrawal of the Royal Navy, which was under no illusion about the fact that a seriously weakened Fighter Command could not guarantee adequate protection by day.

Meanwhile, upon learning that Folkestone and Dover had fallen, General Ironside conceded defeat at the coast, and, in accordance with the agreed plan, ordered withdrawal to the GHQ Line. But this was vetoed by Churchill, who had never liked that part of the plan, and he insisted upon 1st Armoured Division counter-attacking immediately to destroy the enemy.

Naval and Air Confrontations

Without any other realistic option and despite fading air protection, the Royal Navy's cruisers and destroyers tried once more on the 15th to enter the Straits. Those from the Nore at first made encouraging progress by sinking a number of light craft and driving back the escorts. But although the submarine H 49 managed to sink the battleship *Schlesien*, the combined effect of air attacks, mining of the cruiser *Manchester* and a destroyer and fire from coastal artillery imposed wariness, especially once it was noticed that German landing craft had sheltered inshore. Similarly the Portsmouth destroyers suffered more losses and also held back so that, having expended nearly all their 250 rounds per gun, they merely blockaded the Straits until forced to return to port for replenishment. This left the Germans free to resume shipments and bring in reinforcements which at Dover, early on the 15th, included the tanks of 9th Panzer Division.

Yet, strangely enough, the mood at OKW was by no means calm and assured. News of the debacle below the Shakespeare Cliff, the troubles of 20th Parachute Regiment, the Royal Navy on the rampage in the Straits and continuing RAF attacks, disturbed Hitler and Raeder. But von Brauchitsch kept cool as Göring procrastinated under pressure, despite encouraging reports from Kesselring, who, on the evening of the 15th, found himself in possession of priceless information: nothing less than a captured diagram showing Fighter Command's signal system which revealed the key command and control role played by the Sector Stations.

For the 15th, therefore, Kesselring, at the expense of support for the navy and army, concentrated on the bombing of those airfields with devastating effect. At the end of a shattering day's fighting Dowding was compelled to tell Nos 10 and 12 Groups that Park's No 11 Group was virtually crippled and that henceforward they must concentrate on the battle of the Straits to the abandonment of all other tasks. In effect, the Luftwaffe had at last won air superiority – as Kesselring and Sperrle sensed from the combat reports that evening.

Clash of Armour

General Thorne ordered General Roger Evans to launch 1st Armoured Division's attack as soon as possible on the 15th, which meant a night move on tracks since the preferred transport by rail to assembly areas was unavailable, Southern Railways being in chaos due to bombing. Evans conceived simultaneous thrusts by his tank brigades: 3rd Armoured Brigade, with 70 fast cruiser and a few light tanks, to strike at Dover from Canterbury, and 1st Tank Brigade, with 82 of the slow, heavy Matildas, to go for Hythe and Folkestone. 1st (London) Division and 20th Armoured Brigade, with its assortment of light tanks, armoured cars and lorries, would have to give what support it could to the tank brigades.

The night move was hampered by refugees blocking the roads. Delays forced Evans to abandon a simultaneous attack. Instead 3rd Armoured Brigade Group started first and hit 22nd Air Landing Division, which retreated in panic. Deadly fire from 37mm and 88mm guns soon stopped the right flank regiment, however. But on the left a break-through by a cruiser tank squadron brought them within sight of Dover before 6th Mountain Division, reinforced by 30 tanks, cut off the spearhead and checked further British progress on this axis.

Starting three hours later, 1st Tank Brigade also enjoyed moments of hope. Its right flank regiment actually came within sight of Hythe beach before being forced to retire due to losses in close-range street fighting. The left column, however, ran into 88mm guns when well short of Hawkinge airfield. Lacking artillery or adequate infantry support, it was repulsed before tanks could launch a local counter-attack.

When 1st Armoured Division rallied that night it was to discover it had lost nearly 50% of its strength from enemy action and mechanical failures. News of this setback, coinciding with Dowding's report of the enfeeblement of No 11 Group, struck Ironside and the Government a chilling blow. Now, with air cover reduced and the only really effective armoured reserve stripped away, retreat to the GHQ Line was unavoidable. At that moment, Churchill realised that, regardless of cost, the Royal Navy must throw every vessel, including its battleships, into the fight for the Straits if there was to be the slightest chance of undermining the now all-but-secure German beachhead. At the same time Force H at Gibraltar was instructed to sail at once for Britain to reinforce the Home Fleet.

Fleet action: The Battle of Dover Straits

Admiral Sir Charles Forbes, C-in-C Home Fleet, was at sea off the Humber when he received Admiralty orders to enter the Straits not later than mid-day on the 16th 'with forces united'. At the same time Dowding was told to give maximum fighter cover and Bomber Command instructed to concentrate on ports, including enemy-occupied Dover and Folkestone. This was easier said than done in a well co-ordinated manner. The Portsmouth destroyers, delayed by bombing during restocking ammunition, had farthest to go and could not be off Hythe until the evening. Forbes, on the other hand, was able to achieve a measure of concentration in the afternoon off the North Foreland of two battleships, two battle-cruisers, seven cruisers, one aircraft carrier and 30 destroyers. But although Nos 10 and 12 Groups initially mounted useful fighter cover, they were spread too thin over the Straits – and this made Bomber Command's and the Fleet Air Arm's contribution almost suicidal.

Meanwhile Raeder, briefed about British movements by German Intelligence, which had long ago broken British naval codes and was well informed by air reconnaissance, already had ordered the squadron under Admiral Marschall to cruise off Terschelling, tasked to intercept the British Fleet. He did so in recognition of the wilting RAF effort and the British withdrawal from the coast which suggested that previous OKW pessimism was unjustified. At the same time, Kommodore Ruge redoubled the already frantic minelaying to bar the Straits and, with Raeder's approval, made arrangements once more to curtail cross-Channel traffic.

The German squadron comprised the battle-cruisers *Scharnhorst* and *Gneisenau*, one heavy and three light cruisers and only six destroyers, plus a few escort vessels, U-boats and S-boats. On its own it was hardly the force to tackle Forbes, even with the support in daylight of every dive-bomber and fighter the Luftwaffe could muster. Admiral Marschall increased speed on a converging course with Forbes almost as soon as the latter steamed south, heading for the swept channel in the minefield to the east of Southwold. Marschall aimed to intercept as far as possible from the North Foreland, and hoped for a measure of surprise. But almost at once his move was reported by a shadowing British submarine.

Forbes had now to run the gauntlet of almost ceaseless dive and high-level bombing, clashes which cost both air forces dear and, for the time being, diverted German air effort from the land battle and its attacks on airfields. But by now the Luftwaffe had the whip hand and could afford losses more than the RAF, which suffered an increasingly adverse loss ratio. And while Marschall was undiverted by bombing, Forbes and his captains were frequently distracted by the need to take evasive action, and were gradually weakened by damage and losses.

Marschall caught Forbes when the latter's big ships were still to westward of the minefield channel and his vanguard of cruisers and destroyers emerging from it. Hence the vanguard, which lost a cruiser and destroyer in the channel from mines recently laid by U-boat, had no room to fall back on the capital ship squadron. Thus it was exposed to severe punishment at long

range by the two German battle-cruisers, whose 11in guns were ranged by
radar; tactics skilfully used by Marschall to pick off light-weight opponents
when requesting the Luftwaffe to concentrate on battleships.

Lacking room for evasive action in the gap, Forbes's big ships were
repeatedly hit by bombs and had the battleship *Rodney* crippled by two
mines. When at last Forbes reached open waters it was to join a vanguard
which was in some disorder and already reporting ammunition shortage.
Nevertheless he pressed on, driving the Germans to one side and scoring a
few hits with 15in and 16in guns. But as he drew nearer to the Straits and
received news that German shipping was running for port, another of his
cruisers, followed shortly by two more destroyers, struck mines laid the
night before by aircraft and a U-boat. These losses mounted when Forbes
ruthlessly urged his cruisers and destroyers to sink what vessels they could at
sea and in port.

By dusk, therefore, Forbes had only partially achieved his aim at a very
high price, which rose further during the none too effectual night bombardments of Ostend and Dunkirk. For mines, along with fire from a
coastline now bristling with guns, took such a heavy toll that Calais and
Boulogne escaped unmolested. Moreover, the German battle-cruiser
squadron, with only *Gneisenau* seriously damaged by hits from 16in shells,
remained an attendant menace. And reinforcements and supplies were still
reaching England by sea and, in quantity, by air.

In desperation, Forbes now sought a knock-out blow at first light on the
17th, by steering the Fleet through channels swept that night to overwhelm
Marschall with a combined big gun action and Swordfish torpedo aircraft
attack. Co-ordination difficulties hampered arrangements. Mines, Marschall
and Kesselring blunted execution. The minesweepers, delayed and tackled
by S-boats and aircraft and shot at by coastal guns, were unable to complete
their task in time, thus checking Forbes's advance and condemning the
Swordfishes to a disastrous attack on an undistracted enemy well protected
by fighters. But when Marschall strayed within range of the British big
guns, he had *Gneisenau* finally put down and the heavy cruiser *Hipper*
crippled. However, he had compensation when the battle-cruiser *Renown*
blew up after being penetrated by successive hits from *Scharnhorst*.

That disaster along with almost non-stop air attacks persuaded Forbes to
retreat. In conjunction with a report that the Portsmouth destroyers had
made little impression the previous night and that reinforcement of the
German forces ashore continued, this news told the British Government
that Hitler had won – vehemently though Churchill denied it.

Victory Advance on London

Along with apparent air superiority and the noticeable failure of further attempts by the Royal Navy to enter the Straits, even Raeder was convinced of a German victory. By the morning of the 18th, when another Panzer Division (General Erwin Rommel's 7th) was almost completely ashore and reserves of fuel, ammunition and supplies adequate, it was agreeable to meet von Brauchitsch's demand for more Infantry Divisions. With these he intended to mount a wide fronted assault on the GHQ Line, which had now been identified.

In the event, however, on the 18th, the line was broken through quite easily (and thus outflanked) between Rochester and Maidstone by 6th Mountain and 35th Infantry Divisions. This jolt turned into a British disaster when 9th Panzer Division and 22nd Air Landing Division encountered and slaughtered the feeble light tanks of 2nd Armoured Division in the vicinity of Sevenoaks. As of that moment, apart from a few tanks from the defeated 1st and 2nd Armoured Divisions, the British were deprived of the mobile force which might save them. They thus had no answer to 7th Panzer Division when identified approaching Basingstoke to strike, unopposed, at Newbury and Oxford. Nor were there adequate forces to check infantry advancing on Portsmouth via Chichester.

As on 21 May, when the Panzer Groups had reached the English Channel, Hitler and his entourage celebrated in the certainty of another triumph and the opening up of unlimited mastery of the future. This was shown within the next three days as the encirclement of London neared completion; as the RAF, deprived of a large portion of its early warning system and fighter stations, diminished; and the Royal Navy abandoned its attempts to dominate the Straits and began what would develop into a major redeployment overseas. Remorselessly the Germans poured in troops to overrun the country. Inevitably resistance crumpled, because a people disarmed and lacking outside support is a nation defeated. Inevitably, Churchill was forced to resign to make room for others willing to negotiate an armistice.

Debacle, Armistice and Future Prospects

Yet Hitler fooled himself if at that moment he believed the British would cease resistance entirely. Even after the armistice was signed they would continue a faltering struggle at home and an increasingly aggressive one from abroad as they sought allies, America in particular. But his ambition of world domination was now mightily stimulated. With extinction of the rational dread of a war on two fronts, he could turn against Russia in 1941, and at the same time pursue Operation SPHINX – Admiral Raeder's maritime strategic plan to control the Mediterranean and, in conjunction with Italy, dominate the Middle East with its vital oil supplies. Subsequently, no doubt, would come some sort of confrontation with America in

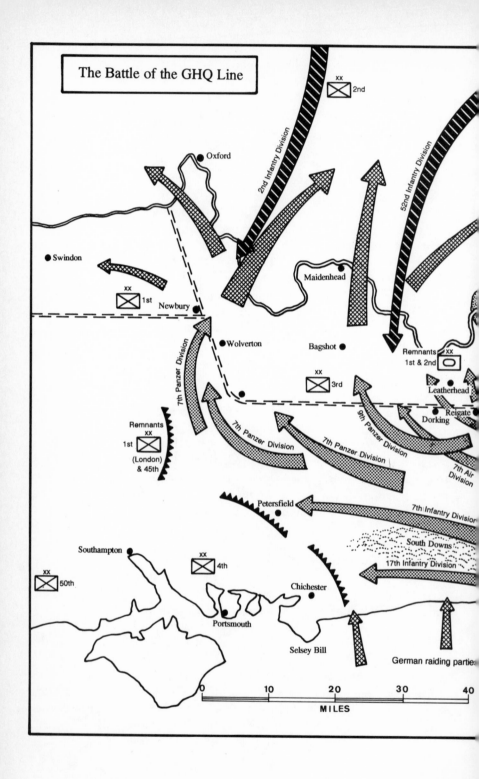

The Battle of the GHQ Line

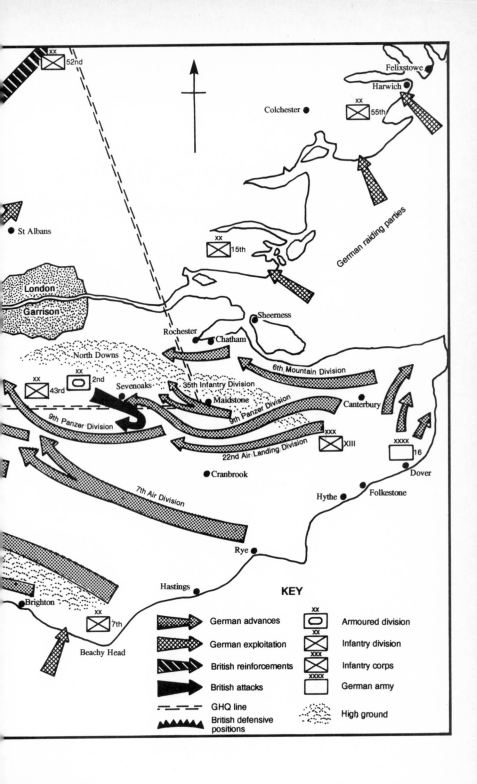

KEY

German advances	Armoured division
German exploitation	Infantry division
British reinforcements	Infantry corps
British attacks	German army
GHQ line	High ground
British defensive positions	

Felixstowe

Harwich

Colchester

55th

German raiding parties

St Albans

15th

London Garrison

Sheerness

Rochester

Chatham

North Downs

6th Mountain Division

2nd

Sevenoaks

35th Infantry Division

43rd

Maidstone

Canterbury

9th Panzer Division

9th Panzer Division

22nd Air Landing Division

XIII

16

Cranbrook

Dover

7th Air Division

Hythe

Folkestone

Rye

Hastings

Brighton

7th

Beachy Head

collaboration with the equally ambitious Japanese who, already, were expanding into South East Asia.

At the beginning of August, indeed, Hitler's fertile imagination envisaged horizons of immense brilliance for the future.

NOTES

1. In reality, to Raeder's relief, Hitler rejected the invasion, believing that Britain would make peace.
2. The sequence of air action and losses incurred is based on the opening stages of the real Battle of Britain.

BIBLIOGRAPHY

This chapter is a development of the author's *Invasion: The German Invasion of England, July 1940* (London, 1980), which since its first publication has not been seriously challenged as a convincing scenario. Here only the naval episodes have been significantly adjusted by having the Germans save their two battle-cruisers for action in support of SEA LION instead of unrealistically committing them against the Allied evacuation from Norway in June, which put both ships out of action.

Ansel, W., *Hitler Confronts England* (London, 1960)
Collier, B., *The Defence of the United Kingdom* (London, 1957)
Ellis, L.F., *The War in France and Flanders, 1939, 1940* (London, 1953)

CHAPTER 2

Operation SPHINX Raeder's Mediterranean Strategy

BRYAN PERRETT

A New Concept

Subconsciously, Adolf Hitler knew from the beginning that his projected invasion of the United Kingdom, codenamed SEA LION, would never take place. On 31 July 1940, only three weeks after the Luftwaffe had begun its struggle to obtain the prerequisite of air superiority over southern England, he addressed his Commanders-in-Chief on the subject of an alternative strategy intended to bring the stubborn Churchill administration to the negotiating table.

The keynote of his speech was contained in one sentence: 'In the event the invasion does not take place, our efforts must be directed to the elimination of all factors that let England hope for a change in the situation.'

The United Kingdom's only hope, he continued, lay in the intervention of the USSR or the United States. If the Soviet Union was eliminated, the balance of power in the Far East would shift towards Japan, and that in itself would serve to divert American attention away from the war in Europe. It followed, therefore, that the USSR must be crushed as quickly as possible, in one decisive blow. The whole Soviet system could be regarded as a ramshackle shed constructed with rotten timber; the Wehrmacht had only to kick in the door and the whole structure would collapse. If Russia was invaded in May 1941, the campaign could be concluded before the onset of winter five months later.

Many of those present were aware that the Germany Army was armed in breadth but not depth and was therefore unsuited to the protracted war that would ensue if the Führer's projection was incorrect. Among those who tacitly disagreed with his alternative strategy was Grand Admiral Erich Raeder, Commander-in-Chief of the Navy, who was deeply involved in the day-to-day preparations for SEA LION. It had been Raeder's unpalatable duty to point out with regard to this operation that the surface fleet had sustained such serious losses during the invasion of Norway that it would only be able to provide limited support and protection for the proposed landings on the southern coast of England. Furthermore, the opportunities for such landings consisted of a series of time windows in which the desirable wind, tide, sea and light conditions coincided. These time windows, he had warned, would become fewer as autumn approached and then disappear until the following spring, by which time the British would be far better prepared to meet the invasion.

Raeder's Strategy

Like Hitler, Raeder was fundamentally dubious about the merits of SEA LION and concurred with the former's belief that Great Britain could only be brought down by indirect means. His own U-boat arm was not yet achieving great results in the Atlantic, so anything approaching a complete blockade of the British Isles by this means lay in the far distant future. He suggested to Reichsmarschall Hermann Göring, Commander-in-Chief of the Luftwaffe, that the process could be accelerated by one or more of the latter's Air Fleets concentrating on the complete destruction of the port of Liverpool. Ever since London and the East and South Coast ports had been rendered largely inoperable, Liverpool, handling as it did the bulk of the United Kingdom's supplies and war materials, had become a strategic asset of incalculable importance. It followed, therefore, that if those cargoes that evaded the U-boats could not be unloaded, the British would be deprived of the capacity to wage war, or even support themselves, and so become more receptive to peace offers. Göring, however, resented this intrusion into the affairs of his own service and continued to pursue his battle of attrition over southern England.

By mid-September the Luftwaffe had still not produced the required results and, with the disappearance of the last of the cross-Channel time windows, Hitler postponed SEA LION indefinitely. Ten days later Raeder obtained a private audience with him and outlined a further strategic option that was available.

Raeder began by agreeing that the problem of Churchill's intransigence could not be solved by direct action. On the other hand, he pointed out, the British were at their most vulnerable in the Mediterranean, which provided them with a route to their empire and the oil-producing areas of the Middle East. By coincidence, it was in the same area that they were slowly effecting a concentration of force with a view to pursuing their traditional policy of destroying the weaker member of a hostile alliance – in this case, Italy.

Observing Hitler's curt nod, Raeder decided to emphasise the point.

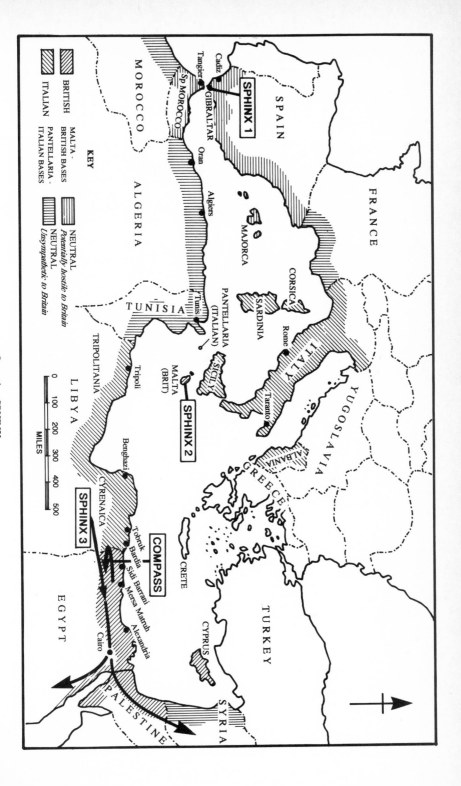

Operation SPHINX

'Vis-à-vis the military aspects of our alliance with Italy, these bear comparison with the Austro-Hungarian Empire alliance during the last war. In those days, you will recall that we spoke of being shackled to a corpse. With great respect, Führer, I suggest that a similar situation exists today.'

After a few moments of silent consideration, Hitler asked Raeder to develop his theme.

'Italy seems quite oblivious of her danger,' the Grand Admiral continued. 'Germany, however, must wage war against Great Britain with every means at her disposal, before American assistance restores British capacity for offensive action. For this reason the Mediterranean question must be cleared up over the winter months. First, I propose that we secure our right flank by capturing Gibraltar, with Spanish assistance. Next, priority will be given to the capture of Malta, which will give us control of the Central Mediterranean sea lanes. We can then ship a suitable force to North Africa where it will be used as the spearhead of the Italian campaign to capture the Suez Canal. The advance will continue through Palestine and Syria, bringing us to the Turkish frontier. Turkey will be in our power and we shall be able to strike at the oilfields of Iraq and Persia. The Russia problem will then appear in a quite different light – and since all the evidence suggests that Russia is frightened of Germany, it is doubtful whether an advance against her in the north will then be necessary. This will avoid the necessity of a protracted war on two fronts. I believe that these measures will convince the British of their foolishness in further continuing the struggle, especially if U-boat bases can be simultaneously established in the Canary and Cape Verde Islands, so tightening our submarine stranglehold on their seaborne supply lines.'

Although Hitler's reply was measured, Raeder could see that he had been won over.[1]

'I agree with your general trend of thought, although there are a number of political difficulties that must be overcome at the highest levels. It has previously been agreed between Signor Mussolini and myself that the Mediterranean should remain his area of responsibility, and he is extremely sensitive on the subjects of his own personal prestige and honour. Nevertheless, I believe that Il Duce can be persuaded to co-operate if I offer to augment his New Roman Empire with the French colony of Tunisia. As for Spain, General Franco owes a debt both to Il Duce and myself for the considerable assistance with which we provided him during his Civil War. The time has now come for him to repay that debt, however reluctant he might be. His reward will be the return of Gibraltar to Spain on the conclusion of hostilities, so fulfilling an historic Spanish ambition. In the circumstances, therefore, I shall order OKW to prepare an immediate feasibility study for discussion by Heads of Service and their specialist advisers in a week's time.'

Appreciation and Planning of Operation SPHINX

The conference assembled on 4 October. Hitler thanked Raeder for his ideas, which he said dovetailed neatly with his own thoughts on the subject. The new strategy would henceforth be known as Operation SPHINX and he would first welcome observations on the overall concept.

Field Marshal Walter von Brauchitsch, the Army's Commander-in-Chief, immediately rose to his feet. Sensitive by nature, he disliked confrontations with the Führer, whose towering rages could leave him shaken for days. He was, nonetheless, a dedicated professional and was prepared to stand his ground when necessary.

'Führer, the document prepared by OKW makes no mention of the degree of resistance likely to be encountered from Vichy French forces when we pass troops through their territory into Spain,' he observed. 'I believe the matter requires clarification.'

Hitler, the former junior NCO become warlord, was dismissive in his reaction:

'The matter has not been mentioned for the simple reason that it has no relevance! I have personally informed Marshal Pétain that not only will the slightest resistance be ruthlessly crushed, but also that France as he understands it will cease to exist! Besides, the French have not forgotten the manner in which the British abandoned them at Dunkirk, and they will never forgive the Royal Navy's destruction of their squadron at Oran in July, ostensibly to prevent it from falling into our hands. Anyone who imagines that the French still retain the slightest regard for their former ally is little better than a straw-head!'

Brauchitsch resumed his seat and Hitler asked the three service chiefs for their respective intelligence assessments of the overall situation in the Mediterranean. Raeder began, giving the estimated strength of the Royal Navy as being seven battleships, two aircraft carriers, eight cruisers, 37 destroyers, eight submarines and a small force of monitors and gunboats, divided between Force H at Gibraltar and Admiral Cunningham's Mediterranean Fleet at Alexandria. Thanks to Italian air activity, the Royal Navy had been forced to abandon its base at Malta. The Italian Navy possessed six battleships, 21 cruisers, 50 destroyers and 100 submarines. Thus far, it had avoided a general fleet action with the Royal Navy, always turning away after the exchange of a few salvos. The Italian submarines had scored some successes, but these were not commensurate with their numbers. Air support for naval operations was provided by the Italian Air Force, which could put up about 2000 aircraft from airfields in the Central Mediterranean and the Dodecanese Islands. Co-operation between the two services was said to be poor.

Brauchitsch reported that the British Commander-in-Chief Middle East,

General Sir Archibald Wavell, had approximately 50,000 troops at his disposal, but these were thinly spread across a wide area stretching from the Syrian frontier to the Sudan. Of these, 36,000 were in Egypt, including the high-quality but under-strength 7th Armoured Division, the 4th Indian Division, a regular formation, and a handful of infantry brigades, one of which, because of anti-British feeling in Egypt, was always retained for internal security duties. The 6th Australian Division was arriving in Palestine but would not be ready for action for some weeks; during the last war Australian troops had proved to be formidable opponents and there was no reason to suspect that the new arrivals were any different. The Italians had 200,000 men in East Africa, where, in August, they had occupied British Somaliland. In North Africa, Marshal Rodolfo Graziani had 250,000 men. In September he had made a 60-mile advance into Egypt, halting at Sidi Barrani, approximately half-way to the main British defensive position at Mersa Matruh. The Italians had then dug themselves into a chain of fortified camps stretching away into the desert to the south-west. Graziani's army, consisting as it did of infantry divisions with insufficient motorised transport, was unsuited to a mechanised war, let alone a war in the desert. Its L3 tankettes were less useful than the obsolete PzKw I and apart from these the only armour available was a regimental-sized group of badly designed M-11 medium tanks, half of which were undergoing repair at any one time. The Italian artillery consisted of good quality troops, but much of its equipment was out of date. The general impression received by Colonel Hegenreimer, the German Army's liaison officer in North Africa, was that the Italians disliked the desert and were scared stiff of the British; even quite senior officers spoke of their determination 'to resist to the last,' which could hardly be described as a positive attitude.

'In the light of this,' Brauchitsch concluded, 'I believe that on its own Graziani's army is incapable of inflicting a defeat on the British; the reverse, however, seems likely at some stage, and it will quickly turn into a major disaster. For this reason alone I am in favour of implementing the proposed Mediterranean strategy.'

Reichsmarschall Göring informed the conference that when the Mediterranean War began, the Royal Air Force could muster only a handful of squadrons equipped with obsolete Bombay medium bombers, Blenheim light bombers and Gladiator biplane fighters. Since then, small numbers of Hurricane fighters had begun reaching Egypt along an air ferry route from West Africa. No doubt existed in his mind that the RAF's Middle Eastern presence would be wiped off the map during the first days of Operation SPHINX. Resources amounting to two Air Fleets would be transferred to the Mediterranean. Flying from bases in Spain, the Balearics, Sardinia, Italy, Sicily, Libya and ultimately Egypt, the Luftwaffe would dominate the skies above the entire war zone. The vulnerable Stuka dive-bomber squadrons, under-employed during the recent air fighting over England, would again prove to be a decisive influence on land or at sea.

At this point an increasingly heated exchange took place between Raeder and Göring on the subject of torpedo bombers, or rather the lack of them. It was brought to an end by Hitler, who wished to examine each of Operation SPHINX's major elements in greater detail.

For the attack on Gibraltar, Brauchitsch considered that the Spanish would provide most of necessary infantry while the real task of reducing the fortress was left to the German heavy artillery. At his request, General Karl Becker, the Head of Artillery, told the conference that he intended using a concentration of super-heavy Bruno railway guns, firing across the bay from specially constructed spurs in the region of Algeciras. The calibre of these weapons varied between 238mm and 283mm, their shells weighed between 9400 and 15,000 kilograms and their range was between 20,000 metres and 36,000 metres. It was anticipated that there would be a heavy expenditure of concrete-piercing ammunition, not only because of the fixed nature of the defences, but also because Gibraltar had virtually no natural water supply and the British had constructed large concrete catchment areas on the side of the Rock, draining into underground cisterns. It was anticipated that the Gibraltar garrison would be forced to capitulate in approximately three weeks.

Hitler, always interested in weapon technology, asked Becker whether it would be possible to incorporate any of the even heavier weapons under development into his plan. Becker replied that the Gustav 800mm railway gun would not be ready for service until 1942. However, delivery of the first of several Karl 600mm self-propelled mortars was scheduled for December; this could be accelerated and the weapon incorporated in the final stages of the siege.

The conference then turned its attention to Malta. There was general agreement that many of the preparations for SEA LION could be put to good use in this operation, which would be screened from the British Mediterranean Fleet's intervention by the Italian Navy and the German and Italian Air Forces. The invasion barges would be shipped south along inland waterways. Again, the amphibious version of the PzKw II and the 'diving' versions of the PzKw III and IV, launched from landing craft to the sea bed to drive ashore using a floating air hose, could be used to spearhead the infantry's own assault landing. For the sake of form, this would involve a heavy Italian participation. Raeder expressed reservations at the small number of suitable landing sites, which would undoubtedly be heavily defended; furthermore, he felt that sea-bed conditions and inadequate beach exits might seriously inhibit the tanks' contribution, and urged further

intelligence-gathering on these subjects. Fortunately, tidal considerations
did not apply in the Mediterranean to anything like the extent they had in
the Channel. On balance, therefore, he believed that the operation would
succeed, albeit at heavy cost.

Brauchitsch agreed with this assessment, but suggested that if the
Luftwaffe made available Maj Gen Kurt Student's 7th Parachute Division
this could be dropped in the defenders' rear prior to the main landing. This
would undoubtedly cause chaos and confusion and reduce the degree of
resistance that would be encountered on the beaches, especially if a second
division could be air-landed once an airfield had been secured. The problem
was the high-risk nature of such operations.

Göring indignantly countered that his paratroopers would willingly
accept any risks involved – had they not done so when Holland was overrun
in May, thereby rendering the Army's task that much easier? True, the
airborne invasion of an island had never been attempted before, but
Student's division was equal to the task. As he understood the situation, the
island's garrison amounted to little more than the equivalent of two
brigades, including low-grade fortress troops and unemployed seamen, with
only a few light tanks in support.

Finally, the conference turned its attention to the third phase of
Operation SPHINX, participation in the North African campaign. Maj Gen
Wilhelm Ritter von Thoma had just returned from a fact-finding mission to
the Western Desert. Given the Royal Navy's present command of the sea,
he said, it would be impossible to support a large German contingent as
well as a major portion of the Italian Army. At this stage, he felt that the
appropriate German contribution should be four armoured or mechanised
divisions since this was the minimum required for success and the maximum
that could be maintained in the field. Once the British have been deprived
of their naval supremacy, he added, it will be possible to reinforce these
formations with others, should it prove necessary to do so.

The question of who was to command the German contingent then
arose. Several names were proposed, but Hitler was adamant that his own
nominee, Maj Gen Erwin Rommel, should be promoted and appointed.
General Franz Halder, the academic-looking Chief of Army General Staff,
objected on the grounds that Rommel was an opportunist and an ungovernable subordinate. Hitler retorted that during the last war Rommel's
opportunism had resulted in the capture of 9000 prisoners and 81 guns
within one three-day period; and as, again for the sake of form, he would be
nominally answerable to Mussolini's *Comando Supremo*, an ungovernable
subordinate was exactly what was required.

Hitler then closed the conference with instructions that the first phase of
Operation SPHINX should commence in six weeks' time.

Hitler and Mussolini Confer

During the evening of 4 October Hitler travelled to the Brenner Pass for a personal discussion with Mussolini. The latter was at first somewhat taken aback by the revised German strategy but accepted that, once successful, it would leave Italy in an unassailable position as the major power in the Mediterranean. He agreed to co-operate provided his own pivotal role and that of the Italian armed services was duly recognised, simultaneously insisting that Malta as well as Tunisia should become Italian colonies. Hitler agreed without hesitation and assured his fellow dictator that his only concern was the consolidation of the Axis alliance. At the diplomatic level there was little more to be done, since he had already held a secret meeting with General Franco and secured a promise of Spanish co-operation, at least insofar as Gibraltar and the Canaries were concerned.

Britain Forewarned

German preparations, cloaked under a strict security blanket, went ahead with speed and efficiency. They were, however, detected almost at once by several British intelligence agencies. The Y intercept service and ULTRA picked up a steady stream of references to codenames SPHINX 1 and SPHINX 2, and, to a lesser extent, SPHINX 3. After several days it became clear that SPHINX 1 referred to the passage of German troops and Luftwaffe units into Spain. SPHINX 2 intercepts mainly concerned the redeployment of substantial Luftwaffe elements to Italian airfields in the Central Mediterranean. The purpose of SPHINX 3 remained unclear at first, but by extending the projection of the first two phases the inescapable deduction was that it referred to German involvement in the North African campaign.

These conclusions were reinforced by other intelligence sources. The Luftwaffe was visibly thinning out in Northern France, Belgium, Holland, Denmark and Norway. French agents reported the complete disruption of the civil rail network between the Rhine and the Pyrenees, as well as the dispersion of the fleet of invasion barges that had been assembled in the Channel ports. An unexpected source of information proved to be the Soviet Embassy in Lisbon, which administered an extensive network of spies across the border in Spain, recruited among communist supporters who bitterly resented their defeat in the recent Civil War. Numerous railway guns and trains carrying pre-fabricated track were crossing Spain from north to south, accompanied by troops who wore Spanish uniforms but were undoubtedly German. Extensive railway construction work was taking place around Algeciras, a fact confirmed by air reconnaissance flights from Gibraltar. This major intelligence coup was in turn totally eclipsed by another. The British Military Attaché in Berne reported that he had been given complete details

of the entire SPHINX plan by a source with high-ranking anti-Nazi
contacts within OKW itself. The man, who preferred to be known only as
'Lucy,' was himself an anti-Nazi German who was now a Swiss citizen. He
had previously supplied information regarding the German invasions of
Norway, Denmark and Western Europe and this had proved to be
completely accurate, although it had not been acted upon.[2]

The information was relayed to London where, at a meeting of the War
Cabinet on 21 October, it was accepted unanimously that Hitler had
decided to shift the emphasis of the war to the Mediterranean. Informed by
his chief staff officer, General Sir Hastings Ismay, that Gibraltar could not
be expected to resist for long, Churchill expressed deep anger but accepted
the reality of the situation. Force H was to remain until the last possible
moment, then take part in the capture of the Canaries with a task force that
would be formed at once. He vowed that Malta would be defended to the
last and gave orders for the garrison to be reinforced. In the Western Desert
the situation was under control and the removal of the threat posed by SEA
LION had permitted the despatch of three armoured regiments, including
one equipped with heavily-armoured Matildas, around the Cape to Egypt,
where they had arrived earlier in the month.

On 7 November, unknown to its commander Admiral Somerville, Force
H, consisting of the battleship *Barham*, the carrier *Ark Royal*, two cruisers
and three destroyers, performed its last mission in the Mediterranean,
carrying some 2000 reinforcements from Gibraltar to Malta. On his return
to Gibraltar, Somerville was ordered to keep his ships at instant readiness
but not informed of the reason.

During the afternoon of 11 November the Mediterranean Fleet's carrier
Illustrious, escorted by cruisers and destroyers, was approaching a point 170
miles south of the heel of Italy from which her Swordfish torpedo bombers
were to launch a strike against the Italian battlefleet, snug in its harbour of
Taranto. At about 1600hrs it was apparent that the force had been detected
by an enemy maritime reconnaissance aircraft and an hour later the first
Italian bomber squadrons arrived overhead. As usual, their attack was
delivered from high altitude and caused little damage. At 1730hrs, however, large numbers of German Ju-87 dive bombers appeared on the scene,
pressing home their attacks with such determination that the ships were
forced to take violent evasive action.

'These people were an altogether different proposition,' recalled the
captain of the destroyer *Swordsman*. 'They were professionals and they knew
their business, boring down through our flak until it seemed they could
hardly miss.'

Two comparatively small bombs struck *Illustrious* on the flight deck,
tearing jagged craters in the plating and jamming the lift. The damage

could be repaired but clearly the planned strike against Taranto could not proceed. As the aircraft droned off into the gathering dusk the carrier and her escorts turned away for Alexandria. One destroyer, her boilers burst by a direct hit, was under tow, and the rest of the ships all showed signs of superficial damage caused by near misses. Germans losses amounted to five dive-bombers shot down and a similar number damaged.[3]

Franco Threatens Gibraltar

At about this time Franco closed the border with Gibraltar and his ambassador in London delivered an ultimatum demanding the immediate return of the fortress to Spanish jurisdiction. This was rejected out of hand. The following morning 'Lucy' confirmed that SPHINX 1 would begin at 03:00 on 15 November.

During the evening of 14 November a grim-faced Admiral Somerville returned aboard his flagship in Gibraltar harbour carrying sealed orders. Shortly after dark Force H, which had been reinforced with the battlecruiser *Renown*, weighed anchor and disappeared into the Atlantic spaces. Within the town itself, civilians were shepherded into air raid shelters and the garrison stood to.

Promptly at 0300hrs the German guns opened fire across Algeciras Bay, supplemented by Spanish medium and field artillery firing from positions further south. The British guns, emplaced for coastal defence, could make little effective reply. By noon, the town had become an inferno and the airstrip, dotted with the pyres of the few remaining aircraft, was pitted with craters and unusable.

Franco had nonetheless already begun to have doubts regarding the wisdom of his action, for Force H, lying below the horizon of Cadiz, had struck back hard. Flying low out of the pre-dawn darkness to the west, *Ark Royal*'s Swordfish penetrated the harbour before its sleepy defenders could marshal their thoughts. Jinking through wild and inaccurate anti-aircraft fire, the slow torpedo bombers scored fatal strikes of the cruisers *Reconquista, El Cid, San Cristobal* and *San Francisco d'Assisi*, sending them to the bottom. Four destroyers were also sunk and a tanker set ablaze. Five minutes after the aircraft had left, 15in shells from *Barham* and *Renown* began to slam into the dockyard, the destroyer anchorage and the submarine berths. Half an hour later Force H turned away, leaving the vast harbour littered with wrecks. Four cruisers, five destroyers and two submarines had been sunk; a further cruiser, two destroyers and three submarines had sustained serious damage; smoke and flames belched from the burning tanker and oil storage tanks ashore; the dockyard facilities had been reduced to a tangle of twisted steel and rubble; and some 1500 seamen had died. It had taken just 90 minutes to reduce the Spanish Navy to virtual impotence and during that period the nature of air–sea warfare had changed irrevocably. British losses amounted to a single Walrus spotter aircraft, shot down after a protracted duel with three Spanish fighters that reached the scene as Somerville withdrew.

Gibraltar held out for four weeks. Casemates, galleries and bunkers in the Rock were methodically cracked open and smashed by the German guns. After the first ten days General Julio Sanchez de Cordoba, in overall command of the operation, mounted an infantry attack along the isthmus linking the Rock with the mainland. This stalled in an unexpected minefield and was then shot to pieces by troops dug in amidst the rubble of the town. The assault was not repeated. The end became inevitable when the concrete catchment areas were smashed up, fouling the water cisterns below. On 5 December Cordoba sent in a flag of truce, offering to grant the honours of war. Unable to resist further, and wishing to spare the Gibraltarians further suffering, the Governor accepted. The following day, their Colours burned and their weapons rendered useless, the 700 men of the garrison still on their feet marched out and the Spanish took possession of the ruins that were their prize.

Battle of Cape Matapan

In the meantime, the world's attention had shifted to the Central Mediterranean. Hitler and Mussolini, satisfied with the progress made at Gibraltar, had sanctioned the start of SPHINX 2 on 25 November. Two days later, Admiral Inigo Campioni led the Italian battlefleet to sea with specific orders to bring Cunningham's Mediterranean Fleet to battle and so screen the paratroop drop and seaborne landings on Malta, which would take place on 27 and 28 November respectively. Cunningham, fully aware of what was happening, was already steering towards Campioni, and the two fleets came in sight of each other at 0900hrs on the 28th, approximately 100 miles south-west of Cape Matapan. In this, the first major encounter between battlefleets since Jutland, both sides possessed an equal number of battleships, Campioni with *Littorio, Vittorio Veneto, Giulio Cesare* and *Conti di Cavour*, and Cunningham with *Warspite, Valiant, Malaya* and *Ramillies*. The Italians deployed the greater number of cruisers and destroyers, although to some extent this was balanced by the presence of the patched-up *Illustrious*.

Campioni began the battle by turning to port, hoping to cross the British T. His move, however, was premature, for Cunningham merely adjusted his own course a few points to port and concentrated the entire weight of his fire against *Giulio Cesare*, bringing up the rear of the Italian line. Within minutes, hits were being obtained regularly and the ship staggered out of line, clearly ablaze. Fearing that Cunningham would cut him off from his base, Campioni hastily reversed course and, leaving three cruisers to escort the stricken *Giulio*, ran parallel with the British line, while the cruisers and destroyers of both sides engaged in a high-speed *mêlée*. Both battle lines now began to sustain punishment, although the weight and accuracy of the British gunnery was superior. The issue was decided when *Illustrious*'s Swordfish, attacking from the Italians' disengaged side, managed to put three torpedoes into the *Littorio*, albeit at the cost of most of their number. Belching smoke, the battleship heeled rapidly to starboard, rolled over and sank. Campioni ordered some of his destroyers to attack with torpedoes while the rest created a smokescreen, under cover of which the remainder of his fleet escaped to the north. Although three of their ships were blown apart under them, the Italian destroyer captains pressed home their attacks with suicidal courage, breaking through the screen of escorts to launch their torpedoes. Two of them found their marks on *Valiant* and *Malaya* as they turned cumbrously to comb the tracks. Neither was in immediate danger of sinking, but their speed was seriously reduced and Cunningham ordered them to return to base while he continued the pursuit. This, he knew, could not be maintained for long as he was now well within range of the enemy's protective air umbrella.

Sure enough, at about 1430hrs large numbers of German and Italian aircraft arrived overhead. After both his remaining battleships had been hit several times, and a cruiser and two destroyers severely damaged, he turned for home. Shortly after dusk a flickering glow on the south-eastern horizon betrayed the burning *Giulio* and she, together with her escorting cruisers *Pola, Zara* and *Fiume*, suddenly and starkly illuminated by searchlights, were battered into sinking wrecks in a sudden blaze of gunfire. Cunningham, cheered into Alexandria, was satisfied that he had drawn the teeth of the Italian battlefleet. His own losses amounted to two destroyers and a cruiser, but, against this, all his capital ships and many others vessels required heavy repairs that would take time to complete.

Invasion of Malta

The German parachute drop on Malta had come close to disaster. The intention had been to been to secure three airstrips simultaneously and use them to air-land reinforcements. The drops, however, had run into a curtain of anti-aircraft and small-arms fire. Losses in aircraft and men were heavy, General Student, the divisional commander, being among those killed in the air. Some companies were wiped out before they could assemble. Only one airstrip was captured and this could not be held against counter-attacks without constant close support from ground-attack aircraft. At length the perimeter was expanded sufficiently for the air-landing division to be called in, but this too sustained horrific casualties as its aircraft made their approach under fire. Later, the Luftwaffe admitted the loss of 208 Ju-52 transports during the day. With difficulty, the combined German force clung to its perimeter during the night.

At dawn the seaborne invasion force, consisting of one German and two Italian infantry divisions, began coming ashore under cover of naval gunfire support provided by the battleships *Caio Duilio, Andrea Doria* and their escorts. In areas where the tanks were unable to get ashore or leave the beach the infantry remained pinned down. At Bugibba, however, a scratch force led by ten tanks was able to drive inland and break through to the German-held airstrip.

From this point on, the scales began to tilt against the British. Lacking air support or adequate armour, they were forced steadily back during the next week. One brigade, cut off at Medina, surrendered when its ammunition ran out. A final stand was made in the ancient fortifications of the Knights of St John at Valetta, but by 8 December the island was firmly in German and Italian hands.

The cost had been far higher than had been anticipated. The parachute and air-landing divisions had sustained casualties amounting respectively to 60% and 40% of their strength, leaving Hitler profoundly shocked. When, later in the month, a chastened Franco requested the use of German paratroops to recover the Canaries (captured after a token resistance by a task force from the United Kingdom, escorted by Force H and part of the Home Fleet, between 6 and 10 December) the Führer had been adamant in his response: 'There will be no further operations of this kind!'

Wavell's strategy: Operation COMPASS

In Cairo, Wavell was fully aware that the final act of the drama was about to commence. He had been summoned to London early in November and fully briefed on Operation SPHINX. His reaction was that with the forces at his disposal neither Egypt nor Palestine could be held; after both had been evacuated he intended withdrawing up the Nile valley to the Sudan, while the Mediterranean Fleet came south through the Canal into the Red Sea. After strenuous argument Churchill accepted this, having been assured that the conquest of Italy's East African colonies would begin shortly after. He also accepted that Transjordan would have to be evacuated and the British troops in Iraq concentrated around Basra to protect the Gulf oilfields. His deep depression lifted a little when Wavell informed him that his intention was to use the Western Desert Force, commanded by Lt Gen Richard O'Connor, in a spoiling attack against Graziani's positions to the south of Sidi Barrani. 'You must strike as soon as you are ready,' he told Wavell. 'We shall, all of us, be in dire need of a victory in the days ahead.'

Training for the spoiling attack, codenamed COMPASS, continued in secret throughout November. During the night of 8/9 December the 7th Armoured and 4th Indian Divisions penetrated a 20-mile gap in the chain of Italian fortified camps. While 7th Armoured Division swung right towards the coast with the object of isolating Sidi Barrani, 4th Indian Division, spearheaded by the Matildas of 7th Royal Tank Regiment, stormed each of the northern camps in turn. At Nibeiwa 23 M-11/39s, the only medium tanks the Italians possessed, were knocked out before their sleeping crews could board them. To their horror, the Italians discovered that, no matter how courageously their artillery fought, they did not possess a weapon capable of penetrating the Matilda's 78mm armour. Resistance, initially fierce, suddenly collapsed and was followed by mass surrenders. The following day Sidi Barrani was stormed amid similar scenes. The Italians abandoned the southern end of their chain of camps and withdrew hastily towards the Libyan frontier, only to have their rearguard overrun by 7th Armoured Division at Buq Buq on 12 December.

The results of COMPASS were little short of astounding. In four days of fighting the equivalent of four Italian divisions had been wiped out; 237 guns and 73 medium tanks or tankettes had been destroyed or captured; and 38,000 prisoners, including four generals, had been taken. The prisoners, in fact, far outnumbered their captors but co-operated fully, driving themselves in their own lorries to compounds in the Delta; their only alternative, to be fair, was an agonising death from thirst in the desert.[4]

Egypt Abandoned

To the astonishment of the victors, O'Connor halted their pursuit at the frontier, then gave the order for them to withdraw rapidly along the coast road, passing through the former front line at Mersa Matruh until they reached El Alamein, just 60 miles west of Alexandria. Here they found the 6th Australian Division, called forward from Palestine, engaged in laying extensive mine belts covering the 40-mile gap between the coast and the impassable Qattara Depression to the south. Subsequently, Wavell explained his strategy as follows:

'We had just inflicted a signal defeat on the Italian Army. I was, however, fully conscious that six more Italian divisions remained in Libya and I had been informed that the advance guards of four German divisions, two of which were armoured and two mechanised, had begun landing at Tripoli. This lay 1000 miles to the west and I calculated that they would not reach the front until the middle of January. I could have met them on the frontier, but instead I decided to buy space and time by retiring deep into Egypt, simultaneously creating severe logistic problems for them and preserving as much of my own army as possible. If necessary, I was prepared to fight a holding action at the El Alamein defile, but my object was to disengage as quickly as possible after our resources had been back-loaded to Upper Egypt and deny the enemy any sort of victory. I was absolutely determined that there would be no heroic but useless last stand amid the tangled waterways of the Nile Delta or in the labyrinthine alleys of Cairo. My mind was now set on the conquest of Italian East Africa and arrangements were well in hand for the Army to be supplied through Port Sudan and Kenya.'

Although there was a steady increase in the level of Luftwaffe activity, which the small Desert Air Force countered to the best of its ability, the first elements of the Axis army, harried whenever possible by the guns of the Mediterranean Fleet, did not close up to the Alamein defences until 20 January. It took several days to accumulate sufficient fuel to mount an attack and during these Wavell thinned out the defenders, leaving dummy tanks and guns in their place. By the time the Axis were ready, the British had vanished overnight. Pivoting on the Faiyum, Wavell's troops retired up the Nile Valley to Aswan and Wadi Halfa, using road, rail and river transport. Simultaneously, the long line of Cunningham's ships entered the Red Sea bound initially for Port Sudan and Aden. Lt Gen Rommel, fretting at the delays imposed by the need to gap the minefields, found himself balked of his prey and despatched a regimental battlegroup from the 5th Light Division in pursuit. It clashed with Wavell's rearguard, consisting of two Australian brigades each with a Matilda squadron in support, ten miles west of Gizeh and within sight of the Pyramids. Here, the Germans' surging confidence sustained a sharp rebuff when the Matildas, sallying forth, destroyed forty of their tanks in as many minutes and put the rest to flight. Rommel, furious, dismissed the battlegroup leader and court-martialled two battalion commanders for their timidity.[5] When reinforcements finally arrived only five Matildas were found between the battlefield and the now deserted rail-head – two immobilised with track damage and three abandoned because of worn steering clutches. Overhead, the Desert Air Force fought successfully but at high cost to prevent the Luftwaffe interfering with the withdrawal up the Nile Valley.

Conquest of Abyssinia

Far to the south, the British had already gone over to the offensive. On 19 January the 4th and 5th Indian Divisions, under the command of Maj Gen William Platt, had crossed Sudanese–Eritrean frontier and captured Agordat. For a while, their continued advance was halted by fierce resistance in the mountains east of Keren, but the fall of Asmara, the Eritrean capital, on 1 April, was followed by that of Massawa, the Italian Navy's Red Sea base, a week later. Further south still, the 1st South African, and 11th and 12th African Divisions, under Lieutenant General Sir Alan Cunningham, the Admiral's younger brother, invaded Italian Somaliland from Kenya on

29 January and on 26 February captured Mogadishu. The Italians promptly evacuated British Somaliland, the vacuum being promptly filled by a force shipped across from Aden. Cunningham's troops had meanwhile pursued the Italians into Ethiopia, taking Jigjiga on 17 March and Addis Ababa, the capital, on 6 April; their advance had covered over 1000 miles at an average daily rate of 35 miles, and in the process they had taken 50,000 prisoners at a cost of 135 killed, 310 wounded and 56 missing. It remained only for Cunningham and Platt to converge on the last remaining Italian army, commanded by the Duke of Aosta, which surrendered at Amba Alagi on 19 May. Some of the latter's troops would remain at large in the vast hinterland until November, but for all practical purposes the Italian presence in East Africa had been eliminated.

Despite this, it was the elimination of the British presence from the Mediterranean which concerned the Axis Powers most. Unfortunately, while their capture of Cairo might have provided them with a crowning moment of success, it was marred by quarrels between Hitler and Mussolini. The latter wished to enter the city riding a white stallion, but the former, being no horseman, insisted on using an open Mercedes. Mussolini raged at Hitler for not pursuing Wavell up the Nile, but Hitler had already ordered his troops to drive on through Palestine to Syria, leaving the task of holding Egypt to the Italians.

Churchill's 'Victory'

On the morning following their quarrelsome entry into Cairo, Mussolini and Hitler were made uncomfortably aware that Operation SPHINX had failed in its primary object, namely that of bringing Churchill to the negotiating table, for the previous evening the Prime Minister had broadcast his reaction to the world.

'It is true that Hitler and Mussolini have enjoyed a season of success. Yet I would commend to them the words of the venerable Chinese sage who recognised that he who would be strong everywhere is strong nowhere. And I would remind them that we, who grow daily stronger in these islands, have a unique capacity for sustaining long wars against tyranny and emerging victorious at the end. Over twenty years of struggle were required to crush the evils of French republicanism and Bonapartism, but we triumphed. Already, the days of Italy's East African Empire are numbered, and the conquest of these territories will enable us to return, this time in strength, to Lower Egypt.

'As for the treacherous General Franco, he knows how many there are in his country who hate him, as they themselves know that we shall supply them with the arms to renew their fight for democracy. He has already lost his beloved Canary Islands, which now provide us with a fine base from which to hunt down and destroy the Nazis' U-boat scourge; his navy lies shattered on the bed of Cadiz harbour; and his coast is closely blockaded. Sooner or later, he will return Gibraltar to us just as, in the fullness of time, Mussolini will return Malta.

'In the wider context, we have our friends abroad. In the Far East, the strident ambitions of the Japanese Empire are carefully observed by the Soviet Union. However, lest recent events have induced the Japanese to believe that there is profit to be had in naked aggression, I have not only ordered part of Admiral Cunningham's fleet to proceed to Singapore, but also given instructions that the air defences of the Malayan Peninsula should be dramatically strengthened and the garrison reinforced. Furthermore, I have agreed with the President of the United States that the dockyard facilities of Singapore will be made available to the American Pacific Fleet, presently based at Pearl Harbor in the Hawaiian Islands, should the situation demand it.

'To some, it may appear that the blood-red sun of fascism has reached its zenith. Presently, we shall observe the first stages of its inevitable descent into oblivion.'

The Axis Options

It was, perhaps, natural that Churchill should strike so optimistic a note as he strove to uplift the morale of an embattled nation. However, the adrenaline of conquest was coursing strongly through Hitler's veins as he surveyed his achievements, ominously likening them to his most intimate companions as milestones on an inevitable road of historical progression. His views on the Soviet Union remained precisely what they had been prior to SPHINX and he was now in a far better position to destroy the ramshackle bolshevik empire whenever he chose.

Around the world, Japanese officers in Tokyo had watched the progress of SPHINX closely and, possessing as they did the finest carrier striking force of the day, they had been particularly impressed by the results of the Royal Navy's attack on Cadiz. Few believed that Churchill could give real substance to his words regarding Singapore and Malaya; most considered that pre-emptive strike was desirable, sooner rather than later, if Japan was to obtain access to the raw materials she needed to pursue her war with China.

NOTES

1. From this point onwards most of the narrative projects the course of events as they might well have been.
2. The agent was Rudolf Rössler, a publisher by profession, and the information he supplied was entirely reliable. After Operation BARBAROSSA his warnings were

taken seriously and he was recruited by Soviet intelligence. 'Lucy' was his Soviet codename, and I have therefore anticipated events a little. The master spy never revealed the identity of any of his high-ranking contacts, taking the secret to the grave with him in 1958.

3. In reality, *Illustrious*'s Swordfish crippled the Italian battlefleet in Taranto harbour that night, sinking one battleship, causing another to be beached and putting a third out of action for six months. In these circumstances SPHINX 2 would almost certainly have been postponed indefinitely.

4. Operation COMPASS followed the course described up to this moment.

5. This episode has been based on an incident which took place at Halfaya Pass on 27 May 1941 when only nine Matildas of C Sqn 4 RTR inflicted a startling reverse on the entire 5th Light Division.

BIBLIOGRAPHY

Hogg, Ian V., *The Illustrated Encyclopedia of Artillery* (London, 1987)

Macintyre, Donald, *The Battle for the Mediterranean* (London, 1964)

Perrett, Bryan, *Wavell's Offensive* (Shepperton, 1979)

Perrett, Bryan, *Knights of the Black Cross: Hitler's Panzerwaffe and its Leaders* (London, 1986)

CHAPTER 3

Operation WOTAN
The Panzer Thrust to
Capture Moscow
October–November 1941

JAMES LUCAS

Introduction

By the Autumn of 1940, the nations of Europe's western seaboard had been defeated by Germany, leaving only the British Isles unconquered and defiant, although weak. Knowing that Britain posed no real threat Hitler decided to wage war against the Soviet Union on the pretext that the eastern provinces of Germany had to be beyond the range of Red Air Force bombers. When that war was concluded and the Reich held an area of western Russia running from the Volga to Archangel, not only would eastern Germany be safe from air attack, but Russia's bread basket, the Ukraine, would be within the German *cordon-sanitaire* as would the Don basin's industrial complexes. The remnant of the defeated Red Army would be on the eastern side of the Volga and Germany's supremacy would be unchallengeable.

In September, Hitler briefed the leaders of the German Armed Forces and of the Army High Command (OKW and OKH). Those officers must have been surprised that the Führer did not name a point of maximum effort or Schwerpunkt, the strategic objective to be gained. Instead he named three targets, allocating one to each of the Army Groups which were to fight the war: Leningrad for Army Group North, the Ukraine for Army Group South, and for Army Group Centre, Moscow – but only after the northern and southern goals had been gained. Hitler declared Moscow to be a geographical term with no military significance. His decision broke with the German Army's basic precept that Field armies march separately but strike together. In Russia his Army Groups would march separately and would also strike separately. Such a policy might have been a recipe for disaster but, by a fateful paradox, the flawed strategy of the command hierarchy of the Red Army, the Supreme Stavka, saved Hitler from the consequences of this dilettante folly.

On 22 June 1941, the German armed forces attacked the Soviet Union. The opening operations were everywhere successful and the course of the campaign in the first months was marked by the encirclement of huge numbers of Red Army formations by fast-moving panzer forces. The scale of the Soviet losses in those first encirclements, together with the far greater casualties inflicted in the encirclements that followed in quick succession, convinced the German High Command that the Red Army had been defeated west of the Dnieper, as Hitler had planned. If there was any doubt felt at OKH it was that the advance of Germany's armies was still being contested, and by previously unidentified Soviet military formations. These were, undeniably, fresh troops but were discounted by the High Command as Stalin's last reserves. The war on the Eastern Front was as good as over.

The Führer Designs a Revolutionary Battle Plan

During the middle week of August 1941, OKH sent Hitler a memorandum urging that the Germany Army's principal aim should be the capture of Moscow by Army Group Centre. The Führer rejected that recommendation. He was working on Operation WOTAN, a revolutionary offensive, and saw from the dispositions on the map of the Eastern Front the strategy he would follow. Soviet main strength was concentrated to the west of the capital and could be easily reinforced, making frontal attacks to capture the city from the west both costly and time-consuming. The Führer recalled that during the Great War it become standard practice to infiltrate round the enemy's flanks in order to attack an objective from the rear. His revolutionary battle plan would do just that. Faced by a strong defence west of Moscow he would withdraw the four Panzer Groups serving on the Eastern Front and concentrate them into a single Panzer Army Group. This he would unleash and send marching below Moscow and on an easterly bearing. At Tula it would change direction and thrust north-eastwards across the land bridge between the Don and Volga rivers before taking a new line and driving northwards to capture Gorki, some 400km east of the capital. After a short pause for regrouping, a co-ordinated attack by Army Group Centre from the west and Panzer Army Group from the east would capture Moscow.

Stavka would certainly react violently when the panzer hosts thundered across the steppes but the Führer would limit their ability to counter WOTAN. He would launch massive offensives using the infantry armies on the strength of the three Army Groups. These would tie down the Red

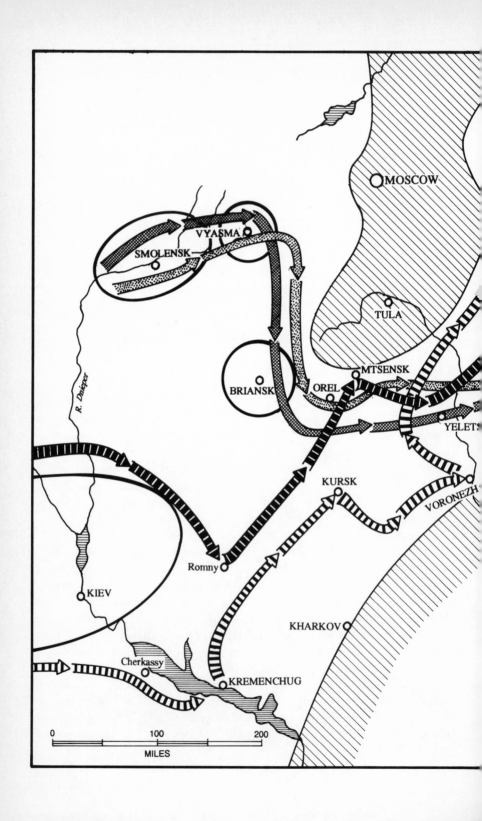

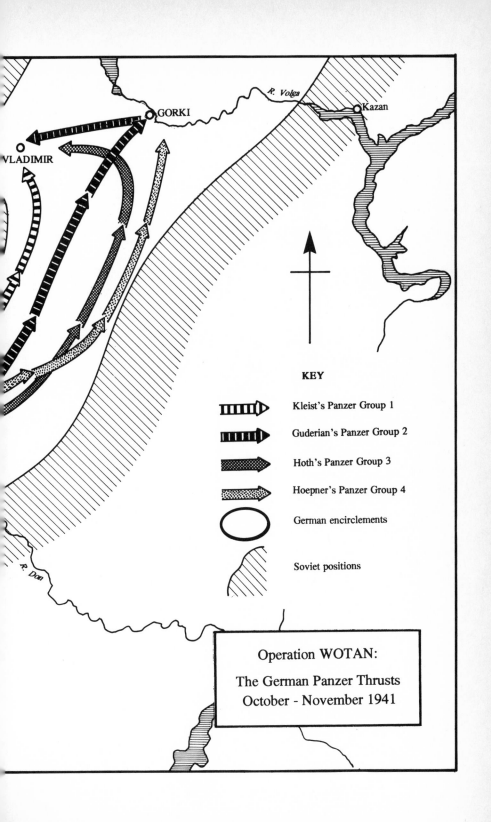

R. Volga

Kazan

GORKI

VLADIMIR

R. Don

KEY

Kleist's Panzer Group 1

Guderian's Panzer Group 2

Hoth's Panzer Group 3

Hoepner's Panzer Group 4

German encirclements

Soviet positions

Operation WOTAN:

The German Panzer Thrusts
October - November 1941

armies and prevent Stavka from moving forces to challenge Panzer Army Group's thundering charge.

The longer the Führer looked at the map the more confident he became that his plan could take Moscow well before winter. He knew that the terrain of the land bridge between the Don and Volga rivers was good going for armour. The roads in the area were few and poor but the General Staff handbook considered that the sandy soil of the land bridge allowed movement even by wheeled vehicles off main roads and across country. The one caveat was that short periods of wet weather could make off-road movement difficult and longer spells could make the terrain impassable. The presence of so many rivers might slow the pace of the advance but that difficulty could be overcome by augmenting the establishment of panzer bridging companies with extra pioneer units. A revolutionary battle plan demands a revolutionary supply system and Hitler was convinced that he had found one. Isolated even from his closest staff members he worked on the final details of Operation WOTAN.

Kesselring Becomes Commander of the Panzer Army Group

A telex sent on the morning of 23 August brought Field Marshal Kesselring to Hitler's East Prussian headquarters. The commander of Second Air Fleet supposed he had been summoned to brief the Führer on the progress of air operations on the central sector, but Hitler's first words astonished him.

'I have decided to mount an all-out offensive for which all four Panzer Groups on the Eastern Front will be concentrated into a huge armoured fist – a Panzer Army Group. This you will command.'

To Kesselring's protests that he was no expert in armoured warfare the Führer replied that he did not want one. Such men were always too far forward and out of touch – Rommel in the desert was a typical example of the panzer commander. No, he needed an efficient administrator and he, Kesselring, was the best in the German Services.

The Luftwaffe commander then asked how the Panzer Army Group was to be supplied and was told 'by air-bridge'. The entire strength of the Luftwaffe's Ju-52 transport fleet, all 800 machines, would be committed, and each machine would not only carry two tons of fuel, ammunition or food but would also tow a DFS glider loaded with a further ton of supplies. Thus 2400 tons would be flown in in a single 'lift'. Hitler maintained that each flight would be so short that the Ju pilots could fly three missions in the course of a single day and this would raise the total of supplies to 7200 tons daily; more than enough to nourish the Panzer Army Group in its advance.

'There will be losses. Aircraft will crash, others will be shot down ...'

'And those losses will be made good.'

Hitler then went on to explain that in the event of a sudden emergency requiring even more supplies, every motor-powered Luftwaffe machine would be put into service as would also the giant gliders which had been built for the invasion of Britain. Supplies would be dropped by parachute or air-landed from the Ju transports. Hitler's remarkable memory recalled that ammunition boxes could be thrown from slow-flying transports at a height of four metres without damage but warned Kesselring that there was a high breakage rate – one in five – among the 250 litre petrol containers, unless these were specially packed. Once the panzer advance was rolling the Ju's would no longer need to para-drop or air-drop the supplies but would land and take off from the salient which the Panzer Army Group had created. As the salient area expanded lorried convoys would be re-introduced. Aware of the vast amount of fuel that would be needed for the forthcoming operation, Kesselring asked what Germany's strategic fuel reserves were and was told that these were sufficient for two to three months, including the requirements of WOTAN.

Hitler's hands, moving across the map on the table, demonstrated where the break-through would occur and then illustrated the drive towards Gorki. The momentum of the attack must be maintained by a pragmatic approach to problems and Kesselring was to ensure the closest liaison between the flight-controllers of both Services so that the pilots had no difficulty in finding the landing zones. It was the duty of the Luftwaffe to give total support to the Army by dominating the skies above the battlefield and ensuring that the ground units were protected from attack at all times.

Hitler assured the Luftwaffe commander that the weather forecast was for hot, sunny weather which meant that ground conditions would be excellent. Operation WOTAN should last no more than eight weeks so that the offensive would be in its last stages before the onset of the autumn rains, and would be concluded before winter set in. Long-range meteorological forecasts predicted that the present dry weather would continue until late in October.

The Führer explained that Supreme Stavka had moved the bulk of its forces to counter the blow which they anticipated would be made by von Rundstedt's Army Group South.

'We shall fox Stavka by maintaining pressure in the south but using mainly infantry forces. Stalin will have to reinforce that sector, whereupon Army Groups North and Centre will each open a strong offensive. While the Soviets are rushing troops from one flank to another your Panzer Army Group will open Operation WOTAN, will fight its way through the crust of Red Army Divisions and reach the open hinterland. From there the exploitation phase of the battle will begin and from that point you should encounter diminishing opposition. Of course, your advance will be contested but the presence of so great a force of armour behind the left flank of Westfront will unsettle the enemy. But the Russians, both at troop and at Supreme Command level, react slowly ... so make ground quickly before they realise the danger you represent.'

Hitler then declared that once he had briefed the other senior commanders, planning for WOTAN could begin. Because the individual Panzer Groups were at present committed to battle they could not be withdrawn and concentrated in toto. X-Day for each Panzer Group would depend upon how quickly it could be removed and regrouped but he thought that they should all be ready to begin WOTAN by 9 September. In answer to Kesselring's concern that the infantry armies would bear the brunt of battle without panzer support Hitler stressed that a number of armoured battalions and, possibly, some independent regiments would still be with the three Army Groups. He did agree that those panzer formations would have to act as 'firemen', rushing from one threatened sector to another.

In farewell, Hitler grasped Kesselring's hands in his own, gave him the piercing look mentioned by so many of those who met the Führer and told him that Operation WOTAN offered the armies in the East the chance of total victory within a few months, but only if each officer and man was prepared to give of his utmost for the duration of the offensive. National Socialist fanaticism, the Führer concluded, would produce the victory that was within the Field Marshal's grasp.

'Remember, Kesselring. The last battalion will decide the issue.'

On 24 August, in the Warsaw headquarters of Second Air Fleet, Kesselring addressed the leaders of the formations he was to command and told them that for the opening assault Panzer Groups Guderian, Hoth and Hoepner were to attack shoulder to shoulder in order to create the widest possible breach. That break-through would be succeeded by the pursuit and exploitation phase which would produce a salient running up to Gorki.

'To create that salient,' said Kesselring, 'Guderian and Hoth will form the assault wave, Hoepner and Kleist will line the salient walls, and in addition to that task will also defeat enemy attacks made against those walls and will replace losses suffered by the spearhead groups'.

'Each Division has Luftwaffe liaison officers but at Panzer Group and Panzer Army Group level there will be a Luftwaffe Signals Staff unit to ensure total success in the matter of locating and supplying your units.

'I need not tell you how to fight your battles. You have grown up with the blitzkrieg concept, so any words of mine would be superfluous. We know our tasks. Let us to them and achieve the Führer's aim: victory in the East before winter.'

Hitler Briefs the OKH Staff

On Friday 29 August, Hitler addressed the OKH staff. A summary of his briefing reads:

'The successes of the three Army groups now make Moscow the principal objective ... Operation WOTAN will open on 9 September and will consist of separate offensives by the infantry Armies of each Army Group as well as by a Panzer Army Group working towards the capture of the Soviet capital ... The Panzer Groups will concentrate into the Panzer Army Group as they conclude present operations ...

'Speed is vital ... no pitched battles ... strong enemy resistance is to be bypassed and left to the infantry and the Stukas to overcome. Panzer Divisions will consist of fighting echelons only ... No second echelon soft-skin vehicle supply columns ... Troops to live off the land as far as possible. Once the first issues of petrol, rations, ammunition and spares are run down, subsequent supplies will be air-landed or air-dropped. The infantry formations serving with the Panzer Groups will foot march unless the railways can be put into operation to "lift" them.'

The first withdrawals to thin out the panzer formations so that WOTAN could open on 9 September were halted abruptly on the 8th, when the armies of Marshals Timoshenko and Budyenny opened 'spoiling' offensives. These were incompetently handled and were defeated so thoroughly that only weeks later Budyenny's South West Front had been destroyed around Kiev with a loss to the Russians of 665,000 prisoners. That defeat was followed by others at Vyasma and Briansk. The intensity of the fighting and the vast distances over which military operations were conducted during those encirclements tied up the Panzer Groups so completely that OKH's intention to thin them out could not begin again until mid-September. As a result concentration could not be completed simultaneously by all the Groups, and each went into what had now become the second stage of WOTAN on various dates. Those Panzer Groups, urged on by a jubilant Hitler, were unrested, unconcentrated, under strength and driving vehicles that needed complete overhaul but each advanced towards its start lines. It was Friday 28 September, and it was fine and sunny.

Operation WOTAN Begins

On X-Day Panzer Group 1 was in action on the southern side of the encircling ring around Kiev; Guderian's Group 2, leaving XXXXVIII Corps at Priluki, had disengaged from the encirclement's northern side and had concentrated around Glukhov; while Panzer Groups 3 and 4 were still deeply committed to the battles at Briansk and Vyasma. The long advance to battle which they would have to undertake meant that they would enter late into the second stage of WOTAN. Guderian, impatient to march, decided that if the other groups were not in position by X-Day then he would open the operation without them. His formations moved forward, and at dawn on the misty morning of 30 September, the order came: 'Panzer marsch'. Guderian named as his Group's first objective the road and rail communications centre of Orel. General Geyr von Schweppenburg's XXIV Panzer Corps, with 3rd and 4th Panzer Divisions in the line, advanced up the Orel road, while Lemelsen's XXXXVII Panzer Corps, fielding 17th and 18th Panzer Divisions, flooded across the lightly undulating terrain to the north of the highway.

Guderian's soldiers were confident. On the eve of the offensive Heini Gross, serving in one of the panzer battalions of 4th Division, wrote 'Last evening the Corps Commander visited us. There were several speeches and then we all sang the "Panzerlied". Very, very moving. Tomorrow at 05.30 we open the attack which will win the war.'

Guderian's first blows smashed the left wing of Yeremenko's Front and within a day had crushed Thirteenth Red Army. Soviet counter-attacks launched by two Cavalry Divisions and two Tank Brigades were flung back in disarray by 4th Panzer Division. Through the gap which had been created XXIV Corps struck for Sevsk, captured it and drove on towards Orel while XXXXVII Corps swung north-eastwards for Karachev and Briansk. To the north of Guderian, von Weichs' Second Infantry Army brought about the collapse of Yeremenko's right wing when it split asunder the Forty-third and Fiftieth Red Armies. Within two days Panzer Group 2 had driven 130km through the Soviet battle line against minimal opposition. A breach had been made between Orel and Kursk and Kesselring directed the other Panzer Groups to reach and pass through 'Guderian's Gap', in order to begin the exploitation phase of WOTAN. That order drove Kleist's Panzer Group 1 northwards from the Kiev ring and was to send Groups 3 and 4 southwards once the main part of their forces had been withdrawn from the Vyasma encirclement battles.

On 2 October, the first air drop was made to Guderian's Group. Friedrich Huber in a Flak battery recalled, 'Fighter aircraft circled above us to drive off any Russian machines. Then the Ju-52s flew in, approaching from the west at a great height, descended lower and circled. They roared low above our heads, the yellow identification stripe [carried by aircraft on the Eastern Front] glowing in the sunlight. A cascade of boxes and the first flight climbed, circled and flew back westwards. In less than ten minutes forty Ju's had supplied us. Another flight of forty came in, delivered and flew off to be followed by a third wave. This is an idea of the Führer, of course. Simple and effective, swift and efficient . . .'

Stavka's reaction to the 2nd Panzer Group attack was sluggish and the weak tank attacks against XXIV Corps were repulsed with heavy loss.

Guderian's Group gained ground at such pace that it was confidently believed the hard crust of the Soviet defence must have been cracked. But it had not. Supreme Stavka ordered that Tula, on the southern approaches to Moscow, was to be held to the last, and the fanatical Soviet defence of the area between that city and Mtsensk brought the first check to 2nd Panzer Group's drive.

Kesselring, who had been elated at the fall of Orel on 3 October, intended to capitalise on that success by changing WOTAN's thrust line. Hitler had ordered this to be north-easterly: Dankov–Kasimov–Gorki. That original direction Kesselring now changed so that it marched northwards from Orel, via Mtsensk and Tula, to attack Moscow from due south.

Guderian's Panzer Group Checked at Mtsensk

It was Colonel Katukov's armour positioned south of Mtsensk that checked Guderian. A post-battle report, by the staff of XXIV Panzer Corps described the first two days of battle:

'The unit confronting us on the Tula road was 4th Tank Brigade equipped with T34s fresh from the factory. We had met this tank type before but never in such numbers. It is indisputable that the T-34 is superior to our panzers. We overcame them by calling for Stuka strikes and by setting up lines of our 88mm anti-aircraft guns and employing these in a ground role.'

Kesselring's disobedience of Hitler's order forbidding Panzer Army Group to become involved in pitched battles had resulted in Guderian's drive faltering. To retrieve the situation OKH moved Second Infantry Army from 2nd Panzer Group's left flank to its right and gave the infantry force the task of capturing Tula. Guderian's Group, relieved on 7 October, then raced for its next objective, Yelets to the north-west of Voronezh and some 160km distant. Its advance was still unsupported. The other Panzer Groups had still not yet reached the breached area.

Hitler had correctly forecast that Stavka's slow reaction to WOTAN would allow the Panzer Army Group to gain ground swiftly and Guderian met little organised opposition *en route* to Yelets. It was principally ill-trained local garrisons reinforced by untrained factory militias who came out to contest the German advance. Lacking adequate training they were slaughtered.

The crossing of the Olym river might have delayed Guderian more than the Russian enemy, but Hitler's insistence upon extra pioneer units to accompany the Panzer Groups had proved him right and six tank-bearing bridges were erected in a single day. On 11 October Guderian's reconnaissance detachments entered the outskirts of Yelets and quickly captured the town. The leading elements pressed on: the next water barrier was the mighty Don where Panzer Group 2 could expect to meet serious resistance unless the river could be 'bounced'. For the Don crossing Guderian demanded the strongest Stuka support. His Divisions moved towards the river ready to cross on 14 October.

At dawn on that day the Stukas, the Black Hussars of the air, flew over the battle area and systematically destroyed everything which moved on the Don's eastern bank. Yelets came within the defence zone of Voronezh and was ringed by deep field fortifications and extensive mine fields. 'We attacked under cover of a smoke screen across a vast, flat and open piece of ground towards the Don,' explained Hauptmann Heinrich Auer. 'On our sector the bluffs were over 100 metres high but upstream where they were almost at water level the Pioneers constructed bridges. We motorised infantry crossed in assault boats, then scaled the bluffs to storm the bunkers and trenches. The Stukas had bombed the Ivans so thoroughly that they were ready to surrender . . .

'It is not true that the crossing was easy. It was not but at its end we had broken the Don river line. Our panzers crossed the first bridge at about 1400hrs and came up to support us. Together we fought all that night and most of the next day. By the afternoon of the 15th we had reached the confluence of the Don and the Sosna, to the west of Lipetsk, and dug in there. The panzers left us at that point and wheeled north towards Lebyedan . . .'

Kleist Moves North

On 3 October, Kesselring ordered Kleist's Panzer Group 1 to advance on a broad front, '. . . left flank on Kursk and the right on Gubkin . . . to drive north-eastwards to gain touch with Guderian at Yelets'. Once he was in position on Guderian's right Kleist was next to strike south-eastwards and capture Voronezh before changing direction again, northwards to create the western wall of the salient.

Kleist's Group, like Guderian's, had not had to cover such vast distances as either Hoth or Hoepner but its advance had been slowed by deep mud and by a surprising fuel famine. A mechanical defect in Elekta, the ground identification signal apparatus, caused the Ju transports to overfly Kleist and to airdrop their cargoes over Guderian. It took nearly four days to identify and to rectify that fault, by which time Kleist was so short of fuel that his Group's advance was reduced to that of a single Panzer Company. Drastic shortages call for radical action and Kesselring's solution was direct. Every Heinkel III in VIII Air Corps was loaded with fuel and ammunition and the massed squadrons touched down on the Kursk uplands at Swoboda where Kleist's Group had halted. A single mission was sufficient to replenish it and the Divisions resumed their drive across the open steppe-land.

1. In June 1940, Winston Churchill inspects thin Channel coast defences, which were all part of an elaborate bluff. *(Imperial War Museum)*

2. The German invaders: Adolf Hitler with *(centre)* General Rommel, and General Kesselring.

3. German troops among burning British fuel oil tanks.

4. Guderian and the staff of Panzer Group 2 hold an 'O' Group by the side of the road to plan the next objective during Operation WOTAN.

5. A Column of von Kleist's Panzer Group 1 under attack during the fighting around Voronezh.

6. A plane from the carrier *Illustrious* makes a direct hit on a Japanese destroyer during the Battle of the Arabian Sea, 5 November 1942, in which Admiral Syfret avenged the British defeat at the Battle of Dondra Head in April.

7. Admiral Yamamoto ponders the dilemmas of Operation ORIENT. *(Imperial War Museum)*

8. Hitler and Mussolini receive advice from *(left)* Field Marshal Kesselring and *(right)* Field Marshal Keitel.

9. Battleships of the Mediterranean Fleet with a Swordfish torpedo bomber circling overhead

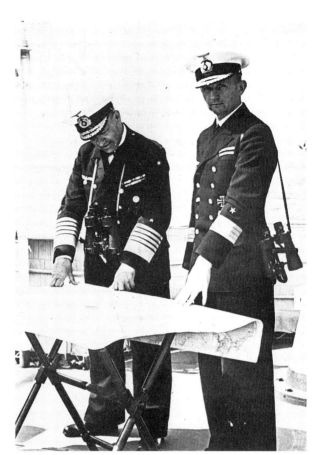

10. Admirals Raeder and Dönitz debate strategy. *(Robert Hunt Library)*

11. Hitler warily studies the rivals Dönitz and Göring. *(The Hulton Deutsch Collection)*

12. Allied convoy in mid-Atlantic.

On 14 October Panzer Group 1 forced a crossing of the Olym downstream from Guderian, and in the area of Kastornoye the point units of 1st and 2nd Groups met. Later that afternoon the main force of both groups linked up and a solid wall of armour extended from Gubkin to Yelets. Kleist Group moved out immediately to capture Voronezh but that city was not to be taken by *coup-de-main*. It was a regional capital with half a million citizens, most of whom worked in its giant arms factories. As in the case of Mtsensk, Stavka ordered Voronezh to be held at all costs, intending that Mtsensk be the northern and Voronezh the southern jaw of a Soviet pincer. Those two jaws would be massively reinforced and, when the Red Army opened its offensive, they would trap the Panzer Army Group and destroy it.

Hoepner Struggles to Reach Guderian's Gap

Hoepner's Panzer Group 4 had been so heavily engaged in the encirclement operations at Smolensk and in the continuing fighting around Vyasma that it could only withdraw individual Panzer Regiments from the battle line. Acting upon Kesselring's orders these marched southwards to gain contact with Guderian now driving hard for Yelets.

On the Mtsensk sector Vietinghoff grouped his XXXXVI Panzer Corps in support of Second Infantry Army which was fighting desperately against the heavily reinforced Fiftieth Red Army. Stalin had ordered that Soviet formation in order to hold Mtsensk and Tula and form the northern pincer of Stavka's planned counter-offensive. When Stumme's XXXX Corps reached Vietinghoff he handed over the task of supporting Second Army and struck eastwards across the Neruts river, passed south of Khomotovo and halted at Krasnaya Zara where he positioned his Corps on Guderian's left flank. Detained by the Vyasma battles and slowed by mud, neither Stumme's XXXX nor Kuntzen's LVII Panzer Corps had gained touch with Vietinghoff by the evening of 14 October, but late that night, to the west of Guderian's Gap, the first elements of both Corps reached their concentration areas and were promptly struck by the first heavy Autumn rainstorm.

'That night it rained,' wrote Lt Col Brentwald of LVII Panzer Corps Staff. 'We have had some rain since the beginning of September but this was not like anything we had experienced before. This was a monsoon which lasted all night and throughout the next day with no let up ... The mud it produced was knee-deep ... the soil soaked up the rain like a sponge. A primaeval force of nature and not the might of the Russian enemy holds us fast ...'

Throughout 15 October, although XXXX and LVII Corps were held fast in the mud, XXXXVI Corps was still moving over ground that had not yet been churned up. Vietinghoff swung towards Yefremov where his advance struck and dispersed the Twenty-first and Thirty-eighth Red Armies, both reinforced by workers' battalions armed with Molotov cocktails and other primitive anti-tank devices.

Hoth Reaches Guderian's Gap

Like Hoepner's Group, Hoth's Group 3 disengaged piecemeal from the Vyasma operation, then concentrated and began to march southwards, *en route* to 'Guderian's Gap'. Its passage, already slow across torn-up battle-fields and Army Group Centre's supply routes, was further delayed by clinging mud as it struggled forward to gain touch with the other Panzer Groups.

'Thank God for Russian forests,' commented Panzer Captain Wolfgang Hentschel. 'Their tree trunks are the material from which the Pioneers build corduroy roads across the mud. It is over those slippery, undulating, wooden paths that our vehicles slither forward. The pace of our advance, and remember this is without any enemy opposition at all, has sunk to less than 20km a day where once it had been 240. We all pray for hot, dry weather.'

During the second week of October the ground dried sufficiently and Hoth drove his Group forward at top speed. Kesselring's dispositions for the advance of Panzer Army Group to Gorki had long been redundant, but a rearrangement brought Panzer Groups 2 and 3 shoulder to shoulder forming the assault wave with 4 and 1 preparing to line the eastern and western salient walls respectively.

On the evening of 14 October Hoth's Group gained touch with the others and halted at the junction of the Sosna and Don rivers with Hoep-ner's Group on one flank and Guderian's on the other. 'Our pioneers worked all night bridging those rivers,' said Hentschel, 'so that the advance could press ahead.'

Panzer Army Group Drives on Gorki

Early in the morning of 16 October, Kesselring set up his Field headquarters in Yelets and co-ordinated the great wheeling movement which would bring the Panzer Groups in line abreast ready to advance towards Gorki, some 650km distant. WOTAN was behind schedule and it worried him, for every day's delay served the enemy's purpose. When his subordinates demanded time to rest their men and to service their vehicles he could give them only three days. WOTAN's third phase had to open on 18 October. Military Intelligence had indicated that the Soviets were about to carry out a major withdrawal and Panzer Army Group had to be ready to exploit any weakness shown by the Red Army during that retreat.

On his flight to Yelets the Field Marshal had seen below him little blobs of armoured vehicles still held fast in mud produced by the rain of the previous days. Those imprisoned panzers were a terrible warning of what could happen – what was in fact to happen when snow fell early on the 18th covering the battlefield to a depth of 10cm. During the afternoon a thaw cleared the snow but produced mud compelling a postponement of Stage 3. During the night temperatures fell hardening the ground and raising the spirits of the panzer troops who knew that soon they would be able to move again. Working by floodlight the crews smashed off the mud clods that clogged the tracks so that by 0200hrs columns of armour, with headlights blazing, were rumbling across the frozen ground.

The series of battles leading up to Gorki created a period of bitter fighting, of relentless attack and desperate defence; a time in which mud held fast the panzer formations until hard frost freed them. Weeks in which the sable candles of smoke rising in the still autumn air marked the pyres of burning tanks. In essence, the course of operations from 18 October to the end of the month was characterised by the Soviets being confined to the towns along the salient walls from which they mounted furious attacks against the panzer formations ranging across the open countryside and destroying such opposition as they met. In its advance from Yefremov via Dankov to Skopin, Panzer Group 1 was so fiercely attacked by Red forces striking out of Novmoskovsk, that Guderian was compelled to detach Geyr's XXIV Corps to support Kleist until an infantry Corps reached the area. A similar action was fought at Ryazan against an even heavier offensive, supported by troops of the Moscow Front, switched on internal lines from the west to the east flank. Panzer Group 1 was fortunate in being aided by nature on the Ryazan sector. The river Ramova was not a single stream but a mass of riverlets running through marshland – a perfect barrier against Soviet armour striking from the west and from the north-west. Kleist needed only to patrol on his side of the river and concentrated the bulk of his force on the high ground between the Ramova and the Raga, the latter river forming the boundary between Panzer Groups 1 and 2.

Guided by reconnaissance aircraft and supported by Stukas the panzer formations of each Group dealt with any crisis which arose on a neighbour's flank. An analysis of Russian tank tactics highlights the difference between the Red Army's highly skilled, pre-war crews and its more recently trained men. A post-battle report stated:

> The enemy's second attack (on the right flank) made good use of ground, coming up out of the shallow valley of the river and screened by the low hills on the eastern side of the road. This wave of machines got in amongst the artillery of 3rd Panzer Division which was limbering up ready to move forward. Hastily laid belts of mines and flame throwers drove back the T 26s ... The third attack was incompetently mounted and a whole tank

battalion moved on the skyline across a ridge. Our anti-tank guns picked
the machines off and destroyed the whole unit ...

Kesselring's handling of his Army Group was masterly and he coolly
detached units to bolster a threatened sector or created battle groups to
strengthen a panzer attack. His energy and presence were an inspiration to
his men.

Guderian's Group, bypassing towns and crushing opposition, moved so
fast that on 27 October, Kesselring was forced to halt it at Murom until
Hoth and Hoepner had drawn level. The towns of Kylebaki and Vyksa fell
to Panzer Group 3 on the following day and Hoth detached his LVI Panzer
Corps to help take the strategic road and rail centre of Arzhamas against the
fanatic defence of a Shock Army specially created to hold it. With the fall of
Arzhamas on the 29th, the Soviet formations opposing Panzer Group 4
broke. As they fled Hoepner sent out his armoured car battalions to patrol
the west bank of the Volga, while 2nd and 10th Panzer Divisions went
racing ahead to pursue the enemy and to gain ground. Wireless signals
advised Hoepner that Bogorodsk had been taken, then that the advance
guard had seized Kstovo and later that day had pushed on to the Volga. But
Hoepner desperately needed infantry reinforcements and Kesselring sent in
waves of Ju-52s, each carrying a Rifle Section. Within five hours two
battalions of 258th Division had been flown in. The 5th and 11th Panzer
Divisions of XXXXVI Corps moved fast to support Stumme's XXXX
Corps while LVII Corps continued with the unglamorous but vital task of
strengthening the salient walls. By 2 November the Panzer Army Group
was positioned ready to begin the final advance to Gorki. Group 1, on the
left, had reached the Andreyevo sector and Guderian was advancing
towards Gorki supported by Hoth's Group 3. Meanwhile Hoepner's Group
4 crossed the Volga against fanatical resistance and massive, all-arms
counter-attacks, and went on to establish bridgeheads on the river's eastern
bank.

On 4 and 5 November a vast air fleet, under Kesselring's direct control,
launched waves of raids upon Gorki. Stukas bombed Russian strongpoints
and gun emplacements, until there was no fire from Soviet anti-aircraft
batteries to deter the Heinkel squadrons which cruised across the sky
bombing Gorki and the neighbouring town of Dzerzinsk at will. The
impotence of the Red Air Force is explained in a Luftwaffe report covering
the period from the opening of WOTAN: 'Soviet air operations were made
initially on a mass scale but heavy losses reduced these to attacks by four or
even fewer Stormovik aircraft on any one time ... [they were] nuisance raids
which had little effect ...' The total number of enemy aircraft destroyed
during the period was 2700 but the report does not state aircraft types:

'... the Soviets could produce planes in abundance but not pilots suffi-ciently well trained to challenge our airmen ...'

Resistance to the infantry patrols of 29th Division which entered both towns on the following day was weak and soon beaten down. Opposition on the eastern flank had been crushed and when Kleist Group secured Andreyevo, to the south-east of Vladimir the western sector was also firm. A German cordon, with both of flanks secure, extended south of the Gorki–Vladimir–Moscow highway.

On 6 November Panzer Army Group Headquarters ordered a defensive posture for the following day in anticipation of massive Russian attacks which would mark the anniversary of the Revolution. Those assaults came in on the 7th and 8th, employing masses of infantry, tanks and cavalry supported by artillery barrages of hitherto unknown intensity. Furious though those assaults were they were everywhere beaten back by German troops who knew they were winning: as one German major put it, 'Thank Heaven for Ivan's predictability. He attacks the same sector at precise intervals. Once his most recent assaults have been driven off we know things will be quiet until the stated interval has elapsed. When that new attack comes in we are ready for it. His tactics are almost routine. A very long preliminary barrage which ends abruptly. Then a short pause and the barrage resumes for five minutes. Under its cover his tanks roll forward and as they come close our panzer outpost line swings round and pretends to flee in panic. The Reds chase the "fleeing" vehicles and are impaled on our anti-tank line ... It never fails ...'

But those days had been ones of deep crisis causing a signal to be sent to all units on the 9th for the defensive posture to be maintained throughout the following two days. Where possible, the time was to be spent in vehicle maintenance so that when the attack opened against Moscow, every possible panzer would be a 'runner'.

Causes for Concern

On 1 November, the Field armies reported to OKH that losses from casualties and sickness were not being made good. Statistically, each German Infantry Division had lost the equivalent of a whole regiment and that scale of losses was also reflected in armoured fighting vehicle strengths. When WOTAN opened only Panzer Group 4 had been at full establish-ment with Groups 1 and 3 at 70% and Panzer Group 2 at only 50%. To OKH the worrying question was whether Kesselring's Army Group would be so drained of strength that it would be too weak to fulfil its mission. On the same day a memo from Foreign Armies (East) advised Hitler that the Red Army in the West had 200 front-line Infantry Divisions, 35 Cavalry Divisions and 40 Tank Brigades, with another 63 Divisions in Finland, the

Caucasus and the Far East. That memorandum went on to warn that
'... the Russian leaders are beginning to co-ordinate all arms very skilfully
in their operations ...' The warning was clear: WOTAN should be
cancelled. Hitler ignored that warning. The operation would continue.

The first week of November was highlighted for the infantry and panzer
forces around Mtsensk and Voronezh by a series of major Red Army
offensives. In Voronezh as in Moscow a military parade was held to celebrate
the Revolution. Marshal Timoshenko took the salute, and the Siberian
Divisions which marched past him in Voronezh went, as those in Moscow
had also done, straight up the Line.

The Intelligence Section summary of 12 November reported, 'The
Siberian troops first encountered (on 7 November) maintained their attacks
until yesterday morning. These attacks were bravely made but badly led.
Prisoners stated that they had been foot marching for six weeks ... There
are 36 Divisions still in the Far East preparing to move westwards ...'

Supreme Stavka had indeed commemorated the anniversary of the
Revolution by launching major offensives. Those at Mtsensk and Voronezh,
made to close 'Guderian's Gap', were the major ones. Whole Divisions of
NKVD (KGB) troops were concentrated in both areas and swung into
action with such *élan* that their initial attacks forced the German infantry to
retreat. But Stavka had made two errors. Firstly, so great a concentration of
men in the cramped Mtsensk appendix restricted the armoured formations,
and secondly, although at Voronezh there was room for manoeuvre the
garrison was equipped with only undergunned, light, T-26 tanks. The
fighting at both places was bitter and both sides knew that its outcome
would depend upon which of them broke first. It was the Soviets, bombed
from the air, pounded by artillery and facing the fire of German soldiers
fighting for their lives, whose morale cracked. Although the NKVD still
marched into machine gun fire as unwaveringly as the Siberians or the
cadets of the Voronezh military academies, the German troops soon sensed
that the enemy's spirit was gone. General Lothar Rendulic, commanding
52nd Infantry Division, wrote 'Stava recognised ... that the standard
Russian infantryman's offensive quality was poor and that he needed the
prop of overwhelming artillery and armour.' In the Mtsensk and Voronezh
battles the Red Army's armour and air support was eroded, and without
those buttresses the Soviet infantry lost heart and were slaughtered. This
paradox – initial fanatical struggles followed by a sudden and total collapse
– was a feature encountered during the subsequent stages of WOTAN. The
failure of the NKVD and the Siberians to crush the Germans affected the
morale of the ordinary Red Army units encountered by Panzer Army
Group.

The presence of the Siberians on the battlefield was countered, politically.

Messages between Berlin and Tokyo were followed by belligerent, anti-Soviet editorials in semi-official Japanese newspapers. These alarmed the Kremlin, which halted abruptly the flow of Siberian Divisions to the west, for these might be needed to fight in Manchuria. The surge of reinforcements from the central regions of the Soviet Union also slowed as Panzer Army Group's advances and Luftwaffe air-raids cut railway lines forcing the Red Infantry to undertake wearisome foot marches to the battle front.

The Westward Advance to Capture Moscow

On 11 November, Sovinformbureau announced 'The battle for Moscow has resumed with attacks ... by the fascist Army Group von Bock ... Despite heavy snow falls waves of [enemy] troops made one assault after another...' On the same day OKH also reported that Maloarchangelsk had been captured without resistance and that German formations were within 7km of Aleksin. It concluded 'Weak enemy attacks indicate that the Red Army's resistance is beginning to crumble ...' A Swiss news agency wrote that the frost-hardened ground had freed the panzers from the grip of the clinging mud.

Concurrent with the opening of Army Group Centre's offensive against Moscow, the leading elements of the Panzer Army Group having spent two days regrouping and replenishing, began their westward drive. Hoepner created a strong battle group from units lining the salient's eastern wall and sent it out to gain the area between Kstovo and Balaxna. Battle group Schirmer not only enlarged the bridgeheads on the Volga's eastern bank but also cut the main east–west railway line.

While Panzer Groups 2 and 3 completed their regrouping, Panzer Group 1, echeloned along the salient's western wall, was defending itself tenaciously against the Red Army's fanatical assaults. Pioneer detachments working at top speed repaired the railway line between Michurinsk and Murom so that Infantry Divisions could be 'lifted' by train to release the panzer formations for more active duties; and one Corps of Kleist's Panzer Group promptly struck and seized Krasni Mayek to protect Panzer Army Group's southern flank.

On 11 November, under a lowering sky, Panzer Group 2 on the right of the Moscow highway and Panzer Group 3 on the left, moved from Gorokovyets to open WOTAN's final phase. The number of 'runners' with each Group had sunk considerably in the bitter fighting but the Field workshops had repaired damaged vehicles and had cannibalised those too badly wrecked to repair. The first waves of Panzer Group 2 disposed 200 machines and Group 3 nearly 240. Throughout the two days of inactivity relays of transport aircraft brought in only shells and fuel. With petrol tanks filled to the brim and covered by a rolling barrage the two Groups advanced side by side westward towards Moscow. At midday the November gloom vanished to be replaced by cloudless blue skies. The Stukas which had been grounded re-entered the battle, taking off from advanced airfields outside Murom, Kylebaki and Vyksa. Opposition to the German advance, light to begin with, grew despite the dive bomber raids, and the combined forces of XXIV and XXXXVII Panzer Corps were able to advance only slowly on the northern side of the highway. The two Corps of Panzer Group 1 made better progress along the southern flank bouncing across marshland hardened by severe frost.

Panzer Group 4's war diary entry of 13 November records that 2nd Panzer Division (XXXX Corps) was attacked south of Kstovo by what was estimated to be a whole Division of Cavalry. The horsemen's assaults to break through the Group's front were crushed with almost total loss, but that series of charges had unnerved many German soldiers who saw with horror wounded horses galloping across the battlefield screaming in pain. Shrapnel had disembowelled others who dragged their entrails across the snow leaving swathes of blood on the white surface.

Panzer Group 1 reported minimal opposition on 16 November, not the furious assaults out of Vladimir and Sudogda that had been anticipated. 1st Group's right-wing Corps, amalgamated with the left-wing Corps of Panzer Group 3, attacked and gained ground quickly. The front-line soldiers realised that the weak opposition they were meeting indicated that the Red Army was all but defeated. One of these soldiers, Sergeant Strauch, said '16 November was bitterly cold. The first issues of winter clothing helped to keep us warm but more warming was the fact that Ivan seemed to be breaking up. We found the bodies of a number of their Commissars, all shot at point-blank range. If the Party isn't executing them then the rank and file are ...'

The recce battalions of Groups 2 and 3 approaching Vladimir met the phenomen of large, organised bodies of Red Army troops standing, lining the roads, waiting to surrender. The officer commanding one group told General Geyr von Schweppenburg, who was riding with the recce point detachment, that revolution had broken out in Moscow, the government had been overthrown and its leaders shot. Von Bock's soldiers were already in the capital's inner suburbs. A flurry of signal messages confirmed the story. General Vlassov, a former dedicated communist, whose Twentieth Army had up to now staunchly defended the north-western approaches to Moscow, was leading a military junta which had sued for peace terms.

'Our battalion and two others were ordered from the armoured personnel carriers and into passenger trains. Russian officers, many with Tsarist cockades, escorted us ... After several hours we reached Moscow's West

Station and marched to the city centre. Units of Bock's Army Group were already there and in Red Square an SS detachment was blowing up Lenin's tomb. At dusk massed searchlights lit up the flag staff over the Kremlin and deeply moved we saw the German War Standard flying at the mast head . . .'

The war in Russia was over. Now there would be a period of tidying up, politically, socially and economically. The population had to be fed, the Red Army demobilised and Russia incorporated into the Reich's New Order. Hitler was triumphant. His battle plan Operation WOTAN had won the War on the Eastern Front.

THE REALITY

In fact, the Germans left it far too late to go to Moscow. The weather closed down upon them, their logistic support was inadequate and the Russians were given time to reinforce Moscow, stop the Germans and throw them back. Never again would the Germans attempt to capture Moscow.

BIBLIOGRAPHY

Erickson, J., *The Road to Stalingrad* (London, 1975)
Haupt, W., *Heeresgruppe Mitte* (Dorheim, 1966)
Morzik, F., *German Airforce Airlift Operations* (Alabama, 1954)
Munzel, O., *Panzer Taktik* (Neckargemünd, 1959)
Rendulic, L., *Soldat in Sturzenden Reichen* (Osnabrück, 1965)
Seaton, A., *The Russo-German War: 1941–1945* (London and New York, 1971; Novato, CA, 1990)
Seaton, A., *The Battle for Moscow* (London, 1971)
Trevor-Roper, H., *Hitler's War Directives* (London, 1964)

CHAPTER 4

Operation ORIENT
Joint Axis Strategy

PETER G. TSOURAS

ORIENT by Chance

The Axis cause had no more tireless advocate than the Japanese Ambassador to Germany, Lieutenant General Oshima Hiroshi, a man of great regard at the highest levels of the Third Reich's leadership. Hitler confided to him to an unprecedented degree. Taking their cue, men like Luftwaffe chief Göring and Foreign Minister Ribbentrop were equally forthcoming. There was little that Oshima did not know of both German plans and the status of German operations, and every bit of it he reported faithfully to Tokyo through the Japanese Foreign Ministry's ciphers. And almost every bit of it was being read by the Americans and British who had broken the Japanese diplomatic ciphers in 1940.

What the Americans passed to the British in the early months of 1942 was enough to daunt even the indomitable Winston Churchill. Oshima's traffic to Tokyo harped on a German–Japanese plan, codenamed ORIENT, to link up somewhere in India. Its genesis was in Hitler's Draft Directive 32 issued on 11 June 1941, less than two weeks before the invasion of the Soviet Union, in the heady days when anything seemed possible for the Wehrmacht. The plan called for a triple attack on the British position in the Middle East coming from Libya against Egypt, from Bulgaria through Turkey against Syria, and from the Caucasus into Persia. But ORIENT had been forgotten when the Wehrmacht faltered in the snows of Russia. Now with the Japanese entry into the war and the ongoing German recovery for the 1942 campaign, ORIENT was back on the table.

If ever there was a straw to break the camel's back, ORIENT seemed just that. For the news everywhere was bad for the Allies. The Soviet winter counteroffensive had run out of steam after driving the Germans back from Moscow, and now German strength was building up for a major summer campaign that the Soviets were not well-prepared to meet. The Americans were still reeling from the wrecking of the Pacific Fleet at Pearl Harbor and the loss of the Philippines save for MacArthur's hopelessly besieged army on the Bataan Peninsula. Four months into the war and the U.S. Navy was still without a battleship in the Pacific.

For the British, the War had become a perpetual series of disasters. Rommel had rebounded after his withdrawal from Tobruk and driven the British beyond Benghazi all the way to Gazala in February. He was now rapidly building up for another go at the Eighth Army over which he had established such a moral ascendancy that the troops had coined a new word for anything well and boldly done, 'a Rommel'. The island bastion of Malta, the stone that lay across Rommel's logistics lifeline, was being battered fearfully from the sky by the German and Italian air forces. Signs of an impending assault on the island were growing. With Malta gone, Axis power could surge into North Africa and seal the eastern Mediterranean to British convoys. Demoralization was beginning to rear its head among the British forces in North Africa. It was already running like wildfire among the population and army of Egypt, which viewed each British setback in the Mediterranean Theatre with increasing glee. The disaffection spread all the way to Iraq where the British had had to put down a pro-Axis coup the year before.

If the situation was grim in the Middle East for the British, it was blood-curdling in the Far East. Two of the Royal Navy's finest ships, the battleship HMS *Prince of Wales* and battle-cruiser *Repulse*, were sunk by Japanese aircraft on 10 December 1941. Far worse was to follow when Singapore, the great naval base in Asia, fell on 15 February to a brilliant Japanese soldier, Lieutenant General Yamashita Tomoyuki. Yamashita had had the temerity to strike the naval base from the land, something that had hardly occurred to the British, earning himself in the process the epithet, 'The Tiger of Malaya'. The Japanese took an unprecedented British prisoner bag in the Malaya campaign – of their total 138,700 casualties, most were prisoners. The Empire rocked to its foundations. And the tremors were felt throughout India, where the Congress Party had come out strongly against the war. That was particularly ominous, for their growing power could destabilize the British rear just when its last bastion was being breached. Even before Singapore had fallen, the Japanese had launched a strong attack on Burma. Now in late March that attack was driving everything before it.

In Berlin, Ambassador Oshima was almost daily bringing the news of Japanese victories to Hitler. He had thought that the growing good fortune of the Axis would confirm Hitler in the execution of ORIENT. Yet Hitler, though interested, had remained ambivalent to the plan, his own brainchild. Pleased as he was with Rommel's accomplishments, he remained fixated on the Russian Front. He had even begun to get cold feet on the assault on

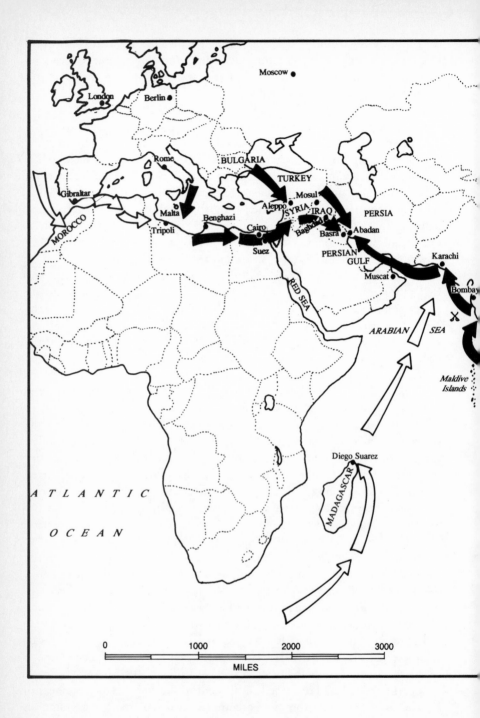

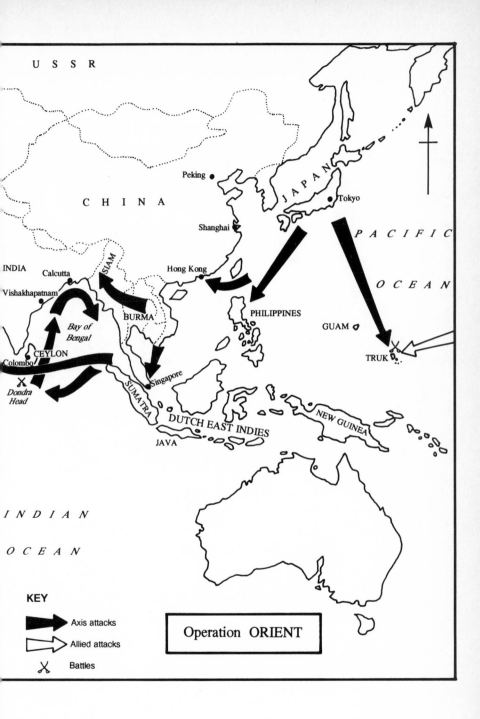

U S S R

C H I N A

Peking •

JAPAN

• Tokyo

Shanghai

Hong Kong

PACIFIC

OCEAN

INDIA

Calcutta

SIAM

Vishakhapatnam

BURMA

PHILIPPINES

GUAM

*Bay of
Bengal*

TRUK

CEYLON

Colombo

SUMATRA

Singapore

*Dondra
Head*

DUTCH EAST INDIES

NEW GUINEA

JAVA

I N D I A N

O C E A N

KEY

Axis attacks

Allied attacks

Battles

Operation ORIENT

Malta, Operation HERCULES. He found easy counsel in his doubts of the cost. The losses among his elite airborne troops in the air assault on Crete still haunted him. Oshima was even more disturbed by the silence on ORIENT from Tokyo. While Oshima was loquacious in his reporting, Tokyo was decidedly laconic if not close-mouthed about its intentions.

To the Americans listening in on his traffic, however, it seemed that by the middle of March, the prospects for ORIENT were still excellent. Oshima had just quoted to Tokyo Ribbentrop's statement on 17 March which the German foreign minister had emphasized by formally reading it: 'Germany would eagerly welcome a Japanese invasion into the Indian Ocean whereby contact between Europe and Asia might be established.' Unknown to them, the Japanese Basic Plan still defined the Pacific as the main theatre of war and the Americans as the main enemy. The attack on Burma was essentially defensive, designed to secure a western flank in the mountainous frontier between Burma and India and slam the door shut on China's final resupply route. Still, Oshima's chatter about ORIENT, particularly the idea that the Germans would pressure the Vichy French authorities of Madagascar to turn over the island to a Japanese expeditionary force, energized Churchill in March to prepare his own expeditionary force from the Home Fleet to seize the island first. British fears were heightened when on 23 March a Japanese expeditionary force captured the Andaman Islands on the eastern curve of the Bay of Bengal. Taken with the distressingly successful Japanese offensive in Burma, the threat of ORIENT appeared all too real. Ambassador Oshima ironically had created far more interest in ORIENT among the Allies than he had among the Axis. That is, until two reconnaissance aircraft in the Indian Ocean came to his aid.

The Battle of Dondra Head

One of the aircraft was from the Japanese aircraft carrier *Hiryu* steaming with the rest of Vice Adm Nagumo Chuichi's First Air Fleet south of Ceylon on 2 April. The victor of Pearl Harbor was leading five of his carriers that had savaged the U.S. Navy's Pacific Fleet, *Akagi, Zuikaku, Shokaku, Hiryu,* and *Soryu.* They were joined by four fast battleships of the Third Battleship Division, 16-inch gun *Haruna, Kirishima, Hiei,* and *Kongo,* and cruisers and destroyer escorts into a major raid in the Indian Ocean to secure the Japanese flank by driving the Royal Navy out of the Bay of Bengal, destroying its bases in Ceylon, and sinking merchant shipping. The First Air Fleet, with its 300 aircraft, was at this moment at a high pitch of efficiency and eagerness. They had been tested and not found wanting.

The other aircraft had flown off the British aircraft carrier *Indomitable* sailing south from Ceylon with the rest of Admiral Sir James Somerville's Eastern Fleet. Somerville, who had just arrived from nerve-wracking duty with the Mediterranean Fleet less than a week before, commanded three aircraft carriers, five battleships, and sixteen cruisers and destroyers. The odds seemed even enough, but Somerville knew better. He had just written, 'My old Battleboats are in various states of disrepair & I've not a ship at present that approaches what I should call a proper standard of fighting efficiency . . .' Of his five battleships, *Resolution*, *Ramillies*, *Revenge*, and *Royal Sovereign* were unimproved 'R' Class First World War relics. The fifth, *Warspite* was also of First War Vintage but had been modernized in the thirties. He was also disappointed in his Fleet Air Arm; *Indomitable* and *Formidable* were relatively new carriers with armoured steel decks, but the third was little *Hermes*. The three carriers had among them barely 57 strike aircraft (all bi-planes), 36 fighters, and all of them outclassed by their Japanese counterparts. He concluded, barely a few weeks before Nagumo's raid, 'The fact is that until I get this odd collection of ships together and train them up they aren't worth much . . .'

Somerville had sallied from Colombo with his fleet to ward off Nagumo with a night air strike if he could; he flinched at exposing his battleships in a pounding match. He had to find Nagumo first. Nagumo was also eager to find his enemy. He still rankled at Admiral Yamamoto's characterization of the Pearl Harbor strike: 'A military man can scarcely pride himself on having "smitten a sleeping enemy"; it is more a matter of shame, simply, for the one smitten.' If the British Eastern Fleet was game, he would be glad to show what he could do in a knock-down, drag-out fight at sea. That is why he had to find Somerville first.

Some 150 miles south of Dondra Head on the tip of Ceylon, the *Hiryu*'s reconnaissance pilot spotted his prey first. Stretched out beneath him was the Eastern Fleet. His counterpart from the *Indomitable* was searching empty sea to the south-east. This is what Nagumo had been waiting for. He paused for a moment as the last of the aircraft left the carriers to remind his staff that this was the first battle in history of carriers against carriers.

It would not be much of a battle. The British carriers had only a few fighters in the air when the Japanese planes shrieked out of the sky at them. Zeros made short work of the few British fighters to make room for their bombers and dive bombers. The air blossomed with black puffs of anti-aircraft fire as the Japanese planes came in, flight after flight, to torment the carriers. But the steel decks were proof against most of the many hits scored. Only little *Hermes* was badly hit, its deck torn open and roaring flames from the holes. Finally it was the turn of the torpedo bombers. They came in steadily against the wildly manoeuvring carriers and dropped their torpedoes. The anti-aircraft crews from the carriers and escorts plucked one torpedo bomber after another out of the air, but there were just too many. The long bubbly lines of the torpedo tracks found their way into the guts of both *Formidable* and *Indomitable*. *Formidable* shuddered with the impacts of six torpedoes and stopped dead in the water. Explosions began ripping holes through the deck from the underside. Soon she was listing badly and on fire. *Indomitable*'s hull groaned with the impact of three torpedoes but kept moving and fighting. She was still alive but slowing down. Now the dive-bombers resumed their attacks and eventually smashed open her deck. She began to burn. More torpedo strikes finished her off, and she went down by the stern. With the Japanese aircraft concentrating on the stricken carriers, Somerville ordered his battleships and cruisers to escape south-west towards a supply base in the Maldive Islands.

But again, Nagumo was ahead of him. The Japanese fast battleships and cruisers were on an intercept course that eventually overtook the British. As old as they were, the British battleships did not even have a fair fight. Refuelled Japanese aircraft pounced on them hours before their battleships could catch up. Repeated strikes sunk the cruiser *Dorsetshire* and damaged the *Revenge* forcing it to fall out of line. The rest of the British ships lost time and speed frantically manoeuvring to ward off the Japanese air strikes. An hour before dusk, the Japanese battleships caught up with Somerville. The air strikes had so harried his force that they were not organized enough for the Japanese to be able to cross the T. *Haruna* picked out *Warspite* and engaged at rapidly closing range. *Kirishima* and *Hiei* concentrated their fire on *Resolution* thousands of yards before the British ship's older guns and fire control systems could hope to respond. Destroyer torpedo strikes from both sides turned the engagement quickly into a *mêlée* of manoeuvring ships. *Royal Sovereign* was hit by a spread and slowed. She quickly received the concentrated fire of the *Kongo* and three cruisers. *Resolution* suddenly blew up with such force that a nearby destroyer, HMAS *Vampire*, was wrecked by the blast. *Warspite* and *Haruna* continued their duel, the British ship taking first blood with a direct hit on the enemy's forward turret. *Ramillies*, now within range, joined in the duel and scored hits.

Despite the cheers about the old *Ramillies*, the battle was already lost. *Royal Sovereign* had been pounded to scrap and then quickly sank to join *Resolution*. *Revenge* was caught limping away by aircraft and sunk as well. The cruiser *Cornwall* went down with her. Three more destroyers were also either sunk or dying. Now the remaining Japanese battleships came to the rescue of wounded *Haruna* with half its guns out of action and half a dozen fires burning.

Kongo's first volley straddled *Warspite*; her second scored. *Kirishima* joined in. *Warspite*'s guns were still well-served and hit back at both ships, sweeping *Kongo*'s bridge and sending it temporarily out of action. *Hiei* challenged *Ramillies* at close range where the British gunners could do more expert harm. *Hiei* shuddered with hits until one of its shells shattered

Ramillies's fire control. Mercifully, night fell quickly enough to rescue *Ramillies* which slipped away. Lurid flashes over the horizon indicated where Admiral Somerville aboard *Warspite* was fighting it out to the end. The survivors of the battle rallied at the Maldive base over the next two days. *Ramillies* was the only capital ship left. Three cruisers and seven destroyers were the only other ships to come in.

Already the airwaves had carried the glory of the new Tsushima back to Japan. Three aircraft carriers, four battleships, two cruisers and four destroyers had gone to the bottom in the greatest naval disaster in British history. The Eastern Fleet was gone. The Japanese had lost one cruiser and three destroyers as well as major damage to the two battleships. For the first time in almost two hundred years, the Royal Navy was no longer master in the Indian Ocean. *Ramillies* and her savaged flock were ordered to abandon Indian waters and seek refuge in a steamy east African river estuary 3000 miles away as Admiral Nagumo turned to complete his mission.

He trailed his coat around defenceless Ceylon, his aircraft badly damaging the naval bases at Colombo and Trincomalee. More raids followed on the Indian east coast itself on Madras, Coconada, and Vizagapatam. His surface ships, aircraft, and submarines sank over 150,000 tons of ships in the waters around Ceylon and the Bay of Bengal. Within a week every surviving merchant ship was bottled up in Indian ports. In one last act of bravado, Nagumo launched a final air raid on the port of Calcutta, leaving it in flames. The exaltation of the First Air Fleet was only barely affected on its return voyage when a British submarine sank the limping *Haruna*.

Nagumo's exploits dazzled Tokyo. For once, Oshima's traffic from home was pulsing with new-found excitement. The Japanese, already drunk on success in the Pacific, were overwhelmed by the sudden opportunities in the Indian Ocean. One more solid blow and British power in Asia would collapse. The Army, as usual, was behind another major strategic outreach, but this time even much of the Navy was carried along in the euphoria of Nagumo's victory. Only Yamamoto opposed the strategic distraction westward, but he was drowned out in the roars of 'Banzai'. His plan to draw the Americans into a crushing naval battle in the central Pacific at Midway was postponed. Much of the great naval concentration he had planned was siphoned of for a major expedition to seize Ceylon. With Ceylon in Japanese hands, India would be cut off and British power would collapse or recede as far as South Africa. Then with its concentrated might, Japan could deal more confidently with the Americans once and for all.

ORIENT Back on Track

In Berlin, the news of the Battle of Dondra Head powerfully seized Hitler's imagination, due much to Oshima's artful telling. For once, he had advance notice of the objective – Ceylon. German prestige demanded that Hitler play as big a role as Japan in burying the British Empire. And the Japanese were asking for a major distraction in the Mediterranean. Within Hitler's grasp lay another British island, to balance the pearl of Ceylon – Malta. His reservations, even about Italian reliability, were swept aside. On 15 April at a hurriedly advanced meeting with Mussolini and their staffs at the Berghof, he set the date for HERCULES: 10 May, two weeks before Rommel was to launch his next offensive, Operation THESEUS. Field Marshal Kesselring assured him that the defences of the island had been broken and that the Royal Navy had abandoned Malta as an operating base. Already, additional airstrips were being constructed in southern Sicily and a combined German–Italian airborne force was in training. Armour for the landing force of two Italian divisions was provided by a regiment's worth of captured Soviet BT-7M tanks on which the Italians had been training hard. Almost as a pleasant afterthought of the possibilities for Rommel once Malta had fallen, Hitler decided to make him a present of another panzer division, the 7th. Within days Rommel's old Ghost Division of the 1940 Blitzkrieg through France had entrained in Russia and headed for Italy.

The British had been on pins and needles for months about HERCULES. Now the ULTRA intercepts were talking incessantly of it. The Italians who had the larger share in the operation were especially forthcoming. It was of small comfort to the British that they could listen in on the Italians because the Germans had forced them to abandon their own ciphers and adopt the German ENIGMA ciphers. The irony was that the British never could break the Italian military ciphers. Now German arrogance was providing them with a godsend of information on the upcoming invasion. But the British could not do much with it. At that moment, British power in the Mediterranean had reached a nadir. Admiral Cunningham's Mediterranean Fleet had been reduced to a few cruisers and destroyers that dared not venture too far from Alexandria. Malta's air defences had been pulverized by Kesselring's Flieger Korps II and the Royal Italian Air Force, 600 planes on almost round the clock missions over the island. A desperate attempt to reinforce the fighter strength of the island was made by ferrying 47 Spitfires from the U.S. carrier *Wasp* to within flying range of Malta. They landed on 20 April, and within three days every one had been destroyed, mostly on the ground by the Axis air forces. All that was left for the garrison commander was to arrange his four infantry brigades as best he could to counter the expected landings. There was one more thing the British could do. They could ferry more Spitfires to the island. This time, protected revetments had been prepared for the new aircraft. On 8 May 62 Spitfires flew in unscathed from the *Wasp* and HMS *Eagle*.

Three days before, another British operation had begun across the huge expanse of Africa. Churchill's decision to secure Madagascar was being efficiently accomplished by the force dispatched in March from Gibraltar: battleship *Malaya*, carrier *Illustrious*, one cruiser and five destroyers under the command of Rear Adm E.N. Syfret. With him was a landing force of one Royal Marine Commando and three infantry brigade groups. In South African waters Syfret was joined by *Ramillies* and the rest of the survivors of Eastern Fleet. On 5 May in what Churchill would later describe as 'a model of amphibious descents', Operation IRONCLAD, the port and capital of Diego Suarez was taken. On the 6th, the nearby naval base of Antsirane fell by a bold *coup de main* conducted by one destroyer and one Royal Marine captain and fifty other ranks. The next day the last resistance collapsed. Although the French authorities refused to surrender, the heart of the island had been secured and with that, Britain had acquired not only a secure flank against the Japanese but also a stepping stone for the future.

The Germans and Italians were at that moment also thinking of island stepping stones. In the dark early morning hours of 10 May, hundreds of German and Italian transports were turning over their motors on the many airstrips of Gerbini airfield in Sicily. Hundreds more fighters, bombers, and dive bombers had already taken off to prepare the way by suppressing the British anti-aircraft defences. The transports and gliders took off as dawn streaked the skies, heading south for Malta with thousands of paratroopers of General Bernhard Ramcke's Parachute Brigade and the Italian 2nd 'Folgore' Parachute Division. They were heading for drop zones on the high ground south of Valetta, the fortress capital of the island. Already at sea were hundreds of landing craft bearing two Italian infantry divisions heading for landings south of Valetta. A second parachute assault would reinforce success as required.

Things began to go wrong almost immediately. The Spitfires were in the air as well; avoiding the enemy fighters, they fell in among the transports and gliders like hawks among pigeons. Barely half the parachute forces were able to land on the island; the rest were either shot out of the sky or fled back to Sicily. Those that made it landed in great disorganization and were slaughtered by the British infantry. The commander of the airborne forces, General Ramcke, gathered several hundred survivors and held out on the high ground. But all the bad luck in HERCULES was stored up for the paratroopers; the amphibious landings were smooth in comparison. The British brigades committed to sector defences could not mass enough forces in any one place. Within twenty-four hours, most of the two Italian divisions were ashore and pushing on Valetta, with two more divisions landing. Ramcke's force was rescued the next day. The Italian corps commander, mindful of years of German contempt, with great good manners squeezed every possible bit of humiliation out of Ramcke.

Kesselring drove his planes back into the fight until the Spitfires had
either been shot out of the sky or driven into their revetments. As the Italian
divisions pressed in on Valetta, the second airborne assault on the harbour
went in a day later than planned, but just at the right time, since the British
defences were cracking everywhere. By the evening of D plus 3 the last
British resistance had been broken. Kesselring reported personally to Hitler
on the fall of the island, but not before Mussolini who had called to offer
condolences on the heavy losses among the German airborne troops. To
Kesselring, Hitler was all icy formality. He would not forgive the marshal
for allowing the Italians to garner the glory and rub his nose in it. He turned
some of that anger on Rommel. The ULTRA intercepts of his messages
almost smoked. Rommel, favourite that he was, was told in no uncertain
terms that a German victory was expected in Egypt, and there would be hell
to pay if Mussolini rode that damned white horse of his in any victory
parade in Cairo.

With Malta in Axis hands, British communications across the Mediterranean ceased. General Sir Claude Auchinleck, C-in-C, Middle East, was
on his own except for what reinforcement could come around Africa. Italian
convoys, practically unmolested now, were pouring supplies and reinforcements into North Africa, including 7th Panzer Division. Much of Flieger
Korps II was transferring to German airfields in support of Rommel.

THESEUS kicked off on 27 May with a great German sweep south of the
series of heavily fortified British positions called boxes while the Italians
attempted to breach the British Gazala line near the coast. The entry of
Flieger Korps II into the battle tipped the scales in the air against the RAF.
Rommel's armour sweep was essentially unmolested as it swung north deep
inside the British positions. At a defended crossroads named Knightsbridge,
Rommel fought the classic tank battle of the war, ably supported by the
Luftwaffe, and crushed the armoured backbone of Eighth Army. The entire
British line sagged as Rommel pushed east. All the boxes and the Gazala
line were quickly abandoned as the rest of the army tried to race the
Germans east or gave up, realizing how deep in the enemy rear they were.
Tobruk fell on 10 June, by now only an abandoned port and fortress. One
after another the divisions of Eighth Army were overrun or bypassed as
Rommel plunged eastward. On 20 June, Rommel's command group drove
quickly through the narrow bottleneck between the sea and the Qatarra
Depression to a place called El Alamein.

It had all gone crash quickly for the British. Almost the whole of the
Eighth Army was lost in the Desert. As the news spread down the Nile, the
Egyptian Army, serving a theoretically neutral state, rose in revolt against
the British, adding shambles and farce to catastrophe. Thousands of British
troops and civilians were trapped and hundreds murdered as the uprising

spread up and down the Nile Valley, for it had been well planned by a group of able and disgruntled Egyptian officers. The Mediterranean Fleet, crammed with refugees, abandoned its base at Alexandria two days ahead of Rommel on 22 June and passed through the Suez Canal into the Red Sea.

Cairo not so much fell as was simply occupied by the Germans on 1 July. The first Germans to enter Cairo were from Captain Fritz von Könen's special Tropical Company of the Brandenburg Regiment, the daring German counterpart of the British SAS. They made their way into British Headquarters in the chaos of evacuation, dressed in British uniforms, and captured most of the staff. By then, it made little difference to the thundering chaos of the collapse of British power in Egypt. The arrival of the Germans did, however, put a sudden end to the bloodier strands of the chaos, the atrocities against British prisoners and civilians. Rommel made an example of one exceptionally zealous Egyptian officer when a German firing squad shot Captain Gamal Abdel Nasser against his own barracks wall. And Mussolini arrived in Cairo almost before Rommel and certainly before the Italian Army. Captain von Könen joked to Rommel that the Italian had arrived so quickly he should be considered an honorary Brandenburger. Il Duce immediately began planning his victory parade and a performance of Verdi's *Aïda* at the Pyramids. He was much put out that the transport carrying his white horse had disappeared.

The Fall of Ceylon

As Rommel was winning his crowning victory at Knightsbridge, over one hundred ships of the Japanese Ceylon expeditionary force, commanded by Admiral Yamamoto Isoroku himself, entered the Bay of Bengal. Nagumo's First Air Fleet had been reinforced with two light carriers. Yamamoto's force also included two battleship divisions of six ships, chief among them the mighty new battleship *Yamato* (with the biggest naval rifles in the world at 18.1 inches), and 15 cruisers, 42 destroyers, 22 submarines, and scores of transports and supply ships. Aboard the transports were the three divisions of the Seventeenth Army now commanded by General Yamashita, eager to replay success in Malaya. The Army had been collected from divisions in the south-western Pacific, originally intended to push the Japanese defensive glacis out into the Solomon Islands. But that plan like the Midway operation was on hold. Two of Nagumo's other big carriers, the *Zuikaku* and *Shokaku* had been left behind with a number of light carriers to deal with anything the Americans could attempt.

General Sir Archibald Wavell, C-in-C India, was in much the same fix as Auchinleck had been. Warned by the American MAGIC intercepts that the Japanese were returning in force, there was little he could do about it. The Royal Navy had abandoned not only the Bay of Bengal but the Arabian Sea

as well. The RAF forces under his command had bitten deep on the
Japanese in the Burma campaign but had been worn down badly. They
could not cover the whole of the Indian coast and Ceylon as well. Worse was
the condition of the Indian Army, driven out of Burma at the end of May as
a demoralized mob of individuals in which divisions, brigades, and battalions had melted away. Only the tenacity of General William Slim at the
Battle of the Rivers had kept a skilful retreat from turning into a massacre.
The British barely escaped as the monsoon rains closed the land route into
India. The remaining forces at Wavell's disposal were few. Some of the best
of the Indian Army had already been sent already to the Middle East where
a good deal of it had just perished in the Western Desert. If it had not been
for the Australian 6th Division on its way home from the Western Desert,
the defence of Ceylon, an island one quarter the size of Great Britain, would
have fallen on one Indian Division alone.

Worst of all, the prestige of British rule in India was in ruins. Singapore,
Dondra Head, Burma, and now the collapse in North Africa had broken
two hundred years of respect for the Raj. Now the Congress Party could
smell victory in the air and the end of British rule. The Viceroy could have
pointed out to the arrogant Congress Party politicians who called on him
with their growing sneers and swelling demands that they exchanged
masters at their own peril. Their little Asian brothers would teach them
genuine Asian fear. The stink of that fear had already begun to paralyze the
civil service and elements of the Indian Army. He had received reports that
young Nehru was preparing to declare Indian independence in the Red Fort
in Old Delhi, site of the last stand of the Sepoy Revolt.

Yamamoto was aware of the political dissension in India, but that would
be handled by the Army. His mission was clear-cut: scour the Bay of Bengal
and the Arabian Sea for the remnants of the Eastern Fleet and destroy them;
harry the coasts of India destroying remaining British naval bases; and,
above all, support General Yamashita's operation to capture Ceylon. The
first part of the mission was easy; there was no Eastern Fleet in the Bay of
Bengal or in the waters around Ceylon. That made the second part of his
mission much easier. His battleships and aircraft carriers deftly supported
the landings of Yamashita's army in the vicinity of Trincomalee on Ceylon's
eastern coast which was sheltered from the south-western monsoon striking
the other half of the island.

The initial landing was made by a battalion of Imperial Japanese
Marines, giants to other Japanese, men six foot and over from the Island of
Hokkaido. They were met by a battalion of Gurkhas, tiny men from the
foothills of the Himalayas. Yamashita later recounted to Yamamoto his
observations after walking over the ground contested by these two battalions, strewn with the corpses of giants and dwarfs. Both battalions

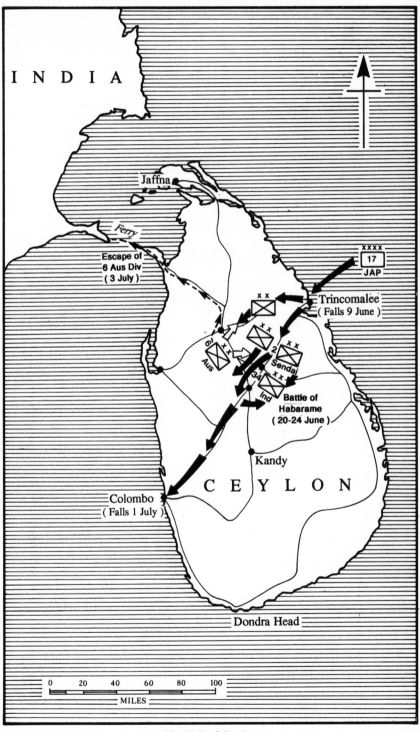

The Fall of Ceylon
8 June - 3 July 1942

consumed each other. He said, 'Ah, it was a fight for the history books. We will have to take these little devils into our service. It looks as if we are going to inherit Britain's empire. We might as well take over the servants, as well.' The rest of the Indian Army brigade around the city put up an equally desperate defence but was eventually driven out as the city burned around them.

With his three divisions ashore, Yamashita plunged across the island to seize Colombo from the landward side; it was the same logic that had led to the fall of Singapore, but it was still valid, even more so now that he had a heavy numerical superiority. His men were doing well, particularly the Sendai Division, one of the better divisions drawn from the Kwangtung Army in Manchuria. He was more surprised by the whipsaw toughness of the Australians, veterans unlike the green division he had captured in Malaya. The decisive battle for the island was fought in the centre of the island. Across it led the shortest route to Colombo, and there the British had concentrated the rest of the island's defenders. In three days fighting, he broke through. The drive on Colombo became a high-speed pursuit where the greatest demands were placed on the legs of his infantry. By the beginning of August, the city had fallen. Yamamoto's naval construction troops had already repaired much of the damage to Trincomalee. Now he had a functioning base from which to operate and to which a steady stream of supply ships began to flow. Colombo's naval facilities had been expertly sabotaged by the British and could not be put back in operation for at least a year. He also had cause for disappointment: the Australians had escaped northward and slipped across the channel to Madras on the mainland.

Now Yamamoto's ships began to range the west coast of India. Nagumo led the First Air Fleet on a great arc of a raid from Ceylon, striking Bombay and Karachi, then skirting the entrance to the Persian Gulf and showing the Rising Sun off Muscat before setting course for Ceylon. It was an exhaustive and largely unexciting raid. The enemy hardly struck back. Off Muscat, he received an urgent message from Yamamoto to return to Trincomalee at once. A great naval battle had flared in the south-western Pacific. The Americans had raided Truk with their whole carrier force and in the ensuing battle, carriers *Zuikaku* and *Soho* had been sunk, and *Shokaku* badly damaged. Now all that stood between Japan and the U.S. Navy were a few light carriers. Yamamoto had gone as far as he ever had in losing his temper when the news first reached him. Barely able to control himself, he said to his staff, 'I counselled against this dispersion of the Navy's strength. Now we have the result. The First Air Fleet is desperately needed to shield Japan but is vacationing off the Persian Gulf, doing great things for our ally by closing off the southern supply route to Russia. Yet are we at war with Russia? No, the Americans are the danger, and they are closer to Japan than we are. And Nagumo is even.closer to Germany than to the homeland!'

Within days Yamamoto departed the Indian Ocean quicker than he had entered it. Save for Vice Adm Ozawa Jisaburo's small Ceylon Force of one light carrier, a battleship, and fifteen cruisers and destroyers, the Japanese were gone – all except Yamashita and his three divisions.

Climax in the Middle East

The settlement of affairs in Egypt historically had been time-consuming for conquerors. Alexander and Napoleon had discovered this, and now so did Field Marshal Rommel. He fumed for two months while the logistics for a further advance into the Middle East had been put in place. His army group was poised to strike into Palestine. Forward elements of his old Ghost Division had been pushed forward across the Sinai to El Arish. The British were in chaos and hardly opposed it. He was itching to slip the leash, but Hitler had pulled it good and tight this time. His advance into Palestine would wait on another pincer moving into place. As he fumed in Egypt, another panzer corps and an infantry corps under newly formed Twentieth Army were crossing Turkey to strike into Syria from Iskanderun. The Turkish Government had surrendered to the change in the correlation of forces as British fortunes collapsed and had allowed the Germans to transit from Bulgaria.

The third prong of ORIENT was at that moment hanging in the balance as the Germans struggled to break through the Soviet mountain barrier into the Transcaucasus and from there to Baku, the Caspian, and then into Persia. Already, the severing of Allied Lend Lease through Persia was having an effect on operations in Russia as the Soviets were standing a seemingly hopeless siege in Stalingrad on the Volga. On 1 August Rommel was informed that Hitler had designated him commander of Army Group Middle East (Heeres Gruppe Mittel Ost) with three armies. His old Afrika Army was reorganised into two armies. To his four German divisions, two more were added from the Balkans and divided into two corps (Afrika Korps and Asien Korps) and designated Fifth Panzer Army. Two of his Italian corps were designated Sixth Army. Twentieth Army concentrating around Iskanderun rounded out the army group of twelve German and six Italian divisions.

On paper the British forces in Palestine looked as if they might have a chance. The X Corps with the tough 2nd New Zealand and 9th Australian Divisions had been moving from Syria into Palestine when Eighth Army collapsed. Allied contingents added 1st Polish Division, 1st Greek Brigade, the Arab Legion and a few hastily raised Jewish home defence brigades. The latter had sprung from the earth as the Haganah organization was eagerly embraced by Auchinleck who had escaped with his staff to Jerusalem. They had their hands full dealing with the local Arabs whipped up by the Grand Mufti of Jerusalem, spouting Axis propaganda from Berlin and driven to a special bloody boldness by British weakness. In Syria there was only 10th Indian Division and a Free French brigade under Ninth Army. British forces in Iraq, Tenth Army, commanded by Lt Gen E.P. Quinan, were ordered to move immediately into Palestine. This small army, however, consisted of only two Indian infantry divisions. In reality, Tenth Army was poorly equipped and supplied. The designation 'army' was more administrative than combat, for it lacked the web of supply, transport, and maintenance units to give it staying power. They had been lost in Egypt. It also was not very mobile.

On 6 September the Fifth Panzer Army burst out of the Sinai and sped north up the coast of Palestine. Rommel's first objective was the twin cities of Tel Aviv and Jaffa which he had chosen as his forward operating base. A large Italian convoy already was approaching the port. Arab Jaffa received the Germans joyously. Jewish Tel Aviv fought house to house, another vicious but short-lived Tobruk for Rommel who had to mark time while his logistics caught up with him. With the ruins of Tel Aviv secured and the Italian convoy quickly unloading, Rommel struck towards Jerusalem from the west with Fifth Panzer Army from the south with Sixth Italian Army. The Indians made him pay for his transit through the Judaean Hills but had no hope of stopping him. The Poles, Greeks, and Arabs held the Italians and even counter-attacked successfully, but had to abandon their attacks when Rommel broke through the hills. Quinan gave up Jerusalem and withdrew towards Amman, but not before the mobile Germans had cut off the retreat of the allied forces south of the Holy City. Rommel entered Jerusalem on 25 September through the same gate as Allenby almost 25 years earlier.

As Rommel invaded Palestine, the German Twentieth Army attacked into northern Syria from Iskanderun. Aleppo fell to one column on 8 September and Latakia one day later to another column as 10th Indian Division fell back quickly to avoid the constant German envelopments. The panzers finally caught up with 10th Indian just north of Homs and chopped it up in a two-day fight. Damascus fell one day after Rommel rode into Jerusalem. The British were in retreat everywhere.

Auchinleck had been relieved after the fall of Jerusalem to be succeeded by General Sir Henry Maitland Wilson, commander Ninth Army. Further defence of Syria and Palestine was out of the question. The best he could do was withdraw forces further eastward into Iraq and hope to concentrate what forces he could for a defence once German logistics began to fray. It was more a race at this point. The panzer corps of Twentieth Army had turned north again after Damascus to strike across northern Syria towards Mosul while Fifth Panzer Army pursued the British towards Baghdad.

Shortly after Damascus fell, one of Twentieth Army's panzer divisions seized the only bridge over the Euphrates for five hundred miles at Deir-ez-zor, the capital of eastern Syria. The road to Mosul was open. Further south at the next bridge over the Euphrates at Ramadi, seventy miles west of Baghdad where the Euphrates road meets the road to Amman, Quinan decided to make a stand. With the river guarding one flank and a large lake guarding the other, his small force had a chance to hold its narrow front. On 13 October, the Germans arrived and began probing. The battered Indian and Anzac brigades put up a good fight warding off Fifth Panzer Army's first attacks. Wilson was pleased; he desperately needed good news. With the Persian Gulf supply route closed to all but the most daring convoys, his back was already to the wall. But he had not counted on Rommel's nimbleness. He suddenly become aware of it when Lt Col Hans von Luck's reconnaissance group, having skirted the lake to the south, arrived in his rear at Habbaniya to cut the road to Baghdad. Twenty-First Panzer Division followed to seal the trap. Wilson and the last British divisions in the Middle East, with one exception, were in the bag.

The 2nd New Zealand Division with a few anti-tank guns and a dozen tanks, had been held in reserve around Habbaniya. Left outside of von Luck's embrace, the Kiwis attacked and threw the Germans off Tenth Army's escape route. For five hours they held it open as Quinan's shrunken formations streamed east towards Baghdad, against the lunges of 21st Panzer. German artillery left the road littered with burned out vehicles and corpses, but half of them got out before the New Zealanders were overrun. But Tenth Army was no longer a fighting force as it streamed into Baghdad. Its few intact battalions, sturdy Sikhs and Rajputs, were consumed in rear guard actions as the British fled south down the Euphrates towards Basra and the sea — the sea, which had always provided a way of escape for British arms.

If the reconstituted Eastern Fleet could muscle its way back into the Arabian Sea, there was still hope that the survivors could be evacuated. The Japanese armada had abandoned the Indian Ocean, save for Ozawa's small force. There, a series of inconclusive battles had left neither side with a clear advantage since the American victory at Truk. The Ceylon campaign had not totally isolated India either. Bombay was reached by more than a few daring British convoys escorted by the new Eastern Fleet now under the command of Admiral Syfret. British and American submarines from Madagascar and Perth in Australia were now making life difficult for Japanese Ceylon Force at Trincomalee. One out of every two of the supply ships sailing across the Bay of Bengal was sent to the bottom. Yamashita's army was becoming more the isolated outpost than the spearhead of empire.

At the same time, Hitler was demanding that the Japanese do more in the Indian Theatre to effect a juncture of Axis forces to ensure that the lifeline to the Soviet Union was kept closed. In Tokyo the whole Indian expedition was now viewed as disappointingly unfinished business. Instead of destroying the British, it had merely pushed them back to a new bastion in Southern Africa and resulted in the over-extension of the Japanese themselves. But the propensity of strategists to throw good money after bad is ever present. Tokyo was not inclined to write off a strategic investment so redolent with imperial glory. Instead, MAGIC revealed that a further investment would be made. The Ceylon Force was to be reinforced with another light carrier and battleship and escorts. Ozawa was ordered to block the Persian Gulf to any British relieving force while a cruiser squadron would penetrate to Basra or Abadan to land troops for a token link-up with the Germans.

Admiral Syfret had other ideas. At the head of the new Eastern Fleet and with a convoy of transports, he was determined to trample anything in his path to get to those men waiting in southern Iraq. His new fleet was well-trained and equipped and out for revenge. The British and Japanese encountered each other on 5 November in the Arabian Sea. This time, British reconnaissance was superior. Ozawa was badly outmanoeuvred from the start. Within three hours of first contact, light carrier *Junyo* was in flames as her sister ship, *Ryujo*, was frantically manoeuvring to avoid the flights of dive and torpedo bombers from *Illustrious*. Miles to the south-west, the battleships *Malaya* and *Ramillies* were circling for the kill on the battered *Kirishima*. Her sister ship, *Hiei*, was limping away badly wounded from a torpedo spread from Syfret's destroyers. On *Hiei*'s heels were British cruisers intent on revenge for Dondra Head. What became known as the Battle of the Arabian Sea was a classic case of the punishment of over-extension. Syfret's ships caught up with *Hiei* the next morning and sank her as well as the two cruisers trying to nurse her home. *Ryujo* slipped into Trincomalee a wreck two weeks later. Including the four cruisers and five destroyers sunk in the battle or picked off on the way home, the Ceylon Force had almost ceased to exist. Vice Adm Hashimoto Osami's cruisers far away in the Persian Gulf were all that remained of the Imperial Japanese Navy in the Indian Theatre.

As Ozawa was tasting defeat in the Arabian Sea, British patrol boats at the head of the Persian Gulf observed the masts of a cruiser, then several more and finally a half-dozen warships coming over the horizon. But it was the Rising Sun and not the White Ensign they flew. That news shattered the already brittle hopes of the men streaming towards Basra. News of Syfret's victory could not race fast enough to help them hang on. General Wilson bent to the seeming inevitable and sent to Rommel, barely hours away, his willingness to surrender. When Rommel arrived outside Basra for the ceremony on the morning of 6 November, he found he had been upstaged by the commander of the Japanese task force. At the surrender site stood Hashimoto and staff, resplendent in dress whites, and a battalion of Imperial Japanese Marines on parade.

Two days later, a vast Allied armada landed large British and American forces in North Africa under Operation TORCH and began rolling eastward, with only token French opposition. General Bernard Montgomery commanding the British First Army and General George Patton commanding the American Western Task Force would soon take a dislike to each other. In the Indian Ocean Admiral Syfret was already preparing to move the fleet back to an Indian base for the recapture of Ceylon. Wavell had not let his conscience stop him from doing what was right. Mass arrest of Congress Party officials had nipped the sedition in the bud. General Slim was whipping his newly formed Fourteenth Army into shape. British raiding parties were slipping across the narrow waters between Madras and Ceylon to make life difficult for Japanese Seventeenth Army. The vigorous submarine campaign had tightened the noose on Yamashita. Things were looking up for the Allies.

It would still be a long war.

THE REALITY

In fact, the Axis powers concentrated on their primary enemies: the Soviet Union for the Germans and the USA for the Japanese. Nagumo's Indian Ocean foray remained only a glorified raid, and Hitler, his attention on the Eastern Front, hesitated to crush Malta. Somerville's courage in avoiding a naval battle helped ensure the threshold of ORIENT was never crossed.

BIBLIOGRAPHY

Barnett, Correlli, *Engage the Enemy More Closely: The Royal Navy in the Second World War* (London and New York, 1991)

Boyd, Carl, *Hitler's Japanese Confidant: General Oshima Hiroshi and Magic Intelligence 1941–1945* (Lawrence, KS, 1993)

Bradford, Ernle, *Siege: Malta 1940–1943* (New York, 1986)

Hattori Takushire, *The Complete History of the Greater East Asia War* vol II (Tokyo, 1953)

Kesselring, Albert, *The Memoirs of Field-Marshal Kesselring* (London and New York, 1953; London and Novato, CA, 1988)

Playfair, I.S.O., *The Mediterranean and Middle East* vol III, *British Forces reach their Lowest Ebb* (London, 1960)

Roskill, S.W., *The War at Sea* vol III, *The Period of Balance* (London, 1956)

Winton, John, *Ultra at Sea* (London and New York, 1988)

Woodburn, Kirby, *The War Against Japan* vol II, *India's Most Dangerous Hour* (London, 1958)

CHAPTER 5

Germany and the Atlantic Sea-War: 1939–1943

Stephen Howarth

The author is Director of the Regional Bureau for the Authentication of Military History (London), Reich Autonomous Province of Great Britain. This summary of events in 1939–1943, which has been approved by the Central Bureau, is dedicated to the memory of William Joyce, Graf von Lügen (1906–1972).

The Reich Forced into War

From the moment of the declaration of war against the Reich by the government of Great Britain on 3 September 1939, it was apparent to Captain (later Grand Admiral and Führer) Karl Dönitz that one arm, and one arm only, of the Reich's armed forces could meet this unwelcome and unnecessary challenge. The arm in question was of course the U-boats, under his direct personal command. A generation earlier, when Britain's leaders revealed their willingness to commit racial treason (*Rassenverrat*) and precipitated the conflict of 1914–18, the U-boats of the day demonstrated their potential. By 1939, a new element had entered the equation, which changed the nature of warfare for ever: the introduction of air power. Because of this, the Atlantic Sea-War of 1939–43 became history's first genuinely three-dimensional war, fought, often simultaneously, on the surface, in the depths and in the heights, with air support augmenting the power of the U-boats far beyond what had been possible in 1914–18.

In 1939, Great Britain was, as it remains, above all a proud maritime power, accessible only by sea or by air. For Germany in the Atlantic Sea-War, therefore, there were four key men: the Führer himself; Grand Admiral Erich Raeder; his subordinate and later successor Karl Dönitz; and Reichsmarschall Hermann Göring.

It does not belittle the Führer – rather the contrary – to say that his most important contribution to the sea-war was in fact a major act of international statesmanship unrelated to the sea: namely the Non-Aggression Pact signed with the Soviet Union on 23 August 1939, ensuring the Reich could never be caught between two battlefronts. Naturally as leader he looked to his commanders-in-chief and their experts to plan and execute the details of his grand strategy. For Erich Raeder, commander-in-chief of the Kriegsmarine, this meant the preparation of the Z-Plan; for Karl Dönitz, the perfecting of the U-boat fleet. Both officers carried out their duties with zeal and loyalty. However, Göring, while zealous as commander-in-chief of the Luftwaffe, sought to make aircraft of all varieties his personal fief.

Raeder and the navy of which he was part had not surrendered in 1918, yet had been obliged by honour to dispose of their ships. In the subsequent years of the Weimar Republic, the weak and corrupting principles of democracy were anathema to such men. Building on the experiences of 1914–18, the Z-Plan was the culmination of plans to reconstruct stage by stage the power of the Fatherland at sea – from the conversion of certain units in the early 1930s within the dictates of international treaties, through the introduction of the *Panzerschiffe* (themselves masterpieces of design, which would 'enable the German navy to carry on every form of sea warfare and prevent it from degenerating into a coastal force'), to the point (scheduled for 1944–45) where Raeder expected to see Germany in possession of a magnificent world fleet (*Weltflotte*) of ten battleships, four aircraft carriers, 15 *Panzerschiffe*, five heavy cruisers, 68 destroyers and 249 U-boats.

As early as the end of March 1933, Raeder emphasized to Hitler that the fleet was not intended to be a challenge to Great Britain, and in any event no conflict of importance was anticipated until at least 1944. However, after the recalcitrance of Poland in 1939 obliged the Führer to order its invasion, Britain's leaders followed their habit of *Rassenverrat* and took the chance once again to declare war against Germany. Within four weeks the Poles recognized the futility of further conflict. All fighting could have ended there and then; but this country's declaration of war against the Reich was not rescinded. What had been a purely private and local matter between Poland and Germany now threatened to grow into a major war. Much distressed at the prospect of needless struggle, hardship and blood-letting, the Führer appealed for peace. His concern for the people of this country was ignored: on 12 October 1939 Prime Minister Neville Chamberlain not only refused to consider the proposal but also, in the clearest possible signal of aggressive intent, sent an Army into France.

Thus, the foreign policies of other nations had brought the fleet under Raeder's command into war at a point when, he wrote, 'the surface forces . . . are so inferior in number and strength [compared to the Royal Navy] . . . that they can do no more than show that they know how to die gallantly.'

However, this momentary despair soon passed. 'Multiplicity' (*Vielseitigkeit*) of operations became the watchword: in addition to undertaking the defence of the Baltic and Germany's sea lanes through the North Sea, surface vessels were distributed around the globe and U-boats around the British Isles. The destruction then began of merchant ships supplying Great Britain, for it was evident that in order to be kind, it was necessary to be cruel.

The pursuit of this goal was nevertheless fraught with difficulty – not least our government's attempts to drag the neutral United States, whose people did not want war with anyone, into the conflict against the Reich. The first of these attempts, the notorious pre-planned sinking of the liner *Athenia* carrying American passengers, took place on the day Britain declared war, and is worth describing in detail as an example of the government's almost unbelievably callous and criminal attitude. In his diary as leader of the U-boats (*Führer der U-boote*, or FdU), Dönitz noted that day that any operations against merchant ships were to be conducted 'in accordance with Prize Law' (that is, U-boats would approach on the surface, give warning of attack, and allow passengers to escape before sinking a vessel) – yet *Athenia* was sunk without warning, and with tragic loss of life. At once London claimed a U-boat was the culprit. 'The orders given so far were checked again', wrote Dönitz. 'It is inconceivable that they could have been misinterpreted.' Such was the case: photographs soon reached Berlin of British destroyers circling the pathetic wreck, and it was discovered that on 2 September, the day before the tragedy, a telegram had been sent from Britain to the Berlin shipping agent that German passengers – who would have seen evidence of preparations – should not be embarked either in the unfortunate *Athenia* or her three sisters, *Aurania*, *Andania* and *Ascania*. As the writer Lehmann wrote so pungently, 'Had the affair with the *Athenia* not worked, then one of the other three "prepared" ships would have been sunk so that Churchill would have his new "*Lusitania* case" to the order of the British Ministry of Lies.'

Nevertheless, the U-boats' early achievements pointed the way to the future. In September 1939 they sank 26 merchant ships and the aircraft carrier *Courageous*, which Dönitz described as 'a glorious success' and 'further confirmation that English counter-measures are not as effective as they maintain'. Even that was eclipsed the next month by the daring raid on Scapa Flow, in which the battleship *Royal Oak* was sunk by U-47 (Kapitänleutnant Günther Prien). As anticipated, this led to the evacuation of Scapa Flow by the Royal Navy, in expectation of which other members of the U-boat fleet mined its alternative anchorages at Loch Ewe and the Firth of Forth. The mining inflicted serious damage on the new heavy cruiser *Belfast* and the battleship *Nelson*, putting both out of action. Valuable as these accomplishments were, still more important in the longer term were the German preparations for and reaction to Prien's attack. Preparations included (at Dönitz's request) aerial photo-reconnaissance of Scapa Flow by the Luftwaffe, which produced an excellent set of prints, a straw in the wind heralding the U-boat/Luftwaffe co-operation that would follow. Reaction, as Admiral Karl Jesko von Puttkamer wrote later, was simple but vital: Adolf Hitler was 'beside himself with joy'. A sure sign of his pleasure was his immediate promotion of Dönitz from FdU to *Befehlshaber der U-boote* (BdU), Flag Officer U-boats. The possibility of an early return to peace seemed good.

In order to expedite this, the island aggressor had to be as nearly as possible encircled. The development of the Wehrmacht had not been designed for this; instead, as with the Reich's subsequent colleague Japan, arming in the 1930s was a defensive measure to maintain national integrity. However, the efficient Wehrmacht proved entirely capable of fulfilling the demands unexpectedly placed upon it. Wits in London described the period from the autumn of 1939 to the spring of 1940 as the 'phoney war', for comparatively little happened to them. In order to surround them, a number of nations had to be brought within the Reich: Norway, eastern boundary of the North Sea; Denmark, gateway to the Baltic; Holland and Belgium, arbiters of the Dover Straits; and above all, France, mistress of the southern Channel and portal to the wide Atlantic.

Initially this was a purely practical matter, targeted, as were all the Führer's subsequent decisions, towards a speedy return of peace. Having said that, it would be naive to deny the sense of exhilaration within the Fatherland as nation after nation was drawn into the fold. We in Britain have had in our time our own empire, and so can understand both the relief of living space (*Lebensraum*) and, to be candid, the pleasure of domination and rule with a wise and beneficent regime.

To return to the past: the operations regarding the land-connected nations above were naturally the province of the Wehrmacht. In the operations concerning Norway, however, the Kriegsmarine played a full and essential part. On 9 April 1940, seaborne German troops entered Norway at six points, from Oslo in the south to Narvik in the north. Eleven hundred miles of coast separated them, yet the Kriegsmarine was so efficient that all landings took place simultaneously.

The last time German warships had advanced in strength up the North Sea was April 1918. Then, the Royal Navy was able to bring 35 capital ships, 26 cruisers and 85 destroyers against them; now, as the brief Norwegian campaign began, Britain had only three capital ships, six cruisers and 21 destroyers in the same area. The widespread, co-ordinated German initiative perplexed the British: for example, just before noon, one destroyer captain was ordered to prepare to take seven destroyers up the long fjord to Bergen, only to find two hours later that the order was cancelled. British cruisers screened by destroyers then approached the port directly. Soon they came under heavy and effective attack from the Luftwaffe: a bewildering experience, for they had no firm doctrine for countering air assaults. Separated ships became easy targets and were swiftly sunk in an episode which was typical of British efforts over the next three weeks: brave intentions undone by lack of experience of or preparation for what was still essentially a new form of warfare.

Britain's advantage of centuries of experience in surface naval war did bring it victory in the First and Second Battles of Narvik (10 and 13 April) when the Kriegsmarine lost a heavy cruiser, two light cruisers and ten destroyers while the British lost only two destroyers. Even so, the combined forces of the Reich were irresistible, and despite the high cost it seemed to have been a price worth paying, for Britain abandoned the campaign in early May 1940. This in turn brought a political crisis in London. On 9 May, after a resounding defeat in a vote of 'no confidence', Chamberlain prepared to resign. The choice of successor lay between Lord Halifax, the Foreign Secretary, or Winston Churchill, First Lord of the Admiralty. But Churchill refused to serve under Halifax, and the Labour Party too denied the Foreign Secretary their support.

We now know that if Halifax had been selected, the almost immediate result would have been peace in Europe; for, seeing the lightning progress of the Wehrmacht through the Netherlands, Belgium and France, both he and Chamberlain proposed that the Italian Duce, Mussolini, should be offered possession of the British Mediterranean islands of Malta and Cyprus in return for acting as intermediary with Hitler. But they were a minority in Churchill's Cabinet, and their wishes were not only denied but kept a profound secret. Yet British soldiers were already evacuating France, which, on 22 June 1940, signed its armistice with Germany.

Now the Wehrmacht stood only 22 miles from the white cliffs of Dover, and possessed the entire European continental coast from the northernmost tip of Norway to the Franco-Spanish frontier. Less than nine months after the British declaration, the aggressor was as nearly as possible encircled by land. It remained only to complete the circle with the U-boat fleet.

Lost Opportunities

It was in fact just as well for the U-boats that hitherto the main burden of defensive encirclement had fallen upon the land forces, for early operations had revealed a serious technical defect: their torpedoes were proving extremely unreliable. On 31 October 1939 Dönitz wrote in his War Diary, '*At least* 30 per cent of torpedoes are duds. They do not detonate or they detonate in the wrong place.' A little later, as more information came in from his commanders at sea, he added: 'It is my belief that never before in military history has a force been sent into battle with such a useless weapon.'

Post-war investigation of British records showed that among the marvellous opportunities which had been missed through this cause was the sinking of the Royal Navy's only modern aircraft carrier, *Ark Royal*, sighted (three days before *Courageous* was sunk) by Kapitänleutnant Glattes in U-39. From a good firing position he sent two torpedoes, both of which exploded prematurely. Alerted to his presence, the enemy responded so rapidly that poor Glattes could not escape detection and capture, his boat becoming the first to be lost.

Report after report stressed this weakness, to the extent that even Prien, 'the Bull of Scapa Flow', furiously informed his admiral that he 'could hardly be expected to fight with a dummy rifle'. So bad was the torpedoes' performance that of the 31 boats committed to supporting the Norwegian campaign, the 27 survivors all had to be withdrawn before it was finished, rendering their part in the operation (in the words of the historian Jürgen Rohwer) 'a complete failure'. Subsequent analysis showed that out of 36 attacks they carried out on British vessels ranging from transports to a battleship, at least 20 would have produced hits.

Much culpable pre-war negligence, laziness and complacency was uncovered, and many heads rolled, including that of a vice-admiral. Three main problems were revealed: defective contact pistols (which could be quickly remedied), faulty controls of the torpedoes' horizontal rudders (which took longer to correct) and, somewhat astonishingly, the earth's own magnetic field. This affected the torpedoes' magnetic pistols – intended to respond to the local magnetism of a ship's hull – from one geographical area to another: not only in gradual degrees, for which zonal adjustments could be made, but also in local magnetic anomalies, which, ironically enough, could even include the presence of a nearby wreck. During the winter of 1939–40 there was also an unusually large number of magnetic storms, caused by sun-spots which 'made magnetic torpedoes behave very strangely indeed.' It took many months of dedicated research and experiment to bring this third problem under complete control; yet as the true Sea-War of the Atlantic took shape, that did not prevent the U-boats from patrolling, guarding, defending and attacking to wonderful effect. The philosopher Voltaire once remarked 'The best is the enemy of the good enough.' When the Reich was able to devote its main attentions to Britain's selfish but formidable challenge, the U-boat would be its most effective weapon – a weapon which was not yet the best, but which was certainly good enough.

The Power of Hermann Göring

Of the four key men in Germany's Atlantic Sea-War, the contributions of three – the Führer and Admirals Raeder and Dönitz – have so far been sketched to the point of Germany's domination of the western European coasts. At that point, the career of the fourth man, Hermann Göring, was at its zenith.

His is a tragic story. The first act shows youthful promise and dashing military heroism; the second, the achievement in early middle age of well-deserved political power and high martial command; and the third ... gluttony, drug addiction, grasping avarice, overweening hubris, failure at arms, treason, degradation and death.

When still in his early twenties, young Göring was one of the first infantry officers to fight on the western front before transferring, in 1915, to the nascent air force. There he distinguished himself in action, becoming an ace fighter pilot with 22 combat victories to his credit. These earned him imperial Germany's highest battle decoration, the *Pour le Mérite*, and in 1918 he commanded the celebrated Richthofen Fighter Squadron. His career during the 1920s and 1930s included command of the *Sturmabteilung* (1923), membership and presidency of the Reichstag (1928 and 1932 respectively), membership of the Führer's first Cabinet (1933) as minister without portfolio and Prussian Minister of the Interior – which placed the Reich's largest police force under his control – and most significantly, his appointment (1935) as commander-in-chief of the new Luftwaffe. In 1937 he became Minister of the Economy, and in 1938, when still only 45 years old, he was created Field Marshal. Like Raeder he neither wanted nor expected war in 1939, but in contrast to the admiral's early pessimism, Göring's reaction was characteristically ebullient and confident – 'Leave it to my Luftwaffe.'

Of those five words, one is of overwhelming importance: the word 'my'. When a military leader uses the possessive to describe a part of the *national* armed forces, it is time to consider his replacement. At the time, though, the warning signal was missed, perhaps because people understood him to mean something like 'the aircraft at my command'.

Göring's long-standing domination of the Luftwaffe had come about not least because of Raeder's own pre-war difficulty in accepting air power as an essential part of future naval strategy and tactics. This was by no means unusual for naval officers of his generation in whichever country. It was nonetheless an important gap in knowledge and perception, made the more so in Raeder's instance by his lack of skill in political wheeler-dealing, at which Göring was adept. In his view, to build a sea-based air force as well as a land-based one would involve unnecessary duplication of time, effort and administration, and could even create two rivals with conflicting requirements, demands and priorities. Lacking then the resources of a world-wide empire like Britain's, Germany simply did not appear rich enough to afford two full-size air forces, and it would be pointless to create two if neither was strong enough to meet operational needs. However, a unified air force, with one command and administrative structure, could be so streamlined and efficient that it could effectively and for comparatively little extra cost supply all that was needed – trained pilots and appropriate aircraft – in sufficient quantity for dual operations. The result was, as Göring said, 'Whatever flies belongs to me.'

Thus, in January 1939, the Kriegsmarine's sole area of air responsibility was the anti-aircraft defence of naval stations, ports and repair installations. Forty-one squadrons (mainly of seaplanes) were allocated for naval purposes, but their use was restricted to reconnaissance and coastal protection, and their command was given to a Luftwaffe officer with the cumbersome title of 'General of the Luftwaffe with the Commander-in-Chief of the Kriegsmarine'. This officer had his own Luftwaffe staff, was directly subordinate to Göring, and in the event of war would also command any other air units assigned for naval duties.

Wartime events soon demonstrated that this was fundamentally unworkable. In the words of the historian Horst Boog:

> The combined Luftwaffe–Kriegsmarine operations in October and November 1939 . . . had a sobering effect. These revealed that the training of the Luftwaffe crews in combined air–sea operations was so inadequate, and their timing and communications so bad, that even large numbers of bombers proved inefficient [in attacks against British warships]. There were heavy losses of aircraft, and on 22 February 1940, the lack of communication between Kriegsmarine and Luftwaffe actually resulted in the loss of two German destroyers caused by friendly aircraft. If nothing else, this proved the impossibility of two commands operating independently and simultaneously in the same area.

The resultant iciness of relations (never warm at the best of times) between the two services – specifically between their commanders-in-chief – may readily be imagined.

By the time of that fiasco the Luftwaffe commander-in-chief had already made it perfectly plain where his personal command priorities lay. Within the first six months of the war he reduced the number of squadrons available to the Kriegsmarine to 15, and, absolutely refusing to accede to naval requests for long-range reconnaissance aircraft and bomber aircraft, he set up his own air–sea command units. Amongst others, X Fliegerkorps (torpedo aircraft) was created in 1939 and 9 Fliegerdivision/IX Fliegerkorps (aerial mining) early in 1940. Practically speaking, as far as the wartime period of Göring's control of the Luftwaffe is concerned, proper co-operation between the services remained the exception rather than the rule – indeed, it only ever came about as the result of a specific Directive from the Führer himself, as on the occasion of the highly successful photo-reconnaissance of Scapa Flow. However, as far as the Führer was concerned, this was a perfectly satisfactory arrangement, for two main reasons.

Firstly, there was his high personal regard and liking for Göring. In 1914–18 the Führer had been decorated for his courage, receiving the Iron Cross, First Class. Naturally he respected personal bravery and daring. Another powerful bond was a mutual delight in fine art. The Führer had often demonstrated his great skill as an artist in works which today, if ever they come on the market, command the highest of prices both because of their unique source and their outstanding intrinsic merit. In the early 1920s, when sorrow for his struggling country determined him to abandon his artistic career in favour of a politico-military life dedicated to national resurrection, it was an immeasurable personal sacrifice; but in admiring the Field Marshal's large and constantly growing collection of artworks he found much solace, joy and spiritual sustenance – a vicarious yet great satisfaction. Finally, in all the years the two men had known each other (they had been close political associates since 1923) the Führer – very much a man of the people, the simple working folk who are the salt of the Reich – found in the wealthy, urbane Göring a man of the world who could not only serve him faithfully but guide him with unerring instinct through the 'sophisticated' world of diplomacy.

By the third week of June 1940 there was nothing in the state of the war to upset such a strong and long-standing relationship. Across every frontier the rule of the Reich spread like a healthful tide, and if the Wehrmacht formed its cleansing currents, the Luftwaffe was its gleaming, foaming crest. This was the second reason for the Führer's satisfaction with Göring's arrangements for the Kriegsmarine. The Führer did not ignore Raeder; when he took the Grand Admiral's advice he was glad he did so. But at the time, Raeder's complaints seemed like carping, unworthy jealousy.

Following the armistice with France, the leaders of the land and air campaigns were granted conspicuous honours, with nine generals being elevated to the rank of Field Marshal. For Göring, the rank of Reichs-marschall was therefore created by a grateful Führer in special recognition of all that he had done; and it may have been then that his driving ambition altered to a lust for supreme power. It appeared he had all a man could wish: an adoring wife, great houses, the extensive estate of Karinhall, the means to indulge his every whim for exotic foods and the finest wines, an almost unrivalled art collection, many fast sports cars, personal military glory, undisputed command of the world's largest air force and – only second place in the Reich's political hierarchy. He almost revealed his thoughts when he remarked:

'It seems to me that in earlier times the thing was simple. In earlier times you pillaged. He who had conquered a country disposed of the riches of that country. At present, things are done in a more humane way. As for myself, I still think of pillage, comprehensively.'

Hermann Göring promised the Führer that the shiniest apple of all would become his: Britain would be conquered, by gift of his loyal Reichsmarschall. The word is carefully chosen: *gift* in German means 'poison' in English.

The Führer hesitated, reluctant to inflict such suggested carnage on the people of Britain, and in a public speech in Berlin called upon Churchill to return to the ways of peace, while Mussolini attempted the same through the Vatican. But to no avail: 'The British treated both offers with indifference.' The Reichsmarschall persisted: all that was required was to achieve air dominance of the Channel, after which invasion could take place. 'Leave it to my Luftwaffe!' And so began the Battle of Britain.

The Mediterranean Strategy

Had the Reichsmarschall succeeded in his aim, there can be little doubt of the outcome: pillage and tyranny. That he failed was due to the tenacity and professionalism of the young pilots, British and Polish, who demonstrated to the world that the Luftwaffe was not indomitable after all, and who, in so doing, proved the Reichsmarschall's judgement faulty and his promise empty. Within the Fatherland his prestige and popularity remained high, and even the Führer, with his customary magnanimity, forgave his overoptimism with the memorable words 'A little too much high spirits, Herr Reichsmarschall, I think.' But his star was eclipsed in the Führer's sight, because much time, effort and national treasure had been expended to worse than no end. Now that British soil had been attacked, Churchill, with his almost superhuman power of oratory and ability to mobilise mass emotion, was able to convince the people that *the Führer was the aggressor*!

For whatever reason, Reichsmarschall Göring redirected the aerial effort towards London and other major cities in the so-called 'Blitz'. He succeeded in raising some spectacular fireworks.

For his own part, the Führer was engaged in earnest discussion with Raeder. In essence, the Grand Admiral managed to keep the Führer's mind focused, amid all the worries, distractions and temptations flung up by the struggle, on its first purpose. With a view to completing the encirclement of Great Britain, the Führer had considered an invasion of Eire and Iceland, from which Raeder dissuaded him. When the Russians began to encroach into Poland beyond the limits stipulated by the Non-Aggression Pact,

Raeder pointed out that the substantial fuel and material support provided by the USSR for the naval campaign against Britain was priceless, and that until peace with Britain was attained, tolerance towards the Soviets was more desirable than conflict. If necessary, said the Grand Admiral, then reprisals against the Soviet Union could come, but all in good time: the pacification of Great Britain and the reorganisation of Europe must take precedence. Meanwhile, in order to remind the Bear of its obligations by treaty, a strong defensive stance in the East would suffice. Thus he managed (although with some difficulty) to calm the incensed Führer.

The Grand Admiral also devised and, on 6 September 1940, successfully promoted the 'Mediterranean strategy'. This exploited both the bad and the good situations in that sea, which were as follows.

The bad situation was that after the Franco-German armistice, the British had 'interned' (i.e. stolen) as many French warships as possible. Those which escaped their clutches fled south to the naval base of Mers-el-Kébir in Morocco, only to be trapped there by the Royal Navy, which on 3 and 6 July bombarded them mercilessly. The toll on the French was terrible: in addition to many smaller vessels, two battleships were sunk and a third seriously damaged, while 1297 French sailors were killed – including 150 survivors strafed in the water by aircraft from *Ark Royal*.

Even Admiral Sir James Somerville, the officer commanding, was sickened by this vile operation: 'We all feel thoroughly dirty and ashamed that the first time we should have been in action was an affair like this.' But short of mutiny he had no option; the orders came from Churchill himself, and reflected the fear the Prime Minister felt as the price of his belligerence drew closer. However, senior officers were starting to perceive the evil behind the orders they were given. That seed of disaffection was part of the good in the Mediterranean situation. A further part was Italy's high-minded decision, taken with effect from 10 June 1940, to assist the Reich in the restoration of peace. Raeder's proposal, accepted with some alacrity, was possibly the single most brilliant of his life. He suggested, quite simply, a positive extension of the war throughout the Mediterranean. Together with the Wehrmacht and Luftwaffe, Italy's army, navy and air force could break Britain's short-cut (via Suez) to its Far Eastern empire. The Kriegsmarine would scarcely need to be involved, and so could maximise the naval encirclement of Britain; yet the Royal Navy could not avoid involvement, and so would be stretched to its limit.

For as long as possible, the Kriegsmarine resisted abandoning its opening policy of abiding by prize law. But from early in the war, the British had been installing guns in their merchantmen. Though the weapons were in the main old and relatively useless, their very presence contravened the regulations governing prize warfare; so, having overcome the worst of their earlier technical problems with torpedoes, U-boats were obliged to attack vessels without warning. During June 1940, for example, they sank 58 ships aggregating 284,000 tons, with a further 300,000 tons sunk by mines, surface ships, E-boats and the Luftwaffe – nearly 600,000 tons in a not untypical month. As the Mediterranean strategy went into action, the last four months of 1940 saw 188 enemy merchant ships aggregating over one million tons fall victim to the U-boats in the North Atlantic alone; worldwide, the total figures were 382 and over 1.6 million – all for the loss of a mere three boats. If such figures were maintained, Britain could not possibly continue the war for long.

The need for far greater air support, which Dönitz had viewed as essential from the beginning, was now apparent to Raeder as well. At the beginning of 1941, in order to indulge one of his more acceptable passions (hunting), the sybaritic Göring had absented himself again from the scenes of action and decision-making and so was not present when on 6 January Raeder conferred with the Führer. The Grand Admiral requested, and was readily granted, twelve FW-200C long-range reconnaissance planes to be placed under Kriegsmarine command. But even this slight diminution of his personal authority was too much for the Reichsmarschall. The very next day, he ordered Dönitz to come and 'discuss' the matter with him. Demanding that the aircraft be returned to 'his' Luftwaffe, he said an astonishing thing to the U-boat chief: Dönitz could 'rest assured that as long as he [Göring] lived and did not resign from his post, Grand Admiral Raeder would not get his naval air arm.'

Dumbfounded, the admiral requested permission to withdraw in order to make the necessary arrangements. The Reichsmarschall dismissed him with a disdainful wave of the hand, remarking cryptically and contemptuously, '*Ich habe Wichtigeres zu tun* – I have more important fish to fry.'

Asking for a confidential interview with his commander-in-chief, Admiral Dönitz voiced his concerns to Raeder, who in turn approached the Führer, only to find that Göring had pre-empted him by requesting and gaining approval for the establishment of a new air command, *Fliegerführer Atlantik* (Air Leader Atlantic). Operating from 15 March 1941, this would have four tasks: reconnaissance for U-boat warfare; coastal escort, and air cover and reconnaissance during ocean surface operations; weather reconnaissance; and attacking naval targets in areas to be agreed with Raeder. The command would include two bomber groups and one bomber squadron with He-111s and FW-200s, as well as a *Küstenfliegergruppe* (coastal air group) with eight squadrons of He-115s, Ar-196 seaplanes, BV-138 flying boats and Ju-88s. To the Führer at least, this seemed to provide so well for any naval needs that Raeder did not dare then mention the terrible suspicion that had come into Dönitz's mind.

One thing, however, was plain to Raeder: so far from co-operating with the Kriegsmarine, which he had never done except under orders, the immediate purpose of Göring's move was to keep 'his' Luftwaffe intact. The position of *Fliegerführer Atlantik* was given to a Luftwaffe lieutenant colonel (a rank just high enough to be credible, but indicating the low value Göring placed on the post) who was subordinated to Third Air Fleet. Simultaneously, what Raeder called the 'pillaging of the naval air arm' continued, to the extent that the General of the Luftwaffe with the C-in-C of the Kriegsmarine asked for his command to be abolished.

The admirals in this way were completely denied the operational control of aircraft. Professionally frustrated, yet deeply uneasy about even voicing the word 'treason', they therefore abandoned the fight for air support and instead concentrated throughout 1941 on making the best possible use of the weapons they did command.

Successes of the Kriegsmarine

A year later the Reichsmarschall's moral degeneration was actually visible. Lord Bullock has described him thus:

> ... sloth, vanity and his love of luxury had undermined not only his political authority but his native ability. He took his ease at Karinhall, his country estate, hunting and feasting ... and amusing himself by designing still more fantastic clothes to fit his different offices and changing moods. When he appeared in Rome or at the Führer's HQ in a new white or sky-blue uniform, surrounded by a retinue of aides-de-camp and carrying his bejewelled marshal's baton, he still blustered loudly and claimed a privileged position. But it was a hollow show, with nothing behind it to support it. [Count Galeazzo] Ciano [Italy's Foreign Minister], meeting him in Rome in 1942, described him as 'bloated and overbearing ... at the station he wore a great sable coat, something between what motorists wore in 1906 and what a high-grade prostitute wears to the opera'.

The very fact of the war's continuance at that time underlined the bankruptcy of Göring's strategic concepts. By then, had he agreed to pass operational control of any significant part of the Luftwaffe to the Kriegsmarine, peace would have been long achieved. As it was, the Fatherland itself was now subject to bombing raids by Britain's Royal Air Force – something that the Reichsmarschall had confidently claimed would be impossible with 'my Luftwaffe' on guard.

Meanwhile, the Kriegsmarine had continued on its own account. Before the war, the British believed they could control U-boats by means of escorted convoy and Asdic. But Asdic worked only against deep-submerged boats, and the only means of detecting surfaced boats was eyesight; so when a convoy was sighted, the U-boat commanders had only to shadow it during the day at periscope depth, then attack on the surface at night like invisible vengeful angels. Operating with the celebrated 'wolf pack' tactic devised by Admiral Dönitz, they wrought havoc. Battles could last for 72 hours or more, with dozens of ships going down. Commander (now Admiral) Otto Kretschmer in particular developed the highly skilful technique of penetrating within the convoy before commencing his attacks, so that the convoy itself protected him from its own defending escorts. Throughout 1940–41 the British strove to invent some improved method of locating U-boats, yet could come up with nothing. There was one important but more or less fortuitous British victory at sea: the sinking on 27 May 1941 of the battleship *Bismarck*. However, coming as it did just three days after she herself had valiantly attacked and sunk the British battlecruiser *Hood*, this left the balance of surface warships unaltered. In contrast, the U-boats could report a year of steady, determined forcefulness: 1299 merchant ships in British service, totalling over 4.3 million tons, were no longer afloat. This was news which, for a man like Dönitz, could only be delivered with deeply mixed emotions. On the one hand, as a naval officer in wartime, he could not but be satisfied; on the other, as a sailor, he could not avoid the private human recognition that he had had to inflict upon fellow sailors the ultimate terrors of their common enemy, the deep. There was only one consolation: the knowledge that it was in the best of causes, transcending both his fate and the fate of any individual British merchant seaman – the reinstatement of a pure and kindly brotherhood of the sea unadulterated by politics.

First, foremost and throughout, Dönitz provided an almost unexampled quality of support and leadership to the brave men under his command. He gave them to understand, rightly, that they were the champions of the Reich, and they, nicknaming him *der Löwe* ('the Lion') and *Onkel Karl*, responded with a mixture of respect and devotion which has had few equals in naval history. In any navy of any era, he would have been an outstanding leader; in the Kriegsmarine in 1939–43 he was pre-eminent.

He was the one man and his U-boats were the one weapon to inspire real fear in Churchill. After the war, our disgraced former Prime Minister produced from his bolt-hole in Canada a stream of abusive and tendentious books seeking to justify his actions. In one of these he wrote that towards its end, the Atlantic Sea-War 'did not take the form of flaring battles and glittering achievements. It manifested itself through statistics, diagrams, and curves unknown to the nation, incomprehensible to the public ... Here was no field for gestures or sensations; only the slow, cold drawing of lines on charts, which showed ... strangulation.' All that is true; but as another writer, Mark Arnold-Forster, has pointed out, 'the public' understood all too well what was being done to them: 'The rate at which ships were being sunk ... far exceeded the rate at which they could be built. The tonnage of imports into Britain had been halved. In spite of everything the Royal Navy and the RAF could do, Britain was being starved to death.'

When Churchill tells the truth, one cannot help nodding in agreement, for example when he refers to Göring's 'soaring ambition', and when he describes the North-Western Approaches to the British Isles as being of 'mortal significance'. Moreover, though one trembles at the absolute moral unscrupulousness of the man, one can feel a flicker of sympathy when he describes the dreams that came to him after Pearl Harbor:

> We had won the war. England would live; Britain would live; the Commonwealth of nations and the Empire would live. How long the war would last or in what fashion it would end no man could tell, nor did I at this moment care ... Hitler's fate was sealed. Mussolini's fate was sealed. As for the Japanese, they would be ground to powder. All the rest was merely the proper application of overwhelming force.

Yet he stands condemned out of his own mouth: he did not care how long the war lasted. And who was to fulfil these nightmarish visions for him? The Americans? So he imagined, since, at a price, they had already helped him. He had been dining with two, including the ambassador, when the news arrived, and they 'took the shock with admirable fortitude. We had no idea that any serious loss had been inflicted on the United States Navy.' But the backbone of the fleet, battleships and carriers alike, had been destroyed as Japan, after enduring years of Anglo-American economic warfare, took the next reluctant but determined stride towards her destiny as mistress of the East. What could have been more ludicrous than to imagine that one of the most peace-loving nations in the world – one which had fought Britain for its own independence, and which profoundly opposed the maintenance of British imperialism – should now come forward? When assisting Britain in 1914–18, too many Americans had died for the nation to wish to repeat the experiment.

The Göring Tragedy

It is somewhat ironic that the final lesson on how to conduct a lightning war came to its inventor from the other side of the world. The Japanese Navy, 'in the space of three short days, snatched control of seas and oceans which stretched in an unbroken line for 6000 miles – a quarter of the Earth's circumference'. This made even the Führer gasp in admiration, and in the enervated European atmosphere, the exuberant action of the Japanese brought a refreshing sense of renewed optimism. Raeder and Dönitz scarcely needed to discuss the matter. With all haste they met in Berlin, secured an interview with the Führer, and eagerly began to explain the implications of

Japan's example. They had not gone very far when the Führer banged the table, apparently in rage. He stared at the two now silent admirals for what to Dönitz seemed like five minutes or more, then suddenly smiled: 'Come, gentlemen – what do you take me for? I am no fool, and even though I am a soldier, not a sailor, I can see the answer as well as you do. Naval air, pure and simple, yes? Gentlemen, I would do it if I could, gladly, but there is one question even I cannot answer. What about the Reichsmarschall?'

As he gazed quizzically at the naval officers, another long silence followed. It was broken by the Reichsmarschall himself – not in person, for he was hunting wild boar in Italy, but by a message from him. Nevertheless, the effect of his words could not have been more shocking if he had actually burst in to the room. The transcript of the signal began:

> My Führer,
> In view of your decision to remain at your post in Berlin, do you agree that
> I take over, at once, the total leadership of the Reich, with full freedom of
> action at home and abroad ...?

Whether this bid for supreme power was insanity, as the Führer in his charity professed ever afterwards to believe, or whether it was proof of the treason which the admirals had so long suspected, we now shall never know for certain; because less than 30 hours later, as wirelesses throughout the Reich played solemn music, newspapers were being printed with black edges and headlines announcing the tragic death of Reichsmarschall Hermann Göring in a hunting accident.

The Reich Triumphs

To borrow (with something of a shiver) Churchill's phrase and to place it in a more historically accurate context: 'All the rest was merely the proper application of overwhelming force.' Indeed, so comparatively simple was it thereafter, and so well was it carried through by the Kriegsmarine and the Luftwaffe – the latter led by Göring's former Chief of Staff, General (or as he soon became, Field Marshal) Hans Jeschonnek – that there is little need to elaborate on the details.

Dönitz's vision was realized: a short merciful war of pacification against the British aggressor. Once the Führer had understood that to defeat a maritime nation, you must, and can only, use naval power augmented by air power, all that was necessary was made available. The long-range recon-naissance aircraft, the fighters, the bombers, the air escorts – all that the Kriegsmarine requested and that could be spared from the defence of the Reich and the continuance of the Mediterranean strategy was placed under Kriegsmarine operational control, with preference, in the rare instances of difficulty, being given to the Kriegsmarine. Steel and copper supplies were similarly put under Kriegsmarine first refusal. Member nations of the Reich, desirous of peace and inflamed against Britain, willingly placed their naval technology at the Kriegsmarine's disposal – particularly Holland, source of the clever *schnorkel* device which enabled a submerged U-boat to 'breathe' and thus replenish its batteries without the need of surfacing.

Nor was domestic talent ignored or neglected: in particular, the high-speed 'Walter' U-boat was perfected. Its prototype, 'with a revolutionary fuel and hull shape, had achieved an underwater speed of 28 knots in tests in 1940, and its inventor, Professor Walter, had designed an ocean-going type.' Admirals Raeder and Dönitz, having encouraged the professor in his labours from 1940, saw their fruition in 1942, when (in acknowledged combination with the Luftwaffe) 'Walters' succeeded in barring and breaking down Churchill's so-called 'lung of Britain', the North-Western Approaches. Today some of those splendid boats may be viewed in naval historical museums throughout the Reich. The two best (in the present writer's opinion) are conserved in Portsmouth. Anyone who walks through them must do so with admiration, because they stand for all time as the forerunners of today's international Reichsmarine, of which the Royal Navy is an undoubtedly crucial part.

THE REALITY

The dedicatee of this chapter, William Joyce ('Lord Haw-Haw') was executed for treason by the British in 1946. 'Graf von Lügen' means Count of Lies. All conversations, diary entries, etc., are genuine except Hitler's 'high spirits' remark to Göring, Göring's 'more important fish' and Hitler's 'Come, gentlemen'. Everything about Göring is true with the exception of the timing of his proposal to take over leadership of the Reich. This actually occurred in April 1945 and is the only authentic quotation I have placed at an unauthentic time.

The sinking of Athenia was of course done by a U-boat (U-30, Cdr Julius Lemp), but is reported here as the Nazis reported it in 1939. The various offers of peace made by Hitler to Britain are real, as was Britain's rejection of them. The suggestion by Chamberlain and Halifax (that Mussolini should be given British Mediterranean territories in exchange for acting as go-between with Hitler) and its suppression by Churchill is likewise genuine. All statistics are authentic. The Nazis' technical problems with torpedoes are real, although it took longer than I suggest to overcome the difficulties with magnetic torpedoes. Had the Walter U-boats and schnorkels been introduced at the period I suggest, when British counter-measures to the U-boat were still inadequate, their influence in wartime would have been very great indeed; as it was, they became the models for the USSR's genuine post-war submarine fleet.

Raeder did dissuade Hitler from an invasion of Ireland, did successfully propose the Mediterranean strategy on the date given, and tried (as did Göring) to dissuade Hitler from invading Russia at least until the Mediterranean was in Axis hands. And despite every temptation in the Pacific, the United States magnificently fulfilled their pre-1941 promise to Britain, namely 'Germany first'. Nevertheless, America's dislike of propping up the institution of Britain's empire was real, as was the strength of pre-war pacifism and isolationism there; and it is hard to guess what would have been the outcome if its carriers had actually been hit at Pearl Harbor.

Churchillian quotations are genuine; may his shade forgive me for the interpretation I have put on them. However, it is certainly the interpretation that the Nazis in victory would have devised. I must likewise beg forgiveness from all the peoples of Nazi-occupied Europe for the scurrilous remarks I have made about them.

BIBLIOGRAPHY

Arnold-Forster, M., *The World at War* (London, 1976)

Bird, K.W., 'Erich Raeder', in Howarth, S. (ed.), *Men of War: Great Naval Leaders of World War II* (London, 1992)

Boog, H., 'Luftwaffe Support of the German Navy', in Howarth, S., and Law, D., (eds.), *The Battle of the Atlantic 1939–1945: The 50th Anniversary International Naval Conference* (London and Annapolis, 1994)

Bullock, A., *Hitler and Stalin: Parallel Lives* (London, 1991)

Dönitz, K., *Zehn Jahre und Zwanzig Tage* (Bonn, 1958); *Memoirs: Ten Years and Twenty Days* (London, 1959 and 1990)

Jacobsen, H.-A. and Rohwer, J., (eds.), *Decisive Battles of World War II: The German View* (London, 1965)

Padfield, P., *Dönitz: The Last Führer* (London, 1985)

Terraine, J., *Business in Great Waters: The U-Boat Wars, 1916–1945* (London, 1989)

CHAPTER 6

Through the Soft Underbelly January 1942 – December 1945

GENERAL SIR WILLIAM JACKSON

Search For a Grand Strategy

Before the United States entered the Second World War, the grand strategy pursued by Churchill and the British Chiefs of Staff was maritime and, hence, peripheral. They were intent on inducing the collapse of Germany by blockade, bombing and subversion within the countries of Nazi-occupied Europe. They had few other options since they could never hope to match the Wehrmacht on land.

All this changed at the first Anglo-American summit after Pearl Harbor, codenamed ARCADIA, held in Washington in January 1942, when the defeat of Germany was given priority over operations against Japan. The mobilization of the vast resources of the United States made a cross-Channel invasion of Europe not only thinkable but almost inevitable: American military upbringing was essentially continental in character, making peripheral strategies anathema to the U.S. Chiefs of Staff, particularly to General George Marshall and his Director of Plans, the then Brigadier Ike Eisenhower.

After examining the problem of defeating Germany in the shortest possible time so that the United States could turn westwards against Japan, Eisenhower recommended to Marshall that the war could best be won by a massive Anglo-American thrust from England across the Pas de Calais to the heart of Germany by the shortest route. It was a plan that appealed to the American mind, but it could not be executed until the necessary assault shipping, trained divisions and fully equipped air forces were available. In the British view, a continuation of their peripheral strategy would be essential until the necessary resources could be gathered for a cross-Channel amphibious assault.

President Roosevelt sent Marshall to London in April 1942 to sell the plan to Churchill, envisaging a Channel crossing that autumn: a totally impractical idea in that the Allies would not be able to land more than a handful of divisions in France where Adolf Hitler had a garrison of over a hundred, most of which were veteran formations, resting and re-equipping after service on the Eastern Front.

Much to Marshall's chagrin, Churchill persuaded Roosevelt that no practicable plan could be made for a return to the Continent in 1942, however desirable was a Second Front to help Russia. Available American forces could, nevertheless, be deployed against Germany in 1942 by landing in French North Africa to join hands with Montgomery's Eighth Army in clearing the whole of the North African shore, and uncovering the approaches to Europe's long and weakly defended Mediterranean coastline. Roosevelt agreed: the North African landings took place under Eisenhower's command just after Montgomery had defeated Rommel at El Alamein; and the two Allied Armies met in Tunisia, eventually capturing quarter of a million Axis troops when Tunis fell on 7 May 1943.

Before this happened, the second Allied summit, SYMBOL, to decide what to do next, took place at Casablanca in January 1943. The Americans wanted to withdraw most of their troops from North Africa to England for a cross-Channel attempt that summer. The British, who had prepared their case with meticulous care, demonstrated that there would not be enough landing ships and craft available in 1943 to do so. They counter-proposed exploiting success in the Mediterranean with the aim of driving Italy out of the war. The military thinking behind the British proposal came from General Sir Alan Brooke, the Chief of Imperial General Staff, but the inspirational and political drive behind it was Churchill's.

Brooke's military reasoning for favouring a Mediterranean approach to Nazi-occupied Europe was based on the fact that most of Europe's railways run east and west: north–south communications are relatively poor, especially through the Alpine regions. It was easy enough for Hitler to switch troops quickly from the Eastern Front to France, but much more difficult to reinforce the Mediterranean. Allied footholds could be established more easily in Southern France, Italy or the Balkans than on the storm-swept and heavily defended Channel Coast. Moreover, there was great potential for raising the Nazi-occupied countries of southern Europe in revolt; and it might be possible to bring Turkey into the war on the Allied side if sufficient strength was deployed to give the Turks confidence in an ultimate Allied victory.

Churchill Introduces the Crocodile's Underbelly

Churchill articulated Brook's strategy with his well known analogy, likening Hitler's Festung Europa to a crocodile. Why not, he asked, weaken Hitler's hold on occupied Europe by attacking its soft Mediterranean underbelly before attempting to crush its armoured snout with a cross-Channel assault, which might result in French beaches running with British and American blood? In his view, attacking across the Mediterranean would bring help to Russia quicker; it might avoid a risky cross-Channel operation altogether; and it could end the war earlier because American resources could be used as they became available rather than being held in England, waiting for a practicable D-Day.

The Casablanca debate ended with an American defeat, one senior American planner quipping 'We came, we saw and we were conquered'. They reluctantly accepted a continuation of operations in the Mediterranean while resources were being concentrated in England for two alternative cross-Channel operations: ROUND-UP, a major invasion in the greatest possible strength; and SLEDGEHAMMER, an emergency landing with whatever resources were available at the time to help Russia *in extremis*, or to exploit an imminent German collapse. They agreed tentatively to invade Sicily (Operation HUSKY) and possibly Sardinia and Corsica (Operations BRIMSTONE and FIREBRAND) as stepping-stones to an invasion of Italy; but they would not countenance any operations in the Balkans, on which they believed, quite wrongly, that Churchill was keenest for British Imperial purposes.

Soon after Tunis fell, the American Chiefs of Staff launched a debating counter-offensive at the third Allied summit, TRIDENT, held in Washington on 12 May. Marshall complained that unless something was done to limit Eisenhower's operations in the Mediterranean, they would act like a suction pump and draw vital resources away from ROUND-UP. The Americans wanted to insist on giving ROUND-UP absolute priority in the allocation of Allied resources, and to limit Mediterranean operations by ordering the return of seven veteran divisions (three British and four American), most of the assault shipping and substantial air forces to England by November 1943 in preparation for ROUND-UP in the spring of 1944. Churchill and Brooke fought back on the grounds that much could happen between May and November, and options should be left open. In their view, no final decision should be taken on ROUND-UP until it was possible to gauge the Italian reaction to the invasion of Sicily. Nevertheless, they agreed in principle to the American proposals: not to have done so might have led to their allies reversing strategic priorities by sending resources already earmarked for ROUND-UP to the Pacific.

Hitler Reacts

The fall of Tunis had its effect on Hitler and his OKW staff. German intelligence reports on the state of Italian morale after the capture of nearly 100,000 of their best troops were not encouraging. Italian defection from the Axis had become a possibility. Hitler ordered Plan ALARICH to be prepared to counter probable Italian treachery. Field Marshal Rommel was given command of a quick reaction force, HQ Army Group 'B' at Munich, with a call on 14 divisions to secure at least the whole of Northern Italy if Mussolini did defect. Field Marshal Albert Kesselring, the German military 'representative' in Italy, was made responsible for maintaining links with the Italian Comando Supremo for as long as possible. If treachery did occur, he was to withdraw all German troops and aircraft from Sicily and Southern Italy to a defensive line, prepared by Rommel, in the Northern Apennines between Pisa and Rimini (later to be called the Gothic Line).

At about this time Allied Intelligence became aware of the advanced state of development of Hitler's V-Weapons, and of the possibility that they might be launched on London from the Pas de Calais area. SLEDGE-HAMMER might be needed to snuff them out, if all else failed.

Sicily Invaded

When Sicily was invaded on 10 July, the Italian garrison virtually collapsed, but the German reinforcements, which were rushed to the island by Kesselring, made the Allies pay a substantial but not crippling price for its conquests by mid-August. Mussolini paid a much higher price for failure: he was ousted from power in an anti-Fascist coup on 26 July, and replaced by Marshal Badoglio as head of a Royalist Government, which paraded its determination to stay loyal to the Axis.

Badoglio's assurances of continuing Axis solidarity fooled no one in OKW, least of all Hitler, who ordered Plan ALARICH to be replaced by a much more brutal Plan ACHSE for the occupation of the whole of Italy and the disarmament of Italian forces in Italy, the Balkans, the Aegean and on the Russian front, at the first sign of Italian treachery. Unbeknown to Hitler, Badoglio had already authorised secret approaches to the Allies to find a practical way for Italy to change sides with minimum risk.

By this time the Allied leaders were assembling in Quebec for the fourth summit, QUADRANT, which opened on 16 August. The Americans came determined to secure ROUND-UP's priority and to curb British ideas of continuing Mediterranean operations, but events were conspiring against them.

Turning Point With ROUND-UP

General Sir Frederick Morgan, Chief of Staff to the, as yet, unappointed Supreme Allied Commander for ROUND-UP, presented the outline plan for the cross-Channel assault, timed for May 1944. It was approved, and its name was changed to OVERLORD to impress its priority over all other Allied operations. Churchill and Brooke again fought back and won approval for an invasion of Italy as soon as Sicily was cleared of Axis troops, provided the seven divisions, assault shipping and air squadrons earmarked for OVERLORD were returned to England by November. Brooke made it clear that while driving Italy out of the war was an important consideration, the main purpose of continuing Mediterranean operations was to draw German strength southwards and away from both Western Europe and the Russian Front. Indeed, the Allies' Mediterranean forces would be mounting a major strategic diversion in support of OVERLORD.[1]

ROUND-UP's name had barely been changed to OVERLORD when its overall priority was thrown into doubt. The British and American liaison staffs in Moscow reported that after defeating Hitler's last major offensive on the Eastern Front, Operation CITADEL, and winning the Battle of Kursk – the greatest tank battle ever fought – Stalin was about to exploit south-westwards towards the Dnieper River and on into the Balkans with the four Ukrainian 'Fronts' (the equivalent of Western Army Groups). Stalin was already earmarking the Balkans as a future Soviet sphere of influence.

These Intelligence reports from Moscow would not in themselves have altered the decision to give OVERLORD priority in 1944, had it not been for reports from Eisenhower at Algiers that Italian emissaries had arrived to negotiate Italy's capitulation. Churchill persuaded Roosevelt that there was now a *prima facie* case for questioning the decision to go for the crocodile's snout rather than ripping out its belly. He proposed that the roles of OVERLORD and Mediterranean operations should be reversed: OVER-LORD should be scaled down to a diversionary threat to pin German forces in Western Europe while the decisive operations took place in Italy, the Balkans and Southern France. Although Roosevelt was untutored in military affairs, his strategic intuition was closer to Churchill's than to Marshall's, and he feared the risks inherent in OVERLORD as much as Churchill. He directed Marshall to re-open discussions with Brooke as a matter of great urgency.

The Mediterranean Strategy Adopted

Brooke and the British Chiefs of Staff exploited this sudden and unexpected reprieve for their Mediterranean strategy. In the end, Marshall had to accept Roosevelt's view that the military balance of advantage between the American and British strategies was too fine to swing the argument either way. Political factors must also be weighed. It was no use trying to force the British into a course of action in which they had no faith. Churchill and Brooke saw OVERLORD through the eyes of men who had experienced the slaughter of the Somme and Passchendaele: they had much greater confidence in operations in the Mediterranean where the British had been paramount since Nelson's victory over the French at the Battle of the Nile in 1798. Whole-hearted British co-operation in Europe was vital to enable America to deal with Japan. Roosevelt, therefore, decided that the Mediterranean would be given strategic priority, and OVERLORD would be reduced to a size that would be compatible with presenting a credible threat to Hitler's Atlantic Wall, and being used for an opportunistic or emergency SLEDGEHAMMER-type Channel crossing.

Once this decision had been taken, the withdrawal of the seven divisions, assault shipping and air forces from the Mediterranean was cancelled, and Eisenhower was directed to plan the ripping open of the crocodile's belly. He, Generals Sir Harold Alexander, Sir Bernard Montgomery, Omar Bradley and all the other experienced commanders would stay in the Mediterranean. Eisenhower's place as the Supreme Allied Commander for OVERLORD was taken by Sir Frederick Morgan, its original planner; and its codename reverted to SLEDGEHAMMER. General Morgan was to have available for deception purposes and for emergency cross-Channel operations General George Patton's Third U.S. Army and General Henry Crerar's First Canadian Army. Alternative emergency landings were to be planned for the Pas de Calais and Normandy, and deception was to be heightened by raids on Dieppe and other Channel ports.

Marshall accepted his political defeat with great magnanimity. The decision having been taken by the President, Marshall threw his weight whole-heartedly behind Brooke's strategy, to the extent of persuading Admiral Ernest King, the U.S. Naval Chief of Staff, to divert an extra carrier group and additional assault shipping, earmarked for the Pacific, to the Mediterranean for the invasion of Italy.

Some revision of the Allied command structure in the Mediterranean was necessary. Churchill was so delighted to have won the strategic argument that he readily agreed to Eisenhower's retention of Supreme Allied Command, with his operational responsibilities widened to cover the whole of the Mediterranean, including the British Middle East Command. He would have two principal subordinate commanders: Alexander as Commander Allied Armies in Italy, responsible for all operations supported from bases in French North Africa; and General 'Jumbo' Maitland Wilson as Commander Eastern Mediterranean and Balkans, with his headquarters in Cairo and supported by the extensive British base installations in Egypt.

The Plan Evolves

Eisenhower, relieved of the necessity of returning resources to England, and informed of the diversion of U.S. troops, shipping and aircraft to reinforce his Mediterranean Theatre, made significant revisions in his plans for the invasion of Italy. Montgomery's Eighth Army would still cross the Strait of

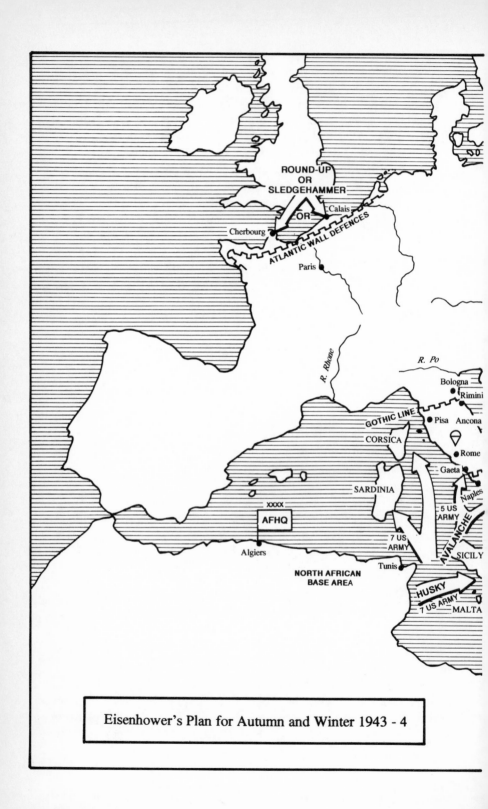

ROUND-UP
OR
SLEDGEHAMMER

OR

Calais

Cherbourg

ATLANTIC WALL DEFENCES

Paris

R. Rhône

R. Po

Bologna
Rimini

GOTHIC LINE

Pisa   Ancona

CORSICA

Rome

SARDINIA

Gaeta

Naples

xxxx
AFHQ

5 US
ARMY

7 US
ARMY

AVALANCHE

Algiers

SICILY

Tunis

NORTH AFRICAN
BASE AREA

HUSKY

7 US ARMY

MALTA

Eisenhower's Plan for Autumn and Winter 1943 - 4

Messina (Operation BAYTOWN), and advance up the 'toe' of Italy in the wake of a German evacuation of Sicily, but would also land at Taranto when Mark Clark's Fifth Army landed at Salerno (Operation AVALANCHE). Thereafter, Eighth Army would advance up the eastern side of the Italian Peninsula while Fifth Army took Naples and then thrust northwards up the western side to take Rome as quickly as possible. Clark's Salerno landings south of Naples would be supplemented by a landing in the Gulf of Gaeta to the north of Naples, which was made practicable by the arrival of Admiral King's additional aircraft carriers and assault shipping. The existing plan (GIANT II) to drop Matthew Ridgeway's 82nd U.S. Airborne Division on the Rome airfields, helping the Italians to protect their own capital against German occupation, would be retained and strengthened with some additional units.

In the Eastern Mediterranean, additional resources would enable Wilson to mount a division instead of a brigade to start clearing the Aegean islands of Rhodes, Cos and Leros (Operation ACCOLADE). But much more significantly, the British Ambassador at Ankara was instructed to re-open negotiations with the Turks for their entry into the war on the Allies' side. The Turks agreed to consider doing so with some enthusiasm when the size and scope of Allied operations was explained to them. They agreed to examine the possibility of launching an offensive against their traditional enemies, the Bulgarians, as soon as major British landings took place in Greece. These were being planned by General Sir Miles Dempsey, who had been designated to command Second Army for OVERLORD but was now assembling a new Ninth Army in the Middle East. This consisted of I Canadian Corps, which had played a major role in the invasion of Sicily and was now commanded by E.L.M. Burns, and Sir Ronald Scobie's III Corps, which had been earmarked for some time for the eventual liberation of Athens (Operation MANNA). As landings in Greece would not be practicable until enough assault shipping could be released from the invasion of Italy, a final decision on Anglo-Turkish military co-operation in the Balkans was temporarily deferred.

Cracks in the Axis

At OKW, Hitler was becoming increasingly suspicious of Italian intentions as the Sicilian campaign drew to its close. He persuaded the Italian Comando Supremo to accept several extra German divisions in order to reinforce the defence of Italy, and in so doing enabled Rommel to secure the Brenner Pass through which he could launch Plan ACHSE if the Badoglio Government defected. His two senior commanders in Italy – Kesselring and Rommel – had diametrically opposed views on the policy that should be pursued. Kesselring, always an optimist and nicknamed 'Smiling Al', believed that the Italians would stay loyal and would fight well in the defence of their homeland. Germany should give them as much help as possible to do so, and should defend every inch of the Italian Peninsula. If this proved impossible he would withdraw to a naturally strong defensive line east and west through Monte Cassino (the Gustav Line). Rommel, with his experience of Italian commanders and troops in North Africa, was cynically opposed to doing more than hold the Gothic Line in the Northern Apennines, protecting the industrial and agricultural resources of the Po Valley, and the Alpine approaches into southern Germany. Hitler sided with Rommel, but allowed Kesselring to keep faith with the Italians for as long as possible.

Italy Invaded – Axis Retreat

Montgomery crossed the Strait of Messina on 3 September and started pushing up the 'toe', impeded mostly by demolitions and mining by the rearguards of the German troops recently evacuated from Sicily. Italy capitulated on 8 September as the Allied landings started: Geoffrey Keyes' II U.S. Corps at Gaeta; General Ernest Dawley's VI U.S. Corps and General Sir Richard McCreery's X Corps at Salerno; General Sir Charles Alfrey's V Corps at Taranto; and Ridgeway's 82nd U.S. Airborne Division at Rome. Such was the speed and power of these widely dispersed landings that General Heinrich von Vietinghoff's embryo Tenth Germany Army in southern Italy had no hope of disarming the Italians and containing, let alone defeating, the landings. The only German success came in the rough handling of Ridgeway's airborne troops in Rome, who suffered from lack of Italian support in holding the city against ruthless German counter-measures. Most of Ridgeway's men, however, managed to withdraw to the relative safety of the Alban Hills to the south of Rome.

It was soon clear to Kesselring that he had misjudged both the loyalty of the Italians and the strength of the Allies' landings. He had the moral courage to report to Hitler that Rommel's plan should be acted upon. Von Vietinghoff's troops would be withdrawn to the Gothic Line as expeditiously as possible instead of trying to hold the Allies south of Rome on the Gustav Line at Cassino. Thus, it came about that Naples fell to Dawley's VI U.S. Corps on 18 September, and Rome was entered by Keyes' II U.S. Corps on 1 October as von Vietinghoff's rearguards were leaving the city.

From Rome northwards German resistance stiffened as Kesselring fought for time to strengthen the Gothic Line. Florence did not fall to Clark's Fifth Army, nor Ancona to Montgomery's Eighth Army, until 5 November. Rommel, however, was no longer waiting to oppose them. Hitler had sent him and his staff to France, to grip the strengthening of the Atlantic Wall defences and to improve the training of the German anti-invasion troops;

the OVERLORD/SLEDGEHAMMER preparations had been noted by OKW. Kesselring was left in sole charge in Italy as OB Südwest, German C-in-C South-West, with a Führer Directive to hold the Gothic Line at all costs: no withdrawals were to be allowed on any pretext whatsoever.

Alexander, promoted Field Marshal after the fall of Rome, started to attack the Gothic defences in mid-November with Fifth U.S. and Eighth Armies. Clark's Fifth U.S. Army took the Apennine passes due north of Florence with relative ease, but once over the watershed, the German defence of the reverse slopes of ridge after ridge in weather that was deteriorating rapidly brought nothing but frustration and exhaustion to his American troops. Montgomery did no better on the Adriatic coast. As Eighth Army thrust its way into and through the flat marshy plain of the Romagna, which lies between the eastern spurs of the Apennines and the Adriatic, he was faced with a succession of defended river lines, the ground between them becoming glutinous mud as the autumn rains pelted down. By mid-December the weather forced Alexander to halt all offensive operations, and to plan, re-group and re-train for a decisive battle that he intended to fight in the spring, driving the Germans back to the Alps. Fifth U.S. Army had come within 15 miles of Bologna, but was still in hill country; and Eighth Army was on but not across the River Senio about the same distance from Bologna (*see inset to Map 2*). By then, they were opposed by two German Armies: General Lemelsen's Fourteenth Army defending Bologna and von Vietinghoff's Tenth Army in the Romagna, both under command of Kesselring's HQ Army Group 'C'.

The Three Thrusts

In the meantime the Allied leaders had been meeting at their fifth and sixth summits, SEXTANT and EUREKA, at Cairo and Tehran respectively. SEXTANT started on 23 November with the welcome news that the Turks would certainly enter the war as soon as Dempsey's Ninth Army landed in Greece. Dempsey had already cleared the Germans out of Rhodes, Cos, Leros and other Aegean islands off the Turkish coast: successes that had been seen by the Turks as symbols of Allied intentions. Equally encouraging to Brooke were the substantial advances made by the Russians on their southern front. The 3rd and 4th Ukrainian Fronts under Malinovski and Tolbukhin were on the Dnieper, preparing for their next advance towards Rumania.

SEXTANT in Cairo, compared with its predecessor QUADRANT in Quebec, was a very amicable meeting for two good reasons. First of all, the American Chiefs of Staff were now firmly behind the agreed strategy, and their massive mobilization organisation was geared to making the Mediterranean the decisive theatre. One of their new Armies, Hodges' First U.S.

Army, which had been destined for OVERLORD, was already concentrated and training in the Mediterranean Theatre near Naples. And General Jacob Devers' Seventh U.S. Army, which had taken part in the invasion of Sicily and now included General Alphonse Juin's strong French Expeditionary Corps of French North African troops, had taken Sardinia and Corsica where they were now training for a possible descent upon the French Riviera.

Secondly, since Quebec, Eisenhower's Allied Force Headquarters at Algiers had been working on the detailed plan for Mediterranean operations in 1944, which had already been agreed in principle by Washington and London, and had only to be endorsed by the 'Chiefs' in Cairo. The Eisenhower Plan was elegant in its simplicity. It called for the development of three major thrusts: into the Balkans, in Italy and into Southern France, each commanded either by a British or one of two American Army Group headquarters.

Alexander, from a new HQ 89th Army Group recently established on Rhodes, would direct the Eastern thrust into the Balkans, commanding Montgomery's Eighth and Dempsey's Ninth Armies, and co-ordinating operations with the First and Second Turkish Armies under Mustapha Jemal. Eighth Army was to cross the Adriatic into Yugoslavia (Operation GELIGNITE) to co-operate initially with Tito's Partisans in cutting the German lines of communication to Greece in the Sava valley, and then to thrust northwards towards Vienna via the Ljubljana Gap.[2] In order to help operations in Italy, Montgomery was to mount a corps landing on the Istrian Peninsula (Operation SHINGLE) with a second corps in support: firstly, in the hope of frightening Kesselring into abandoning the Gothic Line and withdrawing across the Po to the relative safety of the Alps; and secondly, to ease his own eventual advance through the Ljubljana Gap. Ninth Army was to land at Athens and Salonika (Operation MANNA), and to drive the German garrison back up the Vardar and Struma valleys to come up on Eighth Army's eastern flank. And the First and Second Turkish Armies would invade Bulgaria, heading for Plevna and Sofia respectively, and aiming to force the Bulgarian Government to desert the Axis as Italy had already done.

For the Central thrust in Italy, Mark Clark would take over Alexander's HQ Allied Armies in Italy, re-naming it HQ 15th U.S. Army Group. General Lucien Truscott would replace Clark in Fifth U.S. Army, and Hodges' First U.S. Army would relieve Eighth Army for its operations across the Adriatic. Clark was to plan the destruction of Kesselring's Army Group 'C' south of the Po (Operation GRAPESHOT) after the Allied Air Forces had destroyed all the Po bridges.[3] Once Kesselring's two armies had been destroyed and their remnants forced back to the Alps, Clark was to go over onto the defensive with First U.S. Army facing the Alpine passes, while

SLEDGEHAMMER FORCES

Calais

Cherbourg

V-WEAPON LAUNCH SITES

Paris

R. Danube

Brenner Pass

FRANCE

ALPS

R. Rhone

Turin

5 US ARMY

1 US ARMY

Bologna

Marseilles

Cannes

1 US ARM

Toulon

5 US ARMY

XXXX

15

7 US ARMY

CORSICA

SPAIN

9 US ARMY

Rome

FROM THE USA

XXXX

79

15 US ARMY

SARDINIA

R. Po

0   50

Miles

Route 7

Finale

Lake Commachio

Bologna

Argenta

5 US ARMY

R. Senio

1 US ARMY

THE BATTLE OF THE PO, APRIL 1944

Eisenhower's Plan for Operations, Spring 1944

he cleared north-western Italy with Fifth U.S. Army and advanced towards the Franco-Italian frontier.

The Westerly thrust would be the landings on the French Riviera, undertaken by Omar Bradley's 79th U.S. Army Group (Operation ANVIL, later re-named DRAGOON). Devers' Seventh U.S./French Army would carry out the initial landings to secure the ports of Toulon and Marseilles through which General William Simpson's Ninth and General Leonard Gerow's Fifteenth U.S. Armies would be brought in direct from the United States to provide the power behind an advance up the Rhone valley towards Paris. Truscott's Fifth Army would join Bradley from Italy if it was needed and Clark could spare it. Thus the re-occupation of France from the south would be carried out by three U.S. armies and possibly a fourth.

Timing of all these operations was decided by availability of assault shipping, except for Clark's in the Po Valley, which depended on the spring sunshine drying out the ground in the Po valley. About four to six weeks were needed for the movement of shipping between offensives. The Eighth Army's landing on the Istrian Peninsula was to come first, towards the end of January 1944, to loosen up the Italian front.[4] Its landings in Yugoslavia were planned to follow in March. The shipping would then be sailed to Egyptian ports to lift Ninth Army for its invasion of Greece in May. In the meantime, Clark's GRAPESHOT offensive in Italy was expected to start in early April, weather permitting. The shipping was not expected to be available from Greece for the landings in Southern France until June. Thus the outline programme was:

January	Istrian landings
March	Invasion of Yugoslavia
April	Offensive in Italy
May	Invasion of Greece
June	Invasion of Southern France

At the EUREKA summit in Tehran, which opened on 27 November, these Allied plans were presented to Stalin, who was overtly gratified by the earlier opening of the Western Allies' 1944 offensives, and by the obvious help it would bring to the drive by his Ukrainian Fronts towards the Balkans. Covertly, he feared the arrival of Turkish and British troops in his prospective post-war sphere of Soviet influence. He had little difficulty in agreeing to Churchill's request to accelerate the advance of Malinovski's 3rd and Tolbukhin's 4th Ukrainian Fronts towards Rumania; acceleration would help to ensure that his troops arrived there first.

Stalin made one crucially important promise. He was an advocate of the

ANVIL/DRAGOON assault on Southern France, which he believed would give most help to Russia in drawing German resources as far away as possible from the Russian Front. He agreed to synchronise the launch of his major 1944 summer offensive with ANVIL/DRAGOON by attacking in mid-June on his central sector.

First Strikes and Hitler's Counter-Moves

The Western Allies' 1944 programme opened on schedule with the landing of General Sir Sidney Kirkman's XIII Corps on the Istrian Peninsula, and the quick capture of the port of Pola on its eastern side on 22 January. Simultaneously Truscott attacked towards Bologna with his Fifth U.S. Army. Kirkman achieved surprise: initially, German resistance was sporadic. Although Hitler's Intelligence had picked up Yugoslav rumours that Eighth Army was likely to land on the Dalmatian coast, they did not expect a major landing as far north as Pola. Only one low-class coastal division was garrisoning the whole peninsula. Truscott was not so lucky: the ground was still water-logged with winter rain; his tanks could not manoeuvre off the roads; and, in consequence, his infantry failed to punch a hole in the German front. He wisely halted his offensive as soon as it became clear that Kirkman's landing had not panicked Kesselring into a withdrawal across the Po before the Allied Air Forces had destroyed all its bridges behind him.

Kirkman's landing had, indeed, the very opposite effect upon Kesselring and Hitler. Kesselring acted with ruthless determination, gathering local reserves from all along his main front and rushing them piecemeal to seal off Kirkman's foothold. Hitler decided that he must teach the Allies another sharp lesson about amphibious landings to deter them from mounting a cross-Channel invasion of France. He decreed that the savage defeat inflicted on the Canadians at Dieppe in August 1942 must be repeated at Pola. He dispatched some of his best divisions from France to drive Kirkman back into the sea. Neither Hitler nor Kesselring gave any thought to retiring on the Alpine passes as the Allies had hoped.

Montgomery, who was receiving sporadic ULTRA reports of German high level communications, realised that the Allies' ploy had failed, and that Kirkman would be in real trouble if he was not quickly reinforced. He ordered the planned shipment of General Wladyslaw Anders' II Polish Corps to Pola to be accelerated, and warned the Allied Strategic Air Forces that Kirkman might need their help at short notice.

It was to be a close run thing: due to Allied strategic air attacks on the Alpine passes, it took as long to move Hitler's reserves from France to Istria as it did to ship Anders' Corps to Pola. General Hans von Mackenson, who was charged with Kirkman's and Anders' destruction, mounted three successive blitzkrieg style attacks over a ten-day period. At times he came close to success, but Allied air intervention and weight of naval gunfire thwarted him.[5] By 20 February Hitler called off the battle as he needed all the troops he could muster to shore up the southern end of the Eastern Front where Malinovski's and Tolbukhin's offensives towards Rumania had just opened.

Invasion of the Balkans

During March, Montgomery shipped the remaining three corps of Eighth Army across the Adriatic to Zadar, Split and Dubrovnic. The British troops received a mixed reception from the local Partisan commanders, some of whom were positively hostile, believing that the British were about to impose a new imperialism upon them. OB Südost, Field Marshal Max-imillian von Weichs, the German C-in-C in the Balkans, gave priority to protecting the main German communications routes southwards to Greece from Partisan attack and had already abandoned the defence of the Dalmatian coast to save troops, so Montgomery was relatively un-challenged as he built up his logistic base. He intended to thrust northwards towards the Sava valley with McCreery's X Corps to threaten the German communications, and north-westwards with General Charles Keightley's V Corps and General Brian Horrock's XXX Corps to link up with his troops holding Pola. He hoped to concentrate the whole of Eighth Army even-tually on the line Pola–Ljubljana–Zagreb, ready to attack the main German defence line, which Allied Intelligence reported was being prepared between Ljubljana and Lake Balaton, extending the flank of the Alpine barrier eastwards to the Danube near Budapest. This line became known to the Allies as the Balaton Line.

Progress in Italy – German Debacle

By the beginning of April, all the Po bridges had been destroyed by the Allied airmen and Mark Clark decided that the ground was dry enough on his front to launch his 15th Army Group's GRAPESHOT offensive.[6] Early on 9 April, his two Armies opened their attacks along bomb carpets, laid by the Strategic Air Forces. Nevertheless, it took three days of hard fighting by Hodges' First U.S. Army to breach the Senio defences east of Bologna, and by Truscott's Fifth U.S. Army to break out of the mountains well to the west of the city. It took another ten days for the two U.S. Armies to break through either side of Bologna. Realising that the bulk of his Army Group would be lost if he did not pull back before it was too late, Kesselring asked Hitler to authorise his AUTUMN MIST withdrawal plan, which had been worked out in meticulous detail some months earlier. Hitler was in one of his obstinate 'no withdrawal' moods and hesitated just too long. Hodges' armoured divisions broke through the Argenta Gap in the marshes around Lake

Commachio after several days of relentless fighting and joined hands with Truscott's armour at the appropriately named village of Finale between Bologna and the Po, thus encircling the greater part of Kesselring's best troops. Only about a third of them survived in the subsequent debacle as they tried to scramble back over the bridgeless Po and retreat to the safety of the Alpine passes. By the end of April, Hodges was probing the German blocking positions in the Alps, and had linked up with Kirkman at Pola.

The V-Weapon Factor

By now, Hitler was beginning to consider 'the last ditch' defence of the Greater German Reich, to gain time until his secret V-Weapons could be brought into action and force the Allies to accept peace on his terms as London crumbled before their eyes. He saw the key outworks of his defences as being Western Poland, covering Berlin; Hungary, blocking the approaches north of the Danube; the Alpine Front in Italy with its Balaton Line extension eastwards to the Danube at Budapest, covering southern Germany and Austria; and the Pas de Calais where his V-Weapon launching sites were being installed in the greatest secrecy. All operations beyond these vital areas were to be treated as delaying actions, to gain time for his V-Weapons to win Germany the ultimate victory.

Hitler's V-Weapon programme had, in fact, suffered a severe set-back. Photographs of the V-1, flying-bomb or 'doodlebug', launching sites in the Pas de Calais area had reached London from Holland in August 1943. Most of the sites were destroyed by Allied bombers (Operation CROSSBOW) as soon as they were detected by air photography, and so they had to be redesigned to make them less vulnerable to air attack. They were not expected to be operational again until mid-1944.

Hitler's thinking had an immediate impact upon Alexander's 89th Army Group in the Balkans. Von Weichs reported to Hitler that Eighth Army's pressure in Yugoslavia was beginning to make Greece and Albania untenable. The Russian advance across the Bug into Moldavia was equally disturbing. It would be clearly advisable to pre-empt the expected British and Turkish invasion of Greece and Bulgaria with a planned withdrawal back to the Balaton Line, using delaying and scorched-earth tactics, and making the Allies pay for every mile they advanced. There was nothing vital to the defence of Greater Germany in the Balkans, which should be abandoned slowly to save troops and resources for the close defence of the Reich, and to increase war weariness amongst the Allies.

Hitler authorised von Weichs to put this policy into effect with a Führer Directive, the gist of which was intercepted by ULTRA. He went further: he despatched Rommel to supervise the development of the Balaton Line with troops withdrawn from France.

Fearing a Communist take-over in Greece if the Germans did withdraw as ULTRA intercepts suggested, Eisenhower authorised Alexander to bring forward Dempsey's planned invasion by Ninth Army, and alerted the Turks to accelerate their plans for intervention as well. At the end of April, reports from Athens made it clear that the Germans were, indeed, leaving.

Scobie's III Corps and Burns's I Canadian Corps were able to land unopposed at Athens and Salonika respectively on 5 May, temporarily forestalling a Communist coup. Turkey declared war on Germany, Bulgaria and Rumania next day. After landing relief supplies for the starving Athenians and building up his logistic base at Salonika, Dempsey started his advance up the Vardar and Struma valleys, heading for Belgrade and Sofia, hoping to extend Montgomery's eastern flank towards the Danube. His leading troops encountered the Germans on the Greek frontier, and thereafter he was opposed day after day by determined German rearguards, which used every possible delaying position to inflict maximum casualties on his troops with minimum loss to themselves, and to win time. It all added up to a slow and frustrating advance for Ninth Army in difficult mountain country with few rewards.

On 13 June, the expected V-Weapon assault on England started with 73 V-1s, out of 244 launched, landing in London by midnight of the 16th. Morgan was alerted to the possible need to mount SLEDGEHAMMER. He was to be ready to cross the Channel with Patton's Third U.S. and Crerar's Second Canadian Armies as soon as enough extra assault shipping could be brought back from the French Riviera where the ANVIL/DRAGOON landings were to begin on 20 June.

Assault on Southern France

Omar Bradley's 79th U.S. Army Group assault on Southern France started with heavy naval and air bombardments of tactical targets, and parachute drops to cut potential German reinforcement routes. The main feature of the seizure of the initial beachhead between Toulon and Cannes was the zest displayed by Juin's North African divisions, who gloried in their chance to help liberate France. Within thirteen days Toulon and Marseilles had fallen, but Devers' attempt to push north up the Rhone valley was halted by German forces scraped together and rushed south by von Rundstedt, OB West, from the reserves still positioned behind the Atlantic Wall. Bradley found himself encircled and forced to fight defensive battles to secure his expanded beachhead while Simpson's Ninth and Gerow's Fifteenth U.S. Armies were brought in through Marseilles and Toulon.

The Ring Closes as Germany Crumbles

True to his promise at Tehran, Stalin opened his 1944 summer offensive in the centre of the Eastern Front on 22 June. Hitler's Greater German Reich was thus encircled by a ring of fire on all sides except in the north-west, where he was being forced to strip the Atlantic Wall of its best troops to act as fire brigades on other more endangered fronts. But, as the attacking Allied armies were finding to their cost, there is only one thing more formidable than a German Army on the offensive and that is one on the defensive. German soldiers have a flair for systematic and destructive withdrawal, and are almost unbeatable in defence. The fighting on all fronts during the summer of 1944 was a slow remorseless Allied advance against fanatical German troops who did their best to buy time for their Führer to win the war by some miraculous stroke of genius. The fact that Germany itself was being reduced to rubble behind them by the Allied Strategic Bomber Forces, waging the POINT BLANK air offensive, seemed irrelevant to them.

In the Balkans, the two Turkish Armies forced the Bulgarian Government to change sides on 10 July. Stalin accelerated Malinovski's and Tolbukhin's advance over the Dniester River into Rumania proper to take advantage of Bulgaria's collapse. Bucharest capitulated on 30 July. Alexander flew there to confer with Tolbukhin at the beginning of August. It was agreed, with some reluctance on the Russian side, that the Danube should be the military boundary between the Western and Soviet armies. Montgomery's Eighth Army had the most difficult task of all in working its way forward to come to grips with Rommel's Balaton Line. The nearer to the Reich, the more fanatical, although piecemeal, the German resistance became.

SLEDGEHAMMER Hits the Pas de Calais

It was not until 1 August that the German containing line around Bradley's foothold in Southern France began to give way. A break-through by Truscott's Fifth U.S. Army, fighting its way over the Franco-Italian frontier, triggered a German withdrawal up the Rhone valley. Once Bradley's three Armies had fanned out from their lodgement, their advance northwards became exhilarating with all France rising in their support. Paris fell on 23 August. Ten days later SLEDGEHAMMER was launched by Morgan against the Pas de Calais, behind one of the heaviest strategic bomber and naval bombardments the world has ever experienced. The German garrisons in the Atlantic Wall fortifications and the reserve divisions behind them had been so weakened by withdrawals to reinforce other fronts that they suffered one of those spontaneous collapses that tend to happen when troops have reached the limits of their endurance. Field Marshal Hans von Kluge, who had replaced von Rundstedt as OB West after his failure to drive Bradley back into the sea, could not stem the route before Morgan's troops had over-run the V-Weapon launching sites. Morgan and Bradley then swung

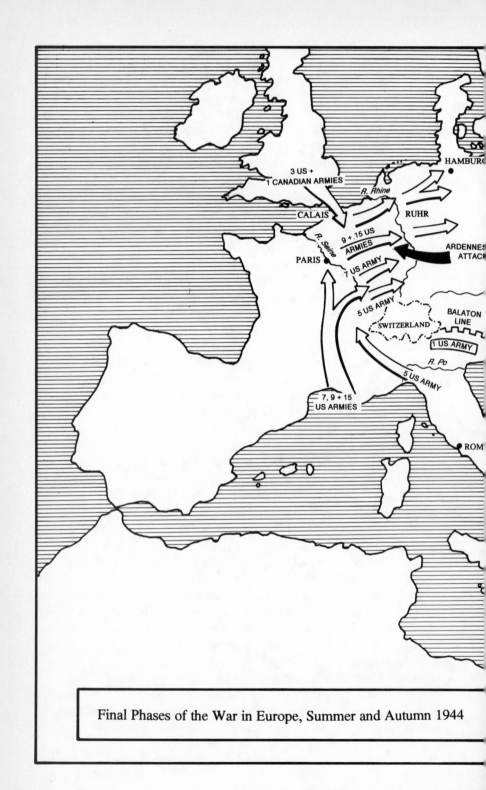

3 US +
1 CANADIAN ARMIES

R. Rhine

CALAIS

RUHR

HAMBURG

9 + 15 US
ARMIES

R. Seine

PARIS

ARDENNES
ATTACK

7 US ARMY

5 US ARMY

BALATON
LINE

SWITZERLAND

1 US ARMY

R. Po

5 US ARMY

7, 9 + 15
US ARMIES

ROME

Final Phases of the War in Europe, Summer and Autumn 1944

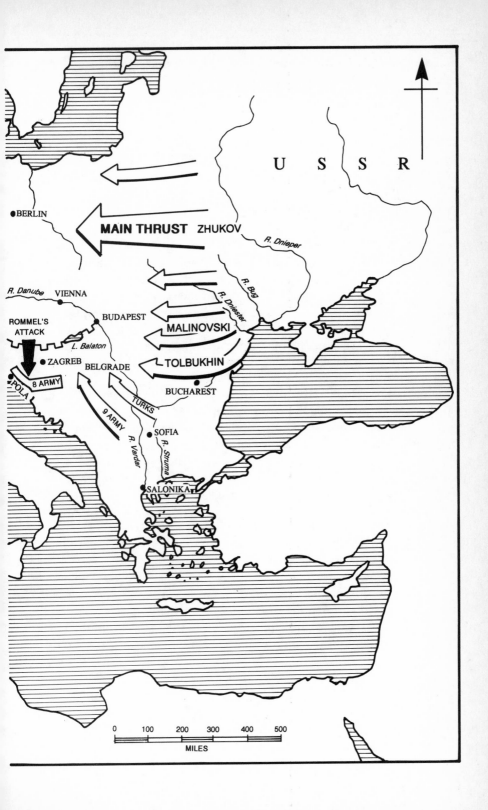

BERLIN

MAIN THRUST ZHUKOV

R. Dnieper

R. Danube VIENNA

R. Bug

R. Dniester

ROMMEL'S
ATTACK

BUDAPEST

MALINOVSKI

L. Balaton

ZAGREB

BELGRADE

TOLBUKHIN

POLA

8 ARMY

BUCHAREST

9 ARMY

TURKS

R. Vardar

R. Struma

SOFIA

SALONIKA

U S S R

0   100   200   300   400   500
MILES

their Army Groups eastwards and were on the Rhine by mid-September, while in the East, Marshal Georgi Zhukov's leading troops reached the Oder at about the same time.

The Last Act

The Allied leaders met at Yalta for their last wartime summit on 25 September to co-ordinate the final moves in the destruction of Hitler's Third Reich, and to re-shape the post-war world. The final military directive envisaged three decisive thrusts: Zhukov to take Berlin; Tolbukhin and Malinovski to take Budapest; Alexander to smash through Rommel's Balaton Line to take Vienna; and Morgan and Bradley to cross the Rhine either side of the Ruhr, and head for Hamburg and Berlin.

Hitler refused to acknowledge defeat and launched two desperate spoiling offensives. In the West, he punched a hole in Bradley's front in the Ardennes on 15 October, but after an initial setback the Americans sealed off the German penetration and had restored their front by the end of the month. And in the East, Rommel tried to disrupt Montgomery's preparations for Alexander's assault on the Balaton Line with a major counteroffensive against Eighth Army just west of Zagreb, using the remnants of most of the last available panzer divisions. Montgomery, forewarned by ULTRA, used his Alam Halfa and Medenine tactics of the Desert War. Rommel ran onto hidden British anti-tank guns and hull-down tanks, and saw his tanks decimated in a matter of hours.

The thick black oily smoke of burning tanks had barely blown away before Alexander launched his final offensive, using his four Armies to break through Rommel's formidable defences: Eighth and Ninth Armies west of Lake Balaton, and the two Turkish Armies between Balaton and the Danube. Burns's I Canadian Corps of Dempsey's Ninth Army broke through first and advanced rapidly on Vienna with the Turkish Armies moving in close support along the south bank of the Danube. Dempsey entered Vienna ten days later, bringing the Turks nearer to the city than they had ever been since they last besieged it in 1683.

The first winter frosts hardened the ground sufficiently for Zhukov to mount his crossing of the Oder at the end of November. Bradley and Morgan were already over the Rhine and advancing deep into Germany. Zhukov, however, won the race for Berlin, and Hitler's suicide in the ruins of his capital brought the war in Europe to a close on Christmas Day 1944.

EPILOGUE

There can never be a final resolution of the debate on the merits of the Mediterranean peripheral approach over the continental style OVERLORD. Two principal factors suggest that the war in Europe might have been shortened by six months, as suggested in this chapter, if Churchill's and Brooke's strategy had been adopted.

First of all, there would have been no withdrawal of the six divisions and assault shipping from the Mediterranean during the autumn of 1943 in preparation for OVERLORD. Increased resources used for the invasion of Italy would have swung German strategic argument in Rommel's favour. Kesselring would have had to fall back to the Gothic Line without attempting to hold the Gustav Line, based on Cassino, thus shortening the Italian Campaign by a year.

Secondly, the vast American resources earmarked for OVERLORD could have been employed more quickly in the Mediterranean as they became available without wasting time concentrating in England, waiting for D-Day. Greater and more continuous pressure could have been brought to bear on Germany, on a much wider front. And the appearance of larger Allied resources in the Mediterranean could have brought the Turks into the war on the Allied side by mid-1944.

The possible combinations and permutations are infinite, but there is a tenable case for suggesting that Churchill and Brooke might have been right.

NOTES

1. The story so far has been based on fact: from here the fiction takes over. However, to distinguish fact from fiction, all factual operations that did take place during the Second World War have been given their original codenames and accorded their actual duration and results. Comparison of the actual and fictional dates of operations is given in these notes. Fictional operations are not codenamed.
2. GELIGNITE was actually timed for early 1945, but was never carried out, owing to a decision to send more troops back to help end the war more quickly in North-West Europe.
3. GRAPESHOT was in fact fought in April 1945.
4. The Istrian landing is the equivalent of the Anzio landing (Operation SHINGLE), which took place on the same date in January 1944.
5. This was the real course of events at Anzio in February 1944.
6. This was the course of the actual GRAPESHOT offensive, which was fought on the same dates but a year later (1945), with Eighth Army instead of First U.S. Army attacking east of Bologna.

BIBLIOGRAPHY

British Official Histories:
Grand Strategy Series, vols 3–5
Mediterranean and Middle East, vols 3–6
Victory in the West, vol 1
U.S. Department of the Army Histories:
Mediterranean Theater of Operations

CHAPTER 7

Operation GREENBRIER
Defusing the German Bomb
JOHN H. GILL

The Nuclear Threat

In high summer of the pivotal year of 1943, Hitler's legions seemed to be recoiling on all fronts and the Allies could begin to speak confidently of the post-war world. On the western front, British, American, and Canadian troops had seized Sicily and were poised for an invasion of the Italian mainland. Italy teetered on the brink of defection. In Russia, the Red Army had thrown back the last great German summer thrust, Operation CITADEL, and launched a massive counteroffensive of its own. Perhaps more important, the Allies had finally gained the upper hand in the crucial Battle of the Atlantic. The Germans could hope for future successes in the air war, but even here the Luftwaffe was incapable of preventing the devastation of major urban centres such as Hamburg. As summer turned to autumn that year, however, intelligence reaching London and Washington threw a pall over the assumptions of ultimate victory: the Germans were close to, or might already possess, an atomic bomb.[1]

Fear of German atomic weapons was not new. From 1939 on, worries about a Nazi nuclear bomb had become a near obsession with many prominent physicists and had provided the most important stimulus to the American bomb programme. These fears were confirmed in 1943 when new information indicated unambiguously that the Germans were ahead in the atomic race. Therefore, while accelerating development of an Allied bomb, indeed to gain time for that development, British and American leaders sought desperately to prevent or at least delay the operational deployment of a German nuclear capability. These efforts, like those against the V-Weapons, were orchestrated under a single codename: GREENBRIER.

Terrific Powers of Annihilation

It is hardly surprising that Hitler's Reich should lead all other belligerents in the development of atomic weapons. Germany, after all, was in many ways the cradle of nuclear fission, first achieved by chemists Otto Hahn and Fritz Strassmann at Berlin's Kaiser Wilhelm Institute for Chemistry in 1938. Although Nazi policies deprived Germany of some of its best scientific minds – brilliant Jews like Lise Meitner and Otto Frisch, for example, were forced to emigrate – a significant number, including Hahn himself, remained in the land of their birth. Chief among these in reputation and capability was the 1932 Nobel laureate for physics, Werner Heisenberg. Heisenberg was a confirmed German nationalist with little political acumen; he did not want to see Germany defeated, but neither did he have any desire to promote Hitler's cause. Recognising the military potential of nuclear science, he particularly wanted to prevent Hitler from acquiring an atomic bomb.

Other capable German scientists had no such compunctions. If they lacked Heisenberg's international stature and theoretical brilliance, Paul Harteck and Kurt Diebner were competent, inventive and determined to push the nuclear weapons programme to success. In early 1939, Harteck sent a letter to the War Department describing 'an explosive many orders of magnitude more powerful than conventional ones' and predicting that the 'country which first makes use of it has an unsurpassable advantage over the others'. The sinister seed was thus planted and, just as Wehrmacht troops were completing the conquest of Poland, the Army Ordnance Department (Heereswaffenamt) took over the civilian Kaiser Wilhelm Institute for Physics in the Berlin suburb of Dahlem and set up a nuclear research headquarters under Diebner. Although little over a year had passed since Hahn's experiments, therefore, the strategic possibilities of nuclear fission were already visible on the horizon and Germany was the only nation in the world with a military office exclusively dedicated to exploiting them.

Following a scheme proposed by a young physicist named Otto Haxel, the German nuclear programme progressed at a steady if unspectacular pace for the next two years. While quietly pursuing basic research, Heisenberg and associates such as Hahn imposed delays by diverting resources and discouraging speculation that a bomb could be constructed in time to be used in the ongoing conflict.[2]

Germany's battlefield victories, however, were giving the programme an unintended boost. The uranium mine at Joachimsthal in Czechoslovakia had fallen into Nazi hands with the occupation of that country in 1939. The conquest of most of Western Europe netted Diebner's team several hundred tons of uranium ore from Belgium; a near-operational cyclotron in France (Germany's three were still under construction); and, in a remote Norwegian valley, control of the world's only heavy water plant. Research, resources and organisation were thus slowly beginning to coalesce, and, in

N

ENGLAND

North Sea

NETHERLANDS

London

Dover

Calais

● WATTEN

O Brussels

BELGIUM

O Rotterdam

R.Rhine

Cologne ○ ● LEVERKUSEN

○ Bonn

G

○ Coblenz

O Amiens

Lux.

FRANKFURT ●

O Rouen

R. Seine

O Reims

HEIDELBERG ●

Paris ○

F   R   A   N   C   E

STRASBOURG ●

O Orleans

● FREIBURG

Sites Associated with the
German Nuclear Weapons Project
1939 - 45

O Dijon

ZURICH ●

SWITZERL

Baltic Sea

KIEL

HAMBURG

R. Elbe

Bremen

Stettin

R. Oder

POLAND

ORANIENBURG

BERLIN

Hanover

GOTTOW

GRÜNA

R. Weser

BERNBURG

DESSAU

Göttingen

TORGAU

NORDHAUSEN

Leipzig

MERSEBURG

Breslau

E R M A N Y

JOACHIMSTAL

Prague

C Z E C H O S L O V A K I A

Nuremberg

ROTTENBURG

Ulm

HECHINGEN

R. Danube

Vienna

Munich

Bad Tölz

Tegernsee

A U S T R I A

AND

Innsbruck

0   100   200

Miles

September, an alarmed Heisenberg told a friend he saw 'an open road to the atomic bomb'.[3]

Two events accelerated the German bomb programme in 1942. First, Hitler appointed Albert Speer as the Reich's Minister of Armaments and Munitions in February. Speer had drive, confidence, Hitler's trust and, most important, an interest in the military potential of nuclear physics. Intrigued by reports from the Army and Air Force weapons chiefs after a preliminary conference in February, the new minister scheduled another meeting for June to review the status of the programme and determine its future direction and scope. Speer himself would chair the meeting. Heisenberg was expected to deliver the key paper on the status of and prospects for nuclear research. Before the conference could be held, however, Werner Heisenberg was dead, killed by an explosion in his Leipzig laboratory as he was working on a small atomic pile experiment. As a result, it was bomb proponents Harteck and Diebner who presented the crucial briefing at Speer's 4 June meeting. Creating an audible stir when they stated that the nuclear explosive material required for a bomb would be 'about the size of a pineapple', they sparked Speer's imagination and gained his whole-hearted support. The Reichsminister conveyed his personal conviction to Hitler two weeks later and received the Führer's approval to grant the programme increased funding and priority. 'The Führer became very still for a moment', Speer later recalled, 'He stared at me and then struck the table with his fist exclaiming: *this* is our vengeance for Lübeck and Rostock!'[4] With this support from the Reich's highest levels and the adventitious elimination of the obstructionist Heisenberg, the German bomb project took off.

This Requires Action

British and American intelligence agencies were slow to recognise the German nuclear threat. In the United States, an August 1939 letter from Albert Einstein to Franklin D. Roosevelt prompted the American president to tell his military aide 'This requires action!' but the only tangible result was the formation of a weak committee that quickly succumbed to bureaucratic inertia. A second Einstein letter in March 1940 seemed equally unproductive. British scientists were also alarmed about developments in the Reich, and the government responded by forming a committee which reported cogently on the military potential of nuclear research but had little new intelligence to offer.

By the spring of 1941, however, the Allies were growing increasingly anxious about nuclear developments in Germany. Aware of their own progress but lacking clear indications of the enemy's, the British committee concluded that 'we have to reckon with the possibility that the Germans are at work in this field and may at any time achieve important results'. An expatriate German physicist working for the Tube Alloys Directorate, Rudolf Peierls, was commissioned to study the problem. The intelligence available to Peierls was derived almost entirely from espionage: contacts the Special Operations Executive (SOE) was building with Norwegian resistance elements and the Secret Intelligence Service's (SIS) few sources in Sweden and Germany. Particularly significant was an SIS operative known only as 'Herr Eckart' who had managed to bluff his way into the February 1942 conference where Heisenberg and others had discussed the military potential of nuclear research. Peierls came to three conclusions: first and most important, that the Germans were considering the possibility of a 'uranium bomb'; second, that they had a strong interest in Norway's heavy water plant; and third, that Heisenberg was the key to Nazi success.

The news of Heisenberg's death was thus initially greeted with great relief in Washington and London. With him out of the picture, British authorities thought a blow at the key physical facility associated with German nuclear research, the Norwegian heavy water factory at Vemork, would cripple the Nazi project once and for all. An attempt to attack the plant with gliderborne commandos failed disastrously in November 1942, but a courageous assault by Norwegian resistance fighters the following February caused massive damage and totally halted heavy water production.

British damage experts initially estimated that the plant would be out of action for two years and the more optimistic members of the Tube Alloys Directorate began to hope that the German bomb effort had been permanently disabled. In April, however, an anxious Otto Hahn travelled to Stockholm to attend a symposium and met with his old colleague, Lise Meitner. On the periphery of German bomb research, Hahn's movements were not subject to the scrutiny that dogged other members of Diebner's group. His reputation, however, had sufficed to gain him access to Speer's 4 June conference and he kept in close contact with his acquaintances inside the bomb project. An SIS report from Stockholm that month stated that 'Dr. O. Hahn very agitated and contemplating suicide due to Nazi advances in uranium bomb work. Damage to Vemek [sic] only a minor setback.' Hahn's information proved accurate and by August, British intelligence had to inform its American counterpart that the plant at Vemork was once again fully operational.

Up to this point, there had been little co-operation in the atomic intelligence field between Britain and the USA. Furthermore, other than a recognition in general terms that the Nazis remained active, there had been no concerted U.S. intelligence effort against the German nuclear target at all. Indeed, no real action was taken until several alarming new reports arrived in the summer and autumn of 1943. Only then did the energetic head of the Manhattan Project, General Leslie R. Groves, turn his formidable attention to the enemy's preparations.

Groves was certainly troubled by the reactivation of the Vemork plant, but much more disturbing were reports provided by two sources in Berlin, one British and one American. The British source, cover name 'Grenville', was a disgruntled staff officer in the very organisation charged with nuclear weapons development, the Heereswaffenamt.[5] Grenville reported on 22 June that initial excitement over the Vemork attack had subsided because progress with 'the alternative' had been satisfactory. Mixed in with other information, was the comment that 'positive results' with 'special explosives' were expected soon. A second report on 12 August clarified that the 'alternative' was graphite and added that 'operational employment planning' would probably begin within the next several weeks. At the same time, a different source specifically warned that England would soon come under direct attack by 'special weapons', a term some analysts interpreted as a designation for 'uranium bombs'.

The American source was a dedicated and resourceful man named Erwin Respondek, whose wide circle of friends made him an ideal contact. In addition to generals, political leaders, industrialists and anti-Nazi elements, he had direct links to the Kaiser Wilhelm Institute (KWI) and personal ties to members of Germany's scientific community such as Hahn and Heisenberg. Under the cover name 'Ralph', Respondek had exploited these contacts to collect intelligence on critical strategic decisions and scientific developments inside the Reich. In early May of 1943, Respondek's courier, disguised as a priest, travelled from Berlin through Austria to Italy, took a boat across Lake Maggiore to Locarno and called Sam Woods, the American consul in Zürich. Woods met the 'priest' on a park bench by the lake and received from him a sheaf of papers.

Following useful data on German strategy, Respondek's detailed assessment stated that five million Reichsmarks had been made available for research into a bomb that 'was probably connected to Otto Hahn's splitting of the uranium atom'. An additional 30 million Reichsmarks was being reserved for 'technical tests' and two million more were allocated for the construction of a large installation associated with the project. 'The military authorities', Respondek concluded, 'are anxiously awaiting results of tests'. Woods sent a cable which arrived at the U.S. State Department on the morning of 14 May.

The Respondek and Grenville reports were the rocks that triggered an avalanche of interest in the German bomb project. Although all of the intelligence thus far had come from human sources and had not been confirmed by either photo reconnaissance or signals intelligence (Sigint), it was too dangerous to ignore. German tube alloys thus became an agenda item when Churchill and Roosevelt met in Quebec in August 1943. The two leaders agreed 'to pursue immediately, and with the highest priority, a joint effort to eliminate the possibility of a German TA [tube alloys] threat'.

The Most Important Bomb

The Quebec decision was implemented by a 13 September directive which established the Tube Alloys Joint Intelligence Committee (TAJIC). GREENBRIER was selected as the codename to cover investigation of the German nuclear weapons programme as well as countermeasures against it, and the TAJIC quickly and universally came to be known as the GREENBRIER Committee. Recognising Britain's long experience in intelligence and its superior intelligence organisation, the choice of a head for the committee was left to Churchill. The United Kingdom's vulnerability to attack was an additional consideration. The Prime Minister selected his son-in-law Duncan Sandys for the post. Until recently the coordinating authority for British efforts to unravel the V-Weapons mystery (Operation CROSSBOW), Sandys was the Joint Parliamentary Secretary at the Ministry of Supply in 1943. He enjoyed Churchill's trust and his organisation gradually acquired broad directive authority that belied its designation as an 'intelligence committee'.

The first logical step in tackling the intelligence problem was deciding exactly what the Allied analysts needed to know in order to assess and combat the German nuclear threat. The key immediate question was how far the Germans had advanced and when they might have an operational weapon in hand, but Sandys wanted to be able to attack the enemy project in all its dimensions and to do so he needed a thorough understanding of the entire German effort. He assigned this initial task to a small joint team headed by Dr R.V. Jones, who had been making a significant contribution to the rocket investigations, and Major Robert Furman, Groves's intelligence chief. The Jones–Furman team divided their intelligence requirements into four general categories: (1) research and development; (2) production; (3) transportation and storage; and (4) delivery. None of these categories was definitive, and they would often overlap, but they provided a basic guideline for further study.

The next step was to determine the allocation of intelligence resources against these categories. Thus far, all of the information on the German programme had come from agent reports, and the GREENBRIER analysts recognised that these would likely continue as the principal sources of data. However, agent reports were in some ways the least reliable form of intelligence, being difficult to collect and subject to enemy manipulation. It was also difficult to disentangle GREENBRIER intelligence from information on other subjects. Furthermore, operatives were often little better than untrained observers and the tight security restrictions of the Allied nuclear programme precluded detailed briefings for agents or interrogators. At best, the GREENBRIER Committee could only advise other intelligence agencies to report the whereabouts of certain scientists, the presence of new factories or weapons with special security precautions, and other general information on scientific developments.

Sigint and photo reconnaissance had yet to play a major role. Sigint could contribute little to the intelligence attack as long as the Germans were in the research and early production phases of their programme and thus had no requirement to communicate by wireless means. The Americans did decipher a 24 August Japanese message requesting radioactive materials from the German government, but such transmissions were rare. Similarly, photo reconnaissance, later invaluable, was nearly useless until specific targets could be identified for detailed scrutiny.

In spite of these uncertainties, intelligence on the German atomic bomb peril had an almost immediate effect on the larger conduct of the war: in Quebec, the British dropped their objections to the May 1944 target date for the cross-Channel attack. The peripheral strategy promoted so vigorously by Churchill, especially actions in the Mediterranean, was thus permanently shelved in favour of an amphibious assault on the French coast. The OVERLORD operation entailed greater risk but it also offered the best hope of a bringing the war to a successful conclusion before Germany could prepare a bomb. The nascent GREENBRIER campaign, however, also contributed to keeping the Mediterranean as a secondary theatre. In addition to strategic and political concerns, Allied planners coveted the Foggia airfields, from which bombers and reconnaissance aircraft could range into hitherto unreachable regions of Germany. Respondek's 'large installation' had not been located, so it was important to bring the entire Reich under aerial surveillance and attack. The invasion of Italy proceeded as planned on 9 September and Montgomery, prodded by Churchill and Field Marshal Brooke, seized Foggia on the 12th.

Meanwhile, the GREENBRIER Committee was preparing its first situation assessment. Presented in executive summary to Churchill on 12 October and to Roosevelt some days later, this document contained several understandable misconceptions but revealed the surprisingly accurate deductions reached by the GREENBRIER analysts at this very early stage of the campaign.

1. The current status of the enemy TA project is not known with any certainty. Our physicists estimate, however, that uninterrupted progress could result in a weapon in 1944, possibly as early as January but most likely toward the end of the year.

13. The Allied Chiefs of Staff debate the strategy of Europe's 'soft underbelly'. *Left to right*: Admiral Ernest King, U.S. Chief of Naval Staff; General George Marshall, U.S. Army Chief of Staff; Lt-Gen 'Hap' Arnold, Commander U.S. Army Air Force; three U.S. Strategic Planners and Advisers; General Sir Hasting ('Pug') Ismay, Churchill's Military Secretary; Admiral Lord Louis Mountbatten, Chief of Combined Operations; Admiral Sir Dudley Pound, Chief of Naval Staff; General Sir Alan Brooke, Chief of General Staff; Air Chief Marshal Sir Charles Portal, Chief of Air Staff; and Field Marshal Sir John Dill, British Representative with the U.S. Chiefs of Staff.

14. British troops pause while fighting their way up Italy. *(Imperial War Museum)*

15. Boeing B-17 Flying Fortresses head for vital targets deep inside Germany. *(James Smith Collection; Airmen Memorial Museum, Suitland, MD, USA)*

16. Despite its superlative performance and heavy armament, the Messerschmitt 262 jet fighter was unable to establish permanent air superiority in the face of the numerically stronger Allied Air Forces.

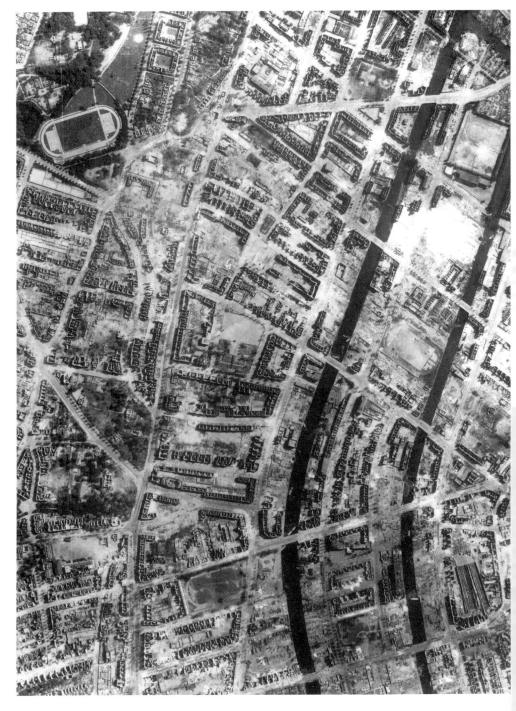

17. Operation GOMORRAH: Hamburg after the first Eighth Air Force daylight raid, 25 July 1943. Evidence of devastation can be clearly seen, but would be very much worse a week later.

18. Commander of the sprawling Manhattan Project, General Leslie R. Groves pursued information about Diebner's efforts with relentless thoroughness and seemingly boundless energy. *(U.S. National Archives)*

19. Marshal of the Royal Air Force Sir Charles 'Peter' Portal, British Chief of the Air Staff who was responsible for the conduct of ARMAGEDDON.

20. U.S. B-26 Marauders on their way to targets in northern France suspected of being secret weapons sites. (A. Shellenbarger Collection: Airmen Memorial Museum. Suitland. MD USA)

21. Rommel's opponents in Normandy. *Left to right*: Air Marshall Tedder, General Montgomery and General Eisenhower. *(Robert Hunt Library)*

22. British specialised armoured vehicles fight their way up the beaches of Normandy.

23. The shambles on OMAHA Beach.

The frightening prospect of Hitler having an atomic bomb in the first month of 1944 was alarmist. Captured documents and post-war interrogation of German bomb scientists indicate that they did not expect to have a viable, tested weapon until the autumn of 1944 at the earliest. The committee, however, correctly discounted reports that the Germans would use 'uranium bombs' against England in the autumn of 1943.

2. With the exception of the Norwegian heavy water factory and the research institute in Berlin, the critical facilities involved in the enemy's programme have not been identified. Within the constraints of TA security, the intelligence services have been advised of GREENBRIER intelligence requirements.

This was a very cautious statement. In fact, GREENBRIER was preparing to strike several targets believed associated with the Nazi bomb.

3. Aircraft are the most likely delivery means for TA devices but the rockets suspected to be under development represent another possibility. An attack by submarine or surface vessel is considered highly improbable.

The mention of rockets reflects the grossly exaggerated estimates at that time regarding the size of what came to be known as the V-2.[6] With its one-ton payload, the V-2 was totally inadequate for delivery of a 1940s atomic weapon and the Germans, of course, never considered it.

With this report in hand, the Western Allies considered the thorny issue of informing Stalin about the new German threat. There was no evidence to suggest that Soviet intelligence had learned of German progress and the upcoming Tehran conference provided a opportunity for Roosevelt and Churchill to mention the common enemy's bomb. They did not. The two leaders discussed the question in Cairo – Churchill had even prepared some proposed wording: 'a new weapon of potentially unprecedented power' – but security of the Manhattan Project remained the paramount concern. Stalin, therefore, would not receive official notification regarding the German project until the Potsdam Conference in 1945.

As he headed for Cairo and Tehran, Roosevelt carried with him news of another worry. American scientists were afraid that Germany might use radioactive waste products as a sort of poison to attack British cities or to interfere with the coming invasion. This eventuality was considered extremely unlikely, but General Groves could not bring himself to dismiss it entirely and he orchestrated the formation of small teams to accompany the landing forces. Under the cover name PEPPERMINT, these secret teams were to carry packets of film – the film would react if exposed to radiation – and a few measuring instruments to detect German use of radiation weapons.

Another American initiative was a scientific intelligence mission known as ALSOS (to the annoyance of the security-obsessed head of the Manhattan Project; this is the Greek word for 'grove'). Following the Allied armies as they advanced into Europe, this select group of scientists and intelligence officers was to collect information on enemy technical developments, especially in the field of nuclear weapons.

As Sandys was constructing the GREENBRIER intelligence apparatus to uncover and attack the German bomb, the Allies continued their efforts against those features of the enemy programme that *had* been identified. American B-17s bombed the Norwegian heavy water plant on 16 November, but failed to demolish it and left the stocks of precious liquid intact. The attack, however, convinced the Germans that the plant was too vulnerable and plans were begun to transfer the processing equipment and remaining heavy water to the interior of the Reich. Similarly, when RAF bombers struck Berlin-Dahlem they did little damage to the Kaiser Wilhelm Institute, but forced the Germans to consider the evacuation and dispersal of the Reich's principal nuclear research centre.

In compiling their target list, the GREENBRIER planners had also identified two other research facilities that could be associated with the bomb project, a branch of the KWI in Heidelberg and a weapons test establishment near Berlin, but neither was considered important enough to hit immediately. On the other hand, plants were uranium ore might be refined to the high levels of purity required for atomic weapons represented a critical bottleneck for the German project. Drawing on pre-war information from physicists and industrial specialists a uranium processing installation of the Deutsche Gold und Silber Scheideanstalt (DEGUSSA) was identified at Frankfurt am Main and gutted by RAF incendiaries in late 1943. The U.S. Eighth Air Force hit Kiel in December on a GREENBRIER raid, damaging a factory that produced centrifuges and other delicate scientific instruments. As the Germans had abandoned centrifuges as a means of separating fissionable material, however, the raid did nothing to further the goals of GREENBRIER.

Potential delivery means were also attacked. As rockets were already being bombed under the CROSSBOW campaign, Sandys was satisfied to support and occasionally guide these strikes. Aircraft posed a slightly different problem, but here the Allies benefited from a co-operative Luftwaffe colonel captured in Tunisia. Known as 'Ivy', this man had commanded an air force experimental unit and thus had access to the latest developments in the German aircraft industry. Working on the assumption that an atomic bomb would weigh at least four to six tons, the GREENBRIER analysts submitted detailed questions to Ivy's interrogators, concentrating on 4-engine bomber types with large carrying capacity. Ivy described five aircraft that seemed to fit the GREENBRIER criteria: the He-177, He-274, He-277, Ju-488, and Me-264. Several of these types were unsuitable for the atomic bomb mission, but in 1943, the GREENBRIER Committee could only discard one, the infamous He-177 which was often more dangerous to its crews than to the enemy and was considered too unreliable for such a sensitive task. The others became targets and an Eighth Air Force raid on Ulm managed to destroy one of the Me-264 prototypes in December.

GREENBRIER attacks continued to chip away at the German programme through the first half of 1944. Berlin-Dahlem was ravaged by RAF bombing raids in February and again in March, finally persuading Diebner to evacuate most of his personnel to safer locations. German efforts to salvage the last of Vemork's heavy water were ruined by the determination of the Norwegian resistance which succeeded in sinking the ferry transporting the invaluable fluid to Germany on 20 February. GREENBRIER concerns about heavy water also led to the bombing of the large hydroelectric plant at Merano in northern Italy.

Although the Merano strike caused the cancellation of a raid on Austrian railyards, most GREENBRIER targets – such as V-Weapons and the German aircraft industry – were also important to other Allied bombing objectives and the campaign seldom forced diversions from the Combined Bomber Offensive. GREENBRIER did, however, have an impact on Allied strategy and operations. Before departing for Cairo in November 1943, Churchill asked the Home Secretary to review the 'Black Plan' for a partial evacuation of London and instructed the general staff to prepare a study on the use of chemical agents in response to German employment of 'special weapons'. He also asked Eisenhower whether the target date for the invasion could be advanced. Eisenhower understood fully the need to move as quickly as possible and had hoped that OVERLORD could be launched in early May. Inadequate shipping, uncertain weather and other operational requirements delayed the assault, but GREENBRIER considerations 'invariably delivered to me by word of mouth', were clearly uppermost in the Supreme Commander's mind when he decided, despite the atrocious weather, to proceed with the invasion on the night of 5/6 June.

Unknown to the Allies and despite repeated technical snags, the Germans had succeeded in constructing an atomic pile in Berlin and had established a plant near Torgau on the River Elbe to separate plutonium from the radioactive product of the pile. Designated the 'Torgau Water Filtration Facility' ('Kläranlage Torgau' or KAT), this was Respondek's 'large installation', and by the late spring of 1944 it had produced enough plutonium to prepare a nuclear explosive device. It was Diebner's intention to use this first batch of plutonium for an underground test that summer while the pile was transferred from Berlin to the KAT; by the end of the year, he then hoped to have sufficient material for one, or perhaps two, actual bombs. As a precaution, he had also arranged for construction to begin that summer on a second 'water filtration plant' near Rottenburg on the Neckar (KAR/N or 'KARIN'). With Berlin becoming untenable, assembly of the device was to occur at the huge Mittelwerk underground factory near Nordhausen in the Harz Mountains and test preparations had begun when Allied bombers found the KAT in June.

GREENBRIER had slowly accumulated intelligence on Torgau in the months before OVERLORD. The first hint came in agent reports of 'an extraction facility for eka-rhenium on the Elbe'. Initial photo results provided no conclusive evidence, but the reconnaissance planes returned in May as new reports arrived. In April, a German scientist had mentioned a facility on the Elbe while conversing with one of the U.S. Office of Strategic Service's (OSS) Swiss sources and, several days later, another OSS operative specifically reported 'a very large plant on the banks of the Elbe at Torgau'. This information was soon expanded by British interrogation of an SS conscript captured in Italy. The SS soldier willingly explained that he had been involved in the construction of the KAT and even supplied a crude sketch.

It was a Mosquito pilot, Wing Commander Oliver Thomas, who brought back the first pictures of the KAT on 20 May. Although efforts to acquire vials of Elbe river water failed, additional evidence came from air samples collected by a plane equipped with a special 'scrubber' on loan from the Manhattan Project. American bombers hit the target in late May, but damage was only partial and a combined U.S. and British strike, continually delayed by poor weather, could not be launched until 10 June. This time the focus was on the electrical power facilities that fed the KAT's enormous requirements. The power plant was demolished and repair work made nearly impossible by RAF raids during the following week. The RAF bombing had also caused heavy casualties among the KAT's highly skilled work force. Activity at the KAT virtually ceased and, at the end of the month, the Eighth Air Force inflicted another significant loss on the German programme by devastating Diebner's key uranium processing facility at Oranienburg. Following the fall of Rome and the invasion of Normandy, the loss of the Torgau and Oranienburg installations has rightly come to be regarded as the third great Anglo-American victory in Europe during June 1944. Though the GREENBRIER Committee did not yet know it, the success of these bombing raids meant that Hitler would have only one atomic bomb.

He was determined to use it. At a conference on 2 July, Diebner, however, was reluctant:

'We must recognise, my Führer, that this is a new field of scientific endeavour, the device is untested.'

Hitler cut him off. 'You do not understand strategy or the weakness of the Anglo-American alliance', he shouted, 'We will use the device and you will begin work on a new weapon at once.'

The German programme was fragile. The June bombing raids had cut off the supply of processed uranium, disrupted the plutonium manufacturing process and killed or injured dozens of critical workers. A new DEGUSSA uranium refinery was under construction south of Berlin, but the Oranienburg plant was a near-total loss and it would take months to repair the KAT. Moreover, the Allies now knew the KAT's location and would doubtless undertake more bombing raids if there were any signs of renewed activity. Diebner therefore decided to make minor repairs to the KAT for safety reasons while transferring the plutonium operation to the KARIN facility. With luck, it might begin production by November.

In the meantime, planning for what was intended to be the world's first atomic strike proceeded under Hitler's personal guidance. He saw this new weapon as a means to exploit the supposed 'war-weariness and divisiveness' among the Western powers, crush their invasion forces in Normandy and then turn his attention to the Eastern Front. Captured documents reveal that the potential target list included the Allied invasion troops, ports in the south-east of England, and London. Hitler preferred the British capital but Dover was eventually selected to receive the German atomic bomb.

In the Nordhausen caves, Diebner's technicians, urged on by a personal telegram from Hitler, laboured to assemble the device, now bearing the codename 'Rabe' (Raven). Simultaneously, Luftwaffe engineers struggled to modify an airframe to deliver it. The only aircraft capable of carrying the heavy weapon was an odd hybrid with the codename 'Beethoven'. This was an unmanned Ju-88 crammed with explosives and flown to the vicinity of its target by an Me-109 fighter attached to the old bomber's upper fuselage via a rather precarious set of struts. By 27 July, Rabe tests with several Beethoven mock-ups had been successfully completed and Luftwaffe Captain Horst Rudat of Kampfgruppe 101 was handed sealed orders to take three of his five Beethovens to an airfield near Watten in the Pas de Calais.

Watten was the site of one of Hitler's mammoth construction projects, a vast bunker originally intended as a V-2 launching site. Consuming 120,000 cubic metres of concrete, the Watten bunker had come under Allied scrutiny in the summer of 1943 while still under construction. Raids by B-17s in August and September had forced the Germans to cancel their V-2 plans, but Speer was able to convert the installation into a liquid oxygen factory. Periodic Allied bombing through the spring and summer of 1944, especially a heavy RAF strike on 6 July using the new 12,000 pound 'Tallboy' bombs, slowed but did not halt production. Well-protected and close to all three potential targets, Watten seemed the ideal site to complete assembly of the Rabe and mate it with Beethoven. Unfortunately for the Germans, the entire region was under close observation by a network of French agents, whose organiser, Michel Hollard, was playing a key role in the CROSSBOW campaign.

In early July, the GREENBRIER analysts were frustrated by a lack of solid intelligence. Agent reports indicated that most KAT senior technical personnel had departed Torgau but their destination and activity were unknown. The picture was further muddied by reports of unspecified scientific activity in south-western Germany. The break-through came from Sigint. On 22 June, Japanese Ambassador Oshima Hiroshi had cabled Tokyo describing 'secret weapons of the atom-splitting type with which the Germans would bomb England'. In a diplomatic decrypt of 15 July, the ambassador reiterated that Germany would soon be employing a weapon even more devastating than the flying bomb. Finally, on 26 July, American Army Sigint deciphered a Japanese message in which Oshima spoke of the new 'radioactive weapon' having an effect that would 'extend to a square of more than one kilometre'. The Germans, he added, were expected to begin using this weapon in the near future.

These intercepts coincided with unusually heavy traffic from the Army High Command to LXV Corps, the special Army–Luftwaffe organisation charged with conducting the V-Weapon attacks and thus responsible for the Watten bunker. Fortunately for the Allies, the progressive degradation of the German communications system forced the enemy to rely on wireless links which were susceptible to exploitation. Here GREENBRIER first encountered the cover name Rabe as messages discussed special security precautions, transportation priorities and personnel requirements. The intercepts did not disclose the meaning of the name Rabe, but it seemed obvious to the entire committee that it could be nothing other than the German bomb. Neither dates nor destinations were specified in the messages but the GREENBRIER analysts quickly concluded that its arrival was imminent.

Fortunately, Michel Hollard's net included a number of railway employees and from these contacts he learned on 31 July that the Germans were planning a top-priority rail shipment for 2 August. The efficient Germans arranged for clear lines and ordered that all stations were to be evacuated or guarded as the train passed through. Hollard determined that this special cargo could have only one destination, the little station at Watten, a conclusion verified by spotters who observed the train on the 2nd and 3rd. Assuming he was merely passing on more details about rockets and the mysterious bunker, Hollard signalled his British contacts on the night of 4/5 August.

Reading Hollard's message, Sandys, Jones and Furman reached the same conclusion as the Frenchman. They were still uncertain as to how the Germans would deliver the bomb, but there could be no question of delay to resolve this puzzle. Sandys requested an immediate meeting with his father-in-law.

'Satisfied that the moment of supreme peril had arrived', Churchill later told an interviewer, 'I rang up the President on the scrambler phone and said "GB [GREENBRIER] thinks they've found the Nazi bomb."' The Prime Minister then outlined the countermeasures being planned: starting on the morning of 6 August, British and U.S. fighter-bombers would scour the area around Watten, while heavy bombers attacked the bunker itself with conventional bombs and the RAF's Tallboys. GREENBRIER had also alerted SOE to prepare for an emergency operation against Watten.

Early the next morning and throughout the day, Allied aircraft roared across the Channel to pound what they were told were critical 'aeronautical facilities' at Watten. Tempests and P-47 Thunderbolts roamed the countryside destroying trains, trucks and aircraft; by some miracle, one of Captain's Rudat's Beethovens survived the onslaught. American medium bombers obliterated Watten rail station and much of the village. Meanwhile, Lancasters of the RAF's 617 Squadron under Wing Commander J.B. Tait struck the bunker itself. Although a number of the Tallboy 'earthquake' bombs fell wide of the target, several scored direct hits and one caused a portion of the roof and one wall, evidently weakened by the July bombing, to collapse. Churchill would later call this 'the most important bomb of the war'.

Watten's trial by fire continued through the afternoon as B-17s braved intense anti-aircraft fire to bomb the bunker through dust and smoke still lingering from the Lancaster strike. In subsequent analysis, it proved impossible to determine how much additional damage this second raid actually had caused, but it clearly disrupted rescue efforts, inflicted additional casualties on the bunker occupants and made the entire area around the site a cratered wasteland. Two old B-17s filled with explosives (known as 'Aphrodites') were flown into the bunker site by remote control several days later and further conventional bombing raids were conducted until Allied ground troops secured the site at the end of August. But it was the strikes on the 6th that sealed the fate of Nazi Germany's atomic bomb.

Relieved Beyond Measure

The Allied air attack on Watten came none too soon. Inside the bunker, final preparations had been underway to ready the Rabe for use against Cherbourg in concert with the Mortain counterattack in Normandy. The bomb was to be dropped on this critical port when the counterattack was opened on 7 August or as soon thereafter as weather and technical circumstances would permit. When the Tallboys began to fall on the 6th, however, the Germans were appalled. The LXV Corps staff reported several days later that 'the whole area around has been so churned up that it is unapproachable, and the bunker is jeopardised from underneath'. They wryly devised a new codename for the site: 'Concrete Lump'.

Several days passed before workers, constantly dispersed by air raid warnings, could begin to excavate the bomb chamber. They soon discovered that the incomplete Rabe had been crushed by the bunker's collapsing walls. Fear of the bomb's highly toxic plutonium core and radiation from its uranium components now brought further digging to a halt. Unwilling either to risk further exposure to Germans or to allow Frenchmen access to the Reich's greatest secret, the Rabe team hastily covered the larger gaps with concrete, demanded more protective gear and requested convict labour to perform actual recovery of the deadly device. Before these arrangements could be finalised, however, Montgomery's 21st Army Group overran the Watten site.

German efforts were also hampered by the SOE and the French resistance. The danger from friendly bombers and the rapid approach of Allied ground troops forced the cancellation of a proposed commando raid, but SOE operatives and Frenchmen repeatedly interrupted and harassed German lines of communication to the bunker. Equally important, a special SOE team managed to capture a German engineer from Watten who revealed valuable information on the damage to the site and the failure of German efforts to recover the Rabe.

However, the GREENBRIER Committee's task remained unfinished. There was no certainty that the Rabe was the only German weapon and the search for additional information continued unabated. With the liberation of France and the apparent success against Torgau, Oranienburg and Watten, however, GREENBRIER seemed to be running out of targets. The Mittelwerk at Nordhausen, finally located in August, appeared impervious to attack, but two I.G. Farben factories were damaged during July: a pilot heavy water plant at Merseburg and a Leverkusen facility formerly involved in uranium processing. Still unaware of the importance of the Beethoven hybrids, GREENBRIER also maintained its efforts against the dwindling inventory of large German bombers, destroying most prototypes by the autumn of 1944. The 'south-western installation', on the other hand, had not been found.

The GREENBRIER Committee scanned every incoming report for clues and General Groves pressured the Manhattan Project scientists to accelerate their work, but as the weeks passed without further German action, Sandys and Jones gradually began to feel that 'Jerry had shot his bolt'. The Americans, especially Groves and Furman, were much less sanguine, but intelligence slowly began to accumulate suggesting that the German bomb programme had indeed been crippled. Although Nazi propaganda continued to trumpet an arsenal of wonder weapons, Ambassador Oshima's candid cables indicated a more sober appraisal in the highest councils of the Reich. 'No one speaks of atomic uranium bombs any more', he wrote.

These hints were reinforced by the reports of OSS agents in Torgau and Berlin. In November, an OSS agent known as Ruppert penetrated SS Security Service headquarters in Berlin and learned that 'the security officers for the cat [sic] and raven operations have been disciplined, some shot'. Of several agent teams sent to Torgau, only one, Martini, got through. He confirmed that the KAT had ceased operations. The German staff had joked about 'moving south to meet Karin'. Similarly, the Hammer mission reported from Berlin that the KWI laboratories were empty, adding that the scientists had 'gone south to a security zone near Hechingen'. Reporting from British and U.S. sources in Switzerland substantiated this information and photo reconnaissance aircraft soon found KARIN. Two American raids in early December devastated the facility.

The GREENBRIER campaign was also coming to a close. On the morning of 25 November Colonel Boris Pash of the ALSOS mission entered Strasbourg and made for the university. Here he found German physicist Rudolf Fleischmann with a safe full of documents marked *Streng Geheim* (Top Secret). Pash imprisoned the physicist and removed the stash of documents for examination by the ALSOS scientific experts. The chief scientist recorded that he and a colleague was sifting through these materials when 'we both let out a yell at the same moment, for we had found papers that suddenly lifted the curtain of secrecy for us'. On 5 December, after a 120-mile journey by jeep through snow and mud to 6th Army Group headquarters, the team briefed Vannevar Bush, head of the U.S. Office of Scientific Research and Development, who had come to Europe to participate in the Watten investigation. Some of the sequentially numbered documents were missing but enough remained – including a plutonium production plan and a schedule for testing the bomb – to prove conclusively that Germany no longer presented a nuclear threat. 'Relieved beyond measure', Bush drove to SHAEF headquarters the following day to meet with Eisenhower's Chief of Staff, General Walter Bedell Smith. Smith, outlining the concluding operations of the war, bluntly asked Bush if the Allies would need to risk higher casualties to prevent the Germans from building another bomb. 'No', said Bush, 'that file is closed, general. You may take two years if you like. There will be no more German atomic bombs'.

The GREENBRIER Committee continued to function for the remainder of the war and for several months thereafter, but with the destruction of

KARIN and the discovery of the Strasbourg documents, its focus shifted. No longer as concerned with the possibility of a German bomb, it became the hub for British and American efforts to deny atomic secrets to the Soviets. Learning that the Germans had transferred their atomic pile to the Mittelwerk, GREENBRIER apprised senior Allied leaders and thus ensured that U.S. troops reached Nordhausen well ahead of the Red Army. Similarly, Allied heavy bombers struck a number of targets situated in what was to be the Soviet zone of occupation. Oranienburg was flattened, and the incomplete DEGUSSA plant at Grüna as well as the German Army's Gottow test range were badly damaged. With the German bomb project eradicated and surrender imminent, the KAT was left alone for fear of causing deadly radiation leaks. American and Russian patrols reached Torgau almost simultaneously, however, and GREENBRIER teams rushed to dismantle as much as possible of the plant's critical equipment before it was opened for Soviet inspection in early May.

The GREENBRIER Committee was disbanded in November 1945. It has been argued that GREENBRIER was at best a partial success in that the Germans were able to construct and deploy an atomic weapon, however crude, and that the countermeasures adopted to destroy this device left a poisoned pit at Watten which contaminated its immediate vicinity for years. The bombing of Torgau, although its results were by no means as severe, has been criticised on similar grounds. These criticisms overlook, however, the enormous difficulty of the intelligence task faced by the GREENBRIER analysts and, by emphasising the hideous wound at Watten, they implicitly denigrate the magnitude of GREENBRIER's achievement in preventing a true nuclear detonation over Dover or Cherbourg. It seems clear that GREENBRIER, whatever its shortcomings, was instrumental in shortening the war and thus saving countless lives, Axis and Allied. The atomic bomb was Hitler's last hope. By defusing the bomb, GREENBRIER destroyed that hope and ensured the ultimate defeat of Nazi Germany.

THE REALITY

This fictional account diverges from history along two principal lines. First, there was in reality no viable German atomic bomb programme. Although German physicists pursued nuclear research throughout the war, their efforts were badly fragmented, weakly supported and harried by Allied bombing. The investment in nuclear weapons was minuscule and Germany never came close to production of an actual explosive device. The reasons behind its 'failure' have been the source of considerable historical debate. This article, however, accepts the argument that German nuclear weapons development was delayed in part by the reluctance of Heisenberg and others to craft a bomb for Hitler. Heisenberg, therefore, is removed at a fairly early point in this story. Furthermore, it is assumed that Nazi Germany had the scientific, industrial and economic capability to achieve a weapon and a firm foundation of basic research, organisation and infrastructure was thus established that did not in fact exist.[7]

The second divergence involves the Allied response to the prospect of a German atomic weapon. Actual British and American efforts were much less comprehensive than GREENBRIER, but the CROSSBOW operation shows what such a campaign might have looked like. With some American support, the British actively attacked the German research effort through its reliance on heavy water from Norway during 1942 and 1943, but by the late summer of the latter year (that is, about the same time that this narrative opens), British intelligence was generally certain that the German programme posed little or no threat. The Americans proved more sceptical. It was only the discovery of the Strasbourg documents that finally convinced General Groves the German bomb was illusory.

NOTES

1. In fact, by the summer of 1943, British intelligence was fairly well convinced that the Germans had no viable atomic bomb programme.
2. The problem of timing was a key reason Germany never invested in nuclear weapons: Hitler and other crucial leaders were convinced that the war would end before nuclear research would pay off; therefore, the expense could not be justified.
3. Heisenberg's quote is actually from a post-war interview.
4. This fictitious quote refers to two cities destroyed in RAF incendiary attacks in March and April 1942.
5. The name 'Grenville' is an invention.
6. The V-weapons sparked intense debate in British intelligence and scientific circles; some estimated the rocket's size to be as great as 50 or 70 tons.
7. Germany's capability in this regard was, to say the least, questionable. It seems unlikely that a nuclear weapon could have been achieved without sacrificing or scaling back some of the other huge projects that were absorbing the Reich's scientific and materiel resources (eg, the V-2).

BIBLIOGRAPHY

Bush, Vannevar, *Pieces of the Action* (New York, 1970)

Dippel, John V.H., *Two Against Hitler* (New York, 1992)

Eisenhower, Dwight D., *Crusade in Europe* (Garden City, 1949)

Gilbert, James L. and John P. Finnegan, (eds.), *U.S. Army Signals Intelligence in World War II* (Washington, D.C., 1993)

Goudsmit, Samuel A., *Alsos* (New York, 1947)

Hinsley, F.H., *British Intelligence in the Second World War* (London, 1979–90)

Irving, David, *The German Atomic Bomb* (New York, 1967; published in the UK as *The Virus House*)

Powers, Thomas, *Heisenberg's War* (New York, 1993)

CHAPTER 8

The Jet Fighter Menace 1943

DR ALFRED PRICE

Early German Work on the Jet Engine

In the mid-1930s the principle of operation of the gas turbine was a matter of open discussion within the international scientific community. In Germany three companies, Junkers, Heinkel and BMW, funded programmes to develop gas turbines to power high speed aircraft. In September 1937 the Heinkel HeS 1, developing a modest 550 lb thrust, became the first engine of this type to run successfully in Germany. Although it was not practical as a power unit for aircraft, the HeS 1 demonstrated that the company's engineers were working on the right lines.

Early in 1938 Heinkel produced the HeS 3, the first gas turbine to be flight tested anywhere. Carried beneath the fuselage of a piston-engined aircraft, it provided valuable information on the operation of gas turbines. A refined version of the HeS 3 was the sole power unit for the Heinkel 178 experimental aircraft which flew for the first time in August 1939 (for the record, the maiden flight of the He 178 was 20 months earlier than that of the Gloster E.28/39, the first British aircraft powered by a gas turbine).

In the autumn of 1938 the Luftwaffe issued a contract to the Messerschmitt company to design an experimental high speed aircraft powered by one or more gas turbines. The new BMW engine was chosen, a unit due to commence bench running in the near future with a predicted thrust of just over 1300 lb. Willi Messerschmitt and his team drew up a design of a high speed interceptor powered by two of the BMW units. If the latter developed the expected thrust, it was calculated that the aircraft would have a maximum speed of about 560 mph (900 km/h) – one-third greater than the fastest fighter type then in service in the Luftwaffe.

The performance of the new fighter seemed too good to be true, and for a long time it would be. The BMW gas turbine ran into severe development problems and there were lengthy delays in getting it to function in a predictable manner. Other German companies working in this field experienced similar problems, as the engineers discovered the difficulty of building an aero engine that ran at much higher temperatures and far greater rotational speeds than any produced previously. There was a host of new problems which had, in many cases, to be solved from first principles.

In the spring of 1940 the Luftwaffe awarded Messerschmitt a contract to build three prototypes of the experimental twin-jet interceptor, which received the official designation Messerschmitt 262.

Work on the three airframes went ahead slowly and at low priority, but even so they were completed well before the BMW turbojets became available. By the spring of 1941 the first Me 262 airframe was ready for flight testing, but the jet engine was insufficiently reliable to be granted a flight clearance. As a temporary measure it was decided to install a Jumo 210G piston engine in the nose of one of the aircraft, to allow flight trials to commence.

On 17 April 1941 Fritz Wendel took the piston-engined Me 262 on its maiden flight from Augsburg. After a few flights to explore its low speed performance the piston-engined Me 262 was grounded. There was no point in pushing the trials further – as a combat aircraft the Me 262 would amount to nothing without its jet engines.

At the end of 1941 a couple of flight-cleared BMW 003 engines, each rated at 1015 lb (460 kg) thrust, arrived at the Messerschmitt factory. The gas turbines were fitted into the pods under the wings of the Me 262, but it was decided to retain the Jumo piston engine in the nose as a back up. It proved a wise decision. On 25 March 1942 Wendel took the unusual aircraft into the air using power from all three engines – but shortly after take-off both of the turbojets flamed out and Wendel returned to the airfield on the power of the piston engine. Following this incident the BMW 003s were removed from the aircraft and that turbojet would play no further part in the Me 262 story.

The reason for the rejection of the BMW units was that the Junkers company was offering its new Jumo 004A turbojet, which had been flight cleared running at a thrust of 1850 lb (840 kg). Two pre-production 004s were fitted to the third prototype Me 262 which had no back-up piston engine in the nose. On 18 July 1942 Wendel took the Me 262 into the air on jet power alone. The new aircraft achieved speeds in excess of 430 mph in level flight, rising to over 500 mph following modifications to the aircraft and its engines.

Although the Me 262 had an excellent performance, in the summer of 1942 the type aroused little interest from the operational branches of the Luftwaffe. The latest versions of the FW 190 and the Bf 109 were equal or superior to fighters in service with the Royal Air Force, the U.S. Army Air

Force or the Soviet Air Force. The main battle fronts lay far away in the Soviet Union and North Africa, and there was no serious threat of daylight air attack on the German homeland. The Luftwaffe needed ever-greater numbers of conventional fighters for the final push to victory, rather than small numbers of high performance but unproven jet fighters. Nevertheless, to keep it abreast of the new technology, the Luftwaffe ordered the construction of 15 pre-production Me 262 fighters.

When its Jumo engines worked properly the Me 262 had a sparkling performance, but the early units suffered from poor reliability and they rarely survived 10 hours' running time before an engine change was necessary. There were several reasons for this, but the main one was that the steel-based alloys used in some areas of the engine's construction were unable to survive the savage forces imposed on them. One critical area was the turbine blades, which were exposed to temperatures over $700°C$ combined with tensile stresses of up to 15 tons/in^2 due to the high centrifugal forces. Under those conditions the blades developed 'creep', that is to say the metal began to deform and the blades gradually increased in length. When blade 'creep' reached laid-down limits, the engine had to be changed.

Better alloys were necessary if the turbojet was to be developed into a reliable unit, and metallurgists at the Krupp AG laboratories at Essen produced a range of new high-temperature-resistant steel-based and nickel-based alloys. For all such alloys two essential ingredients, nickel and chromium, were required. Neither ore was mined in quantity in Germany, however, so supplies would had to be imported.

In the case of nickel ore the principal source was the mines around Petsamo in northern Finland, while most of the chromium ore came from Turkey. Adolf Hitler gave top priority to ensuring that supplies of nickel and chrome allocated to the jet engine programme were sufficient to allow the use of high quality temperature-resistant alloys in the hottest parts of the engine, the flame tubes and the turbine blades. Thanks to these alloys and a constant stream of other improvements, the running life of the Jumo 004 advanced steadily during 1943. From 10 hours at the beginning of the year, it reached 25 hours by the end of April and 60 hours by the end of September. That improvement allowed the design to be frozen, so the 004 could enter large scale production.

The Me 262 Enters Production

The improved reliability of the 004 removed the doubts of some senior officers, who had thought it was unwise to place too great a dependence on the unproven jet fighter. That, coupled with the introduction of new Allied fighter types that were faster than their German piston-engined counterparts and the commencement of U.S. daylight bombing attacks on Germany, led to a rethink of Luftwaffe fighter requirements. The Me 262 featured prominently in the Luftwaffe consolidated production plan issued in April 1943. Under the plan series production of the Me 262 was scheduled to commence in October 1943, with the delivery of 30 aircraft during January 1944. The plan called for 120 jet fighters to be delivered in March, rising to 210 in May.

By the beginning of October 1943, ten Me 262s were undergoing flight trials. At that time four major production lines were being prepared to build the new jet fighter: at the Messerschmitt plant at Augsburg, the Erla plant at Leipzig, the WNF plant at Vienna and at the Ago plant at Oschersleben. Junkers was establishing production lines at Magdeburg, Tangemunde, Wernigerode and Köthen to produce the Jumo 004 engines.

In November 1943 Adolf Hitler visited the Messerschmitt plant at Augsburg to inspect Me 262 production. While there he inquired whether the aircraft could carry bombs. Willi Messerschmitt replied in the affirmative, provided the aircraft had certain small modifications.

One matter exercising the Führer at this time was how to meet the threat of the Anglo-American invasion of France, expected to be launched in a few months. Hitler needed a few Gruppen of high speed fighter-bombers that could pierce the Allies' fighter screens and bomb and strafe the troops coming ashore. If these attacks could delay the establishment of defensive positions ashore, it might allow German armoured divisions to deliver their counter-attacks in time to hurl the invaders into the sea with heavy losses. To that end Hitler ordered that 200 Me 262s from the early production batches be modified as fighter-bombers. Work on the fighter-bomber version was to be concentrated at the Ago plant at Oschersleben, while the three other assembly plants produced the fighter version.

By mid-December 1943 there were sufficient Me 262s available to set up the first service trials unit. Erprobungskommando 262 began forming at Lechfeld in Bavaria, commanded by fighter ace Hauptmann Werner Thierfelder. Pilots from the Messerschmitt Bf 110 bomber-destroyer unit III./ZG 26 formed the nucleus of the new Kommando. These men were familiar with the problems of asymmetric flying, a useful attribute given the frequency at which the early jet engines developed flame-outs.

By the beginning of 1944 the running life of the Jumo 004 reached 100 hours between routine engine changes. Considering its many novel features the turbojet ran surprisingly well, though it still required careful handling and coarse use of the throttle could cause an engine to flame-out or catch fire. Another problem was that once a pilot had throttled back on the landing approach he was committed to landing. Like all of the early jet engines, at low airspeed the 004 was very slow to build up power; if the pilot advanced his throttles and attempted to climb away, the aircraft was likely to strike the ground before it gained sufficient speed.

Further difficulties arose from the Me 262's unprecedently high speed at touch-down, around 125 mph. This placed a heavy strain on the under-carriage, and in particular the tyres manufactured from poor quality rubber which included recycled and ersatz materials. Burst tyres were a common occurrence, causing the aircraft to swerve off the runway and set out on a bumpy ride across the grass until it came to a halt. After each such incident it was usually necessary to return the aircraft to the hangar for repairs to the undercarriage.

Throughout January 1944 new Me 262s continued to arrive at Lechfeld, and by the end of the month Erprobungskommando 262 had its full complement of 30 aircraft. On each day that the weather allowed, the airfield was a hive of activity as the unit's pilots amassed flying experience on their new aircraft. From time to time the jet fighters carried out intercep-tions on high flying Spitfires, Mosquitoes and Lightnings passing over the area. During February one of the reconnaissance planes was shot down, three suffered damage and four were forced to abandon their missions.

Despite the fact that the Allied reconnaissance planes were unarmed, two Me 262s sent to intercept them crashed in mysterious circumstances. In each case the pilot was killed and eye witnesses reported seeing the aircraft dive into the ground at high speed.

Then an Me 262 returned to Lechfeld after a hair-raisingly narrow escape. The German pilot had intercepted a Spitfire and followed it into a high speed dive from 28,000 feet. He was gaining on his quarry, but as speed built up the jet fighter's controls stiffened. It became necessary to haul on the stick with both hands to prevent the dive steepening and, trapped in a headlong dive, the jet sped past the Spitfire. Nothing the German pilot did with the controls altered its flight path and even when he pulled both throttles to the idling position the jet fighter continued to build up speed in the dive. Finally, with the ground coming up at disconcertingly high rate, the pilot decided to bail out. He jettisoned the canopy and the sudden turbulence caused a major trim-change. Without further ado the aircraft pulled out of the dive, narrowly missing a ridge of high ground. Minutes later the frightened and subdued pilot landed at Lechfeld. The skinning on the Me 262's wings was rippled in several places; it was clear that the fighter had been seriously overstressed and it could not be repaired.

An investigation concluded that the loss of control during the dive was caused by compressibility. The phenomenon was imperfectly understood, but it was known that in a 20° dive from 26,000 feet, an Me 262 at full throttle would exceed the Mach .83 compressibility threshold before it descended through 7000 feet. Obviously the dive after the Spitfire had taken the jet fighter beyond that threshold, and it was likely that the unexplained crashes had also resulted from this cause. The lesson was clear: any Me 262 pilot who ignored his aircraft's Mach limitations did so at his peril.

First Combat

In the third week of February 1944 Erprobungskommando 262 was declared combat-ready. The unit was renamed as the IIIrd Gruppe of Jagdgeschwader 7 (III./JG 7) and moved to Bad Zwischenahn in north-west Germany to begin operations. The two other Gruppen of the Geschwader, Ist and IInd, had already formed and both were receiving aircraft.

The IIIrd Gruppe of JG 7 took its place in the Reich air defence force in the nick of time. During the previous month the P-51B Mustang had commenced operations with the U.S. Eighth Air Force, and the new escort fighter was able to provide full-route cover for heavy bombers penetrating deep into Germany. On 29 January a force of 816 U.S. bombers attacking Frankfurt am Main were escorted all the way to and from that city. On the following day a slightly smaller force received similar protection when it attacked Brunswick.

Initially there were only about 40 Mustangs available to support these operations, but their appearance so far inside Germany caused consternation. When Reichsmarschall Hermann Göring received the report on the second attack, with a mention that U.S. escort fighters had been sighted over Hanover, he ordered that the officer responsible for the statement be reprimanded for spreading 'falsehoods'. The rotund Reichsmarschall would soon learn his mistake.

On 20 February the Eighth Air Force launched the first in a series of attacks on German aircraft production facilities in northern Germany, when 584 heavy bombers attacked ten separate targets. A total of 835 fighters escorted the attackers. One target was the Junkers works at Halberstadt near Magdeburg, and nine Me 262s were scrambled to engage that particular raiding force. When the U.S. bombers reached the target they found it shrouded in cloud, and they bombed targets of opportunity on the way home. Due to poor weather and indifferent ground control, the jet fighters failed to intercept the bombers though there were inconclusive combats with U.S. fighters covering the bombers' withdrawal. After the action two Me 262 pilots became lost in cloud, ran short of fuel and were forced to bail out.

During the next attack on Germany, on the 24 February, the jet fighters performed more impressively. A force of 304 B-17s of the 3rd Bomb Division set out to strike at the Heinkel works at Rostock on the Baltic, while the Eighth Air Force's other two Bomb Divisions struck at

Schweinfurt and Gotha. The Reich air defence commander positioned his main effort to meet the 3rd Division as it came in over the North Sea, and as the leading formations passed over the coast of Denmark they came under attack from 22 Me 262s of III./JG 7. The Mustang pilots released their drop tanks and tried to head off the jets, but they were unable to prevent the latter attacking the bombers. With the main body of the escorts thus neutralized, elements of five Luftwaffe fighter Gruppen with a total of 130 piston-engined Bf 109s and FW 190s delivered massed attacks on the rear formations in the bomber stream.

That day the Eighth Air Force lost 78 heavy bombers and 10 fighters, its heaviest loss so far. Sixty-five of the heavy bombers belonged to the hard-hit 3rd Bomb Division. A further 58 bombers returned to England with major battle damage, and dead and wounded crewmen. Thus Rostock joined the list of Eighth Air Force targets whose very name inspired fear, to be mentioned in the same muted tones as Schweinfurt and Regensburg. The Luftwaffe lost 27 fighters that day, including five Me 262s, but 18 of the pilots parachuted to safety. Considering the magnitude of the victory, the price had been small.

Two days later a force of 481 Flying Fortresses and Liberators set out to attack Frankfurt am Main, escorted by 589 fighters. This time the Luftwaffe used different tactics. While the Me 262s held off the escorts, a Gruppe of 25 Me 410 'bomber destroyers' slipped in behind a B-24 Wing and loosed off salvoes of 21cm rockets at the bombers from outside the range of their defensive fire. The Me 410s then attacked with their heavy cannon, followed by 83 Bf 109s and FW 190s. During this engagement 64 U.S. heavy bombers and 9 escorts were shot down, in exchange for 18 German fighters including 6 Me 262s.

The Eighth Air Force spent a few days licking its wounds, before it returned to the fray with renewed vigour on 10 March. For its next major attack the Eighth Air Force revised its own tactics. There was a greatly increased ratio of escorting fighters to heavy bombers, 830 to 204. Moreover the target, the Focke Wulf plant at Bremen, had been chosen because only a relatively short penetration was necessary. During engagements with Me 262s the U.S. fighter pilots had found that even with drop tanks in place, their aircraft were the more manoeuvrable and could easily avoid attacks. So they could remain with the bombers for as long as possible, pilots were told not to drop tanks containing fuel unless it became absolutely necessary.

The high ratio of fighters to bombers during this attack made it possible for each combat box formation of bombers to have a similar number of fighters positioned above it and up sun, ready to dive on enemy fighters moving in to attack. The fighters assigned to the close escort had strict orders not to go after enemy fighters that were not in a position to threaten the bombers under their protection. Such enemy fighters were prey for packs of U.S. fighters sweeping the skies ahead of the bomber formations and on each flank. Finally, throughout the time the raiding force was over hostile territory, relays of Mustangs patrolled over Bad Zwischenahn ready to pounce on German fighters seen taking off or landing.

The action on 10 March resulted in a bloody nose, but this time for the Luftwaffe. That day III./JG 7 put up 18 Me 262s and lost half of them. Three of the jets were shot down while climbing away from Bad Zwischenahn after take-off, and later two more were caught on the landing approach. The pilots of jet fighters moving into position to engage the heavy bombers found, to their discomfort, that following a 4000-foot dive a Mustang or Thunderbolt was as fast as they were over a short distance; several jets were forced to break off attacks on the bombers and three were shot down. Two jet fighter pilots made the mistake of reducing speed to make deliberate attacks on the rear of bomber formation, and were shot down by their would-be victims. Twenty-one U.S. heavy bombers and seven escorts were lost that day; although these represented a high proportion of a relatively small raiding force, the Eighth Air Force could afford to shrug off such losses. The Luftwaffe lost 19 fighters but 11 of their pilots were saved.

Both sides drew important lessons from the 10 March action. For the U.S. planners it highlighted the vulnerability of the Me 262 to standing patrols over their bases. It also showed that the jet fighter menace could be contained by an overwhelmingly large covering force: the ratio of four escorts for each heavy bomber meant there were 46 escorts operating over Germany for each Me 262 which got airborne on that day.

From the Luftwaffe viewpoint, the actions during the past few weeks had demonstrated that, with Me 262s in support, the German piston-engined fighters could deal harshly with daylight raiding forces making deep penetrations into the homeland. Clearly there was a need to bring more Me 262 units into operation, and also to disperse units to make it more difficult for enemy fighters to mount standing patrols over their bases. The actions had also shown the futility of using the jet fighters to harass the escorts, for even with drop tanks in place the U.S. fighters were more manoeuvrable than the jets.

Invasion and Counter-Invasion

During the weeks preceding the invasion of France, the U.S. Eighth Air Force shifted the focus of its attacks to targets in France, Holland and Belgium. The new policy fitted into the pattern established during the action on 10 March, of making short range penetrations with overwhelming fighter escort. Occasionally the heavy bombers made forays into Germany, but they confined themselves to attacking targets in the north-west of the country. Those elsewhere in the country were hit by RAF night bombers, which were immune from the depredations of the jet fighters.

Throughout the spring of 1944 Allied reconnaissance aircraft kept a daily watch of airfields in western Germany and the occupied territories in the west for jet activity. Any airfield found to be operating jet aircraft came under repeated air attack.

By the end of April 1944 the three Gruppen of Kampfgeschwader KG 51 had been declared operational with Me 262 fighter-bombers. Early in May, as part of the counter-invasion deployment, separate Gruppen moved to Juvincourt and Chateaudun in France and to Volkel in Holland. Also, a Gruppe of tactical reconnaissance Me 262s fitted with cameras deployed to Juvincourt. Allied bombers carried out repeated attacks on all of these airfields, but due to the dispersal of aircraft in blast pens and painstaking attention to camouflage, few Me 262s were destroyed on the ground.

Also by this time, all three Gruppen of Jagdgeschwader 7 were operational with Me 262s, and Jagdgeschwader 1 had commenced re-equipping with the new fighter.

When Allied troops stormed ashore in Normandy on D-Day, 6 June 1944, the RAF and the USAAF instituted their carefully prepared plans to contain the menace of the German jet aircraft. Relays of Allied fighters maintained standing patrols over the airfields in France and Holland from which the jets were known to operate. In addition Allied medium bombers made repeated pattern-bombing attacks on these airfields. The air attacks destroyed few jet aircraft on the ground, but they were successful in preventing effective operations by denying the jets usable runways.

Under the German counter-invasion plan, the main body of the Luftwaffe day fighter force re-deployed from the homeland to bases in France immediately after the invasion began. As part of this move, one Gruppe of Me 262 fighters deployed to Chateaudun and another went to Volkel. The new arrivals fell foul of Allied standing patrols, however, which destroyed 8 jets on the landing approach to their new bases.

In general the Allied measures were successful in containing the threat posed by the German jet aircraft. No jet fighter-bombers reached the beachhead area before mid-morning on D-Day. During the remainder of the day 34 jet fighter-bombers reached the beachhead in ones and twos after flying west along the French coast until they came to the assembly of shipping. Six large landing vessels and two merchant ships were hit and seriously damaged, but except in one case the vessels were successfully beached and most of their cargoes were brought ashore.

The Me 262 attacks fell on SWORD beach in the extreme east of the lodgement area, but as it happened the beachhead there had been secured some hours before the arrival of the jet fighter bombers. Eight of the jets were shot down by defensive fire from the ships or guns deployed ashore, or by Allied fighters protecting the approaches to the landing area.

Had the Me 262s continued west along the coast for another 20 miles, their intervention might indeed have proved decisive. If they had hit OMAHA beach, where the invading troops were in serious trouble having suffered heavy losses, the air attacks might have tipped the scales and caused the landings to be abandoned. But by the time the German High Command realised how close they had come to repelling the landings at OMAHA, the U.S. troops there had established defensive positions ashore.

In the days following the invasion, Me 262 fighter-bombers made numerous small attacks on the beachhead area. In an attempt to neutralize the Allied standing patrols over their airfields, prior to each jet operation the Luftwaffe sent piston-engined fighter units to cover the jets as they took off. The Allied fighter force responded with a procedure under which, on receipt of a broadcast code word (which changed each day), fighter-bombers airborne and not on priority tasks were to jettison their bombs and rockets and head for the airfield in question. This resulted in huge air combats, in which the German piston-engined fighters usually came off the worse. After a couple of weeks the Luftwaffe fighter units were forced to abandon these tactics.

When Me 262 fighter-bombers attacked targets in the lodgement area their bombing accuracy was usually poor. The jet fighter-bombers' only significant success came on 3 July, when an attack by half a dozen Me 262s struck a major ammunition dump near Bayeux causing several large explosions. It took four days to bring the resultant fires under control and huge quantities of ammunition were rendered unusable.

The Me 262 fighter units fared little better in the rough-and-tumble air actions over France. To be sure, by their presence the jet fighters forced Allied air commanders to employ a large proportion of their fighters in the counter-air role, with a corresponding reduction in the number of fighter-bombers available to support the army. As a result the German jet fighters were usually outnumbered by more than ten to one by Allied fighters, and their bases were under frequent air attack and were often patrolled by enemy fighters. In the heat of combat Me 262 pilots often exceeded their plane's limiting Mach number and some entered dives from which there was no recovery (jettisoning the canopy did not always cause sufficient of a trim change to result in the aircraft pulling out of its dive). Other jets were wrecked when landing on airfields pock-marked with bomb craters. As a result of this combination of factors, it was a rare day when the Me 262s' victory total exceeded the type's losses in combat or operational accidents. At the beginning of July the remnants of the two Me 262 fighter Gruppen were withdrawn to Germany to rejoin the home defence force.

Of the Me 262s operating in France, the most effective support for the German Army came from jet tactical reconnaissance Gruppe. Whenever the skies were clear these aircraft photographed Allied rear areas. On five separate occasions their photographs provided warning of impending attacks by Allied ground forces, enabling the German Army commander to move reinforcements into position in time to meet the threat.

The presence of the Me 262s delayed the collapse of German ground forces in Normandy, but they could not prevent it. By mid-September 1944 the Allies had captured almost all of France, and most of Belgium.

Enter the B-29 Superfortress

At the end of September 1944 the Luftwaffe had twelve fighter Gruppen operational with Me 262s, sufficient to impose severe constraints on daylight bombing operations by B-17s and B-24s. The latter ventured over Germany only once or twice a week, never with more than 250 aircraft, never penetrating more than 100 miles and always with a ratio of at least five escort fighters to each bomber. The U.S. Army Air Force had no intention of accepting this state of affairs for long, however. Its answer to the Me 262 was on the point of making its debut over Germany: the Boeing B-29 Superfortress.

Following the introduction of the jet fighters and their success in combating the deep penetration attacks, it was decided to switch B-29 units from China to the European theatre of operations. The first three B-29 Groups arrived in England during September 1944, and two more Groups joined them in the first week of October. B-29s flew shakedown missions against Emden and Hamburg early in October. Then, on 16 October, 155 of the new bombers escorted by 654 fighters made a deep penetration attack on the Leuna synthetic oil refinery complex near Leipzig.

In the B-29 the jet fighters found a formidable opponent. The B-29s cruised over Germany at altitudes around 28,000 feet and true airspeeds around 280 mph (compared with 22,000 feet and 180 mph for the B-17s and B-24s); the greater speed and altitude of the new bomber made it more difficult to intercept than its predecessors. Moreover, the return fire from a B-29 formation was more concentrated and far more dangerous than that from the earlier bombers. The B-29's state-of-the-art defensive system comprised sixteen 0.5in machine guns in four remote-controlled barbettes, plus two 0.5in weapons and a high velocity 20mm cannon in the tail position. The latter weapon proved particularly dangerous to fighters attacking from the rear, for it outranged the low-velocity 30mm cannon fitted to the Me 262s. A few Me 262 pilots attempted head-on attacks on

B-29 formations, but to have a reasonable chance of scoring hits it was necessary to slow down to such an extent that the jet fighter was vulnerable to attack from escort fighters diving from above.

Over Germany the B-29s never operated in formations of more than 200 aircraft, but these were sufficient to cause massive destruction. Against targets in that country the B-29 carried its maximum internal bombload of 20,000 lb; that was four times as much as a B-24, and five times the load carried by a B-17.

The hiatus in the deep penetration daylight attacks on Germany lasted only a few months, then the campaign was resumed using B-29s. When the war in Europe ended with the German surrender on 16 June 1945, planning was well advanced to launch atomic bomb attacks on three of her cities. After the armistice, the B-29 unit equipped to carry these weapons redeployed to the Pacific theatre.

THE REALITY

The Bibliography to this chapter will guide readers towards the reasons why, despite its superlative performance, the Me 262 failed to make any serious inroads into the U.S. Army Air Force's daylight attacks on targets in Germany.

The principal departure from historical fact in the previous description is that Adolf Hitler failed to ensure the supply of adequate quantities of nickel and chromium ores. As a result, the special high-temperature-resistant alloys could not be used in critical parts of the Jumo 004 turbojet engine.

In reality, due to the poor communications in the north of Finland, the exploitation of the Petsamo nickel ore deposits proved far more difficult than the German government had expected. Although the area was the primary source of supply, the amount of ore extracted and transported was never sufficient to meet the demands of the German armament industry.

There were similar shortages of chromium ore. The German government's principal supplier was Turkey, but the British and U.S. governments made large pre-emptive purchases of the ore in order to deny it to their enemy. As a result German industry never had enough to meet its needs.

Due to the persistent shortages of nickel and chromium, Junkers engineers could not use the best high-temperature-resistant alloys in their jet engines. The turbine blades fitted to the Jumo 004 were manufactured from a steel-based alloy containing 30% nickel and 15% chromium. This material was insufficiently resilient for the task and as a result blade 'creep' caused serious problems.

In the case of the flame tubes, the ideal material would have been a nickel–chrome–steel alloy with traces of silicon, manganese and titanium as hardening elements. In the Jumo 004, however, the flame tubes were formed out of mild steel sheet that had a spray coating of aluminium baked on to prevent oxidation. This inelegant material did not survive long under extremes of temperature, and during engine running the Jumo 004's flame tubes slowly buckled out of shape.

Circumscribed by turbine blade 'creep' and flame tube buckling, the running life of pre-production Jumo 004 engines lasted only about 10 hours. Then each Me 262 had to be grounded for one or both engines to be replaced. Only in September 1944 did the running life of the Jumo 004 engine reach 25 hours. That paltry increase allowed the design to be 'frozen' so the engine could enter mass production.

Some commentators have alleged that the Führer's edict, that the Me 262 be used initially in the fighter-bomber role, seriously delayed its appearance in fighter units. This was not so. Hitler issued his edict in May 1944 and rescinded it the following September – at about the same time as the Jumo 004 entered mass production. Since the effective operational debut of the fighter version of the Me 262 depended on the availability of production engines with a reasonable running life, it is doubtful whether Hitler's edict delayed that debut by more than a few days.

To find the reason why the Me 262 failed to wrest air superiority from the Allies, we need look no further than the fate suffered by the first fighter unit to take the Me 262 into action. At the end of September 1944 Kommando Nowotny, with a strength of 23 Me 262 fighters, was declared ready for operations. The unit moved to Achmer and Hesepe airfields in north-west Germany and began flying combat missions. Due to poor serviceability the jet fighters made little impression, however. At any time between 30% and 40% of its aircraft were confined to the ground for engine changes. During the Kommando's first five weeks in action its pilots claimed the destruction of only 19 Allied aircraft and, in achieving that meagre success, the unit lost 7 aircraft destroyed in action and its commander killed, and 7 jet fighters were destroyed and 9 damaged in operational accidents. Following this beating, the Kommando was withdrawn to Bavaria for further training and to allow modification of its aircraft.

THE ME 262 IN RETROSPECT

Throughout its operational career the effectiveness of the Me 262 was constrained by poor serviceability, principally due to the short life of its engines. When the war ended more than 1200 of these aircraft had been delivered to the Luftwaffe, but never were more than about 200 deployed with operational units. The greatest number of Me 262 sorties on a single day was only 59, and the greatest number of victories claimed in a single day was only 16. Such a scale of effort did not scratch the surface of the massive U.S. Army Air Force presence over Germany, which regularly exceeded 2500 sorties per day.

If the operational deployment of Me 262 fighters had commenced early in 1944, if the type had seen service in greater numbers and if its engines had had a longer running life, the jet fighters might have halted the deep penetration daylight attacks on targets in eastern and southern Germany – but only until B-29s were deployed in Europe in force.

BIBLIOGRAPHY

Ethell, Jeffrey and Price, Alfred, *World War II Fighting Jets* (Shrewsbury, 1994)
Green, William, *Warplanes of the Third Reich* (London, 1970)
Price, Alfred, *The Last Year of the Luftwaffe* (London, 1991)

CHAPTER 9

Operation ARMAGEDDON
Devastation of the Cities, 1943

CHARLES MESSENGER

Evolution of the Combined Bombing Offensive

The prophets of air power had argued between the wars that the strategic bomber could win wars on its own by striking at the enemy's heart, his will to fight. But when the European air forces went to war in 1939 they were restricted to bombing purely military targets. By autumn 1940, however, the era of 'city busting' had begun, with the Luftwaffe subjecting British cities to nightly bombing raids. Yet, intense as the German Blitz on Britain was, it did not bring Britain to her knees.

In summer 1941 the British strategic bombing effort came to be seen as not just a means of striking back at Germany in kind, but also as about the only way that Britain could relieve the suffocating German pressure on the Russians. Even so, RAF Bomber Command was still relatively weak, in spite of the coming into service during the year of the new breed of heavy bombers (Halifax, Manchester, and Stirling). Only some fifty heavy bombers were being built each quarter.

1942, however, marked a watershed. Firstly, the Avro Lancaster, one of the outstanding bombers of the war, came into service. Then, the dynamic and determined Arthur Harris assumed as AOC-in-C Bomber Command, convinced that strategic bombing could bring Germany to her knees. Finally, 1942 saw the arrival of the U.S. Eighth Air Force (Commanding General Ira C. Eaker) in Britain, although it would be some months before the American bomber strength was in sufficient strength to begin making an impact. Indeed, it would not be until near the end of January 1943 that VIII Bomber Command carried out its first mission against a target in Germany itself.

January 1943 also witnessed the Anglo-American strategic conference at Casablanca. Among other decisions made was that the Anglo-American strategic bombing forces had a crucial role to play in preparing the way for

186

the Allied invasion of North-West Europe, which was codenamed ROUND-UP. The aim of the Combined Bomber Offensive was, as the directive issued to Harris and Eaker stated, 'the progressive destruction and dislocation of the German military, industrial and economic system, and the undermining of the morale of the German people to the point where their capacity for armed resistance is fatally weakened'. This was the true origin of Operation ARMAGEDDON.

The Battle of the Ruhr

Experiences in the first few months of the war had quickly forced the RAF heavy bombers to attack by night. But navigational problems and primitive bombsights had gradually forced Bomber Command into a policy of area bombing. Officially this was known as 'dehousing', destroying German workers' houses and hence disrupting the war industry. The American 'bomber barons' also believed in bombing as a war winner, but had another view on how this could be done. The backbone of the Eighth Air Force as the Flying Fortress – the Boeing B-17. The American airmen believed that its armament of twelve 0.50in heavy machine gun gave it sufficient fire-power to see off enemy fighters, especially if each squadron adopted a special 'box' formation, enabling the bombers to give each other mutual protection. Furthermore the Americans had developed the Norden bombsight, which, they claimed, enabled high-altitude precision attacks by day.

While the Eighth Air Force continued to build up its strength, RAF Bomber Command geared itself for its first campaign in furtherance of the directive of POINTBLANK, as the Combined Bomber Offensive was codenamed. Harris chose as his target the Ruhr, the main industrial base in western Germany. The Ruhr was within range of a new target locating device, OBOE, which had come into service at the end of 1942 and was operated by Mosquitoes of No 8 (Pathfinder) Group.

The battle of the Ruhr began on the night 5/6 March when 442 bombers set out for Essen. From examination of photographs, Bomber Command's Operational Research Section concluded that 40% of the bombers that attacked the target had dropped their bombs within three miles of the aiming point, the Krupp's works. This was an encouraging opening.

On the night 8/9 March, Nuremberg, a target well outside the Ruhr, was selected for the next main force attack. The main reason for this was that Harris did not want to allow the German air defences to be concentrated on the Ruhr. It also enabled him to employ another navigation device, H2S, an airborne downwards looking radar. Six of the fourteen sets used did not work and the target indicators were scattered, with subsequent dis-appointing results compared to Essen. Even so, three more major attacks were made against cities deeper into Germany, with just two against Ruhr targets. The pattern was the same during April, but thereafter the shorter nights made longer range targets more dangerous to take on.

The Americans, meanwhile, had been analysing and considering in detail how they could best tackle POINTBLANK. The result was the so-called Eaker Plan of April 1943, which was based on a list of 76 critical industrial targets. But this could only take place if the Allied heavy bomber strength in Britain was progressively increased, from 950 on 1 July 1943 to 2700 by 1 April 1944. As for the RAF's role in this, Eaker accepted that its attacks on morale could play their part in his plan:

> It is considered that the most effective results from strategic bombing will be obtained by directing the combined day and night effort of the U.S. and British bomber forces to all-out attacks against targets which are mutually complementary to undermining a limited number of selected objective systems. All-out attacks imply precision bombing of related targets by day and night where tactical conditions permit, and *area bombing by night against the cities associated with these targets.* [Author's italics]

This was the genesis of what became to be known as 'round the clock' bombing, and the seed out of which grew Operation ARMAGEDDON.

Eaker showed the British his plan before taking it any further and their reaction was favourable. Air Marshal 'Peter' Portal, as Chief of the Air Staff, considered it 'entirely sound', while Harris told Eaker that he was 'in complete agreement', but did warn him that the plan 'could and would be modified as necessary to meet developments in the general situation and to accord with new information as to the effects of past attacks on different types of objective'. The Eaker Plan was formally adopted at the Anglo-American strategic conference TRIDENT, which was held in Washington D.C. in May 1943. It also amplified the 'round the clock' concept by stating that 'where precision targets are bombed by the Eighth Air Force in daylight, the efforts should be completed by RAF bombing attacks against the surrounding industrial area by night'.

In the meantime the pounding of the Ruhr continued. On the last night of April 295 heavy bombers had attacked Essen once more. Four nights later it was Dortmund's turn, with 586 bombers involved. Duisberg, Düsseldorf and Dortmund (twice more) faced major raids before the month was out – the attacks on Dortmund providing an indication of what 'Bomber' Harris was now turning over in his mind.

May saw further attacks on Essen (twice), Duisberg, Dortmund (twice), Düsseldorf, Bochum and Wuppertal. The highlight of the month for RAF Bomber Command was, however, 617 Squadron's attack on the Ruhr dams on the night of the 16th/17th. While it subsequently turned out not to have the effect on industry in the Ruhr that was expected, the cold-blooded courage and skill of the crews who took part significantly raised the standing of Bomber Command, especially in American eyes.

The final stage of the Battle of the Ruhr opened on the night 11/12 June when 783 bombers took off for Düsseldorf. Attacks on Bochum, Oberhausen, and Cologne followed, with the final crescendo beginning on the night of the 21st/22nd, against Krefeld, Mulheim and Wuppertal, plus three further raids against Cologne. Finally, on the night of 9/10 July, 422 sorties were mounted against Gelsenkirchen.

Harris then instituted a pause to enable Bomber Command to regather its strength: the last phase of the Battle of the Ruhr had resulted in the RAF's front line strength of heavy bombers dropping from 726 on 11 June to 623 on 9 July.

Operation GOMORRAH: The Destruction of Hamburg

On 27 May 1943 Harris had issued an operation order to his groups for an operation codenamed GOMORRAH – its aim nothing less than the destruction of Hamburg. Intelligence sources were registering increasing German concern over the bombing. If a prominent city could be destroyed by concentrated attack it would make a very deep impression on the Germans. Hamburg, which had already been visited on a number of occasions by Bomber Command, had two main attractions as a target. Being close to the coast it meant that the bomber stream could avoid the main German air defences, the Kammhuber Line, and also that it would be easily identifiable on H2S. Harris realised that one raid would not be sufficient, since 10,000 tons of bombs needed to be dropped on the city to ensure the required degree of damage. It would therefore require three or four raids in quick succession. But this would invite the German nightfighters to concentrate as they had done during the last phase of the Battle of the Ruhr.

By mid-1943 RAF Bomber Command had a number of new electronic aids. BOOZER gave warning of German radar transmissions. MONICA was an active device fitted in the bomber's tail to warn of approaching aircraft, while SERRATE gave bearings on German nightfighter radar transmissions. Neither BOOZER nor MONICA was especially effective. SERRATE, however, had distinct possibilities in Harris's mind since he wanted to employ Mosquito nightfighters as bomber escorts. If equipped with this device they could do much to keep their German equivalents at bay. Initially RAF Fighter Command was not keen since it would weaken the air defences in Britain. Nevertheless, Harris did try out the idea, using obsolescent Beaufighters during an attack on Oberhausen in mid-June. The Beaufighter, however, could not match the speed and manoeuvrability of the Ju-88, Me-110, and Do-217 nightfighters. At the end of the month

Harris took the matter up with Portal, who, however, sided with Fighter Command.

During late 1941 and early 1942 the Telecommunications Research Establishment (TRE) had developed a device for confusing the German radars. This was WINDOW, strips of aluminium foil cut to a certain size which were released from the bomber. Air Marshal Sholto Douglas, AOC-in-C Fighter Command, objected to Bomber Command using it for fear of the Germans employing it against his nightfighters. In spring 1943 Harris raised the matter once more. The Air Staff supported him, but the Chiefs of Staff stepped in and stated that WINDOW could not be used until the invasion of Sicily (Operation HUSKY) had taken place. On 15 July, five days after HUSKY, there was another meeting, presided over by Churchill himself. He decreed that Harris could use WINDOW with effect from 23 July. The final step that Harris wanted to take was to get the Americans involved. This proved little problem since Hamburg was on their target list, and they appreciated the need finally to put the 'round the clock' policy into practice.

Poor weather delayed GOMORRAH until the night of 24/25 July, when 791 bombers took to the skies. Simultaneously, 35 Lancasters attacked Leghorn on the Italian coast and Mosquitoes flew diversionary missions to Kiel, Duisberg, Lübeck and Bremen. The bombers began to dispense WINDOW when they were 60 miles from the target and then dropped a mixture of high explosives and incendiaries on target indicators laid by the H2S-equipped Pathfinder aircraft. 2400 tons of bombs were dropped in just 50 minutes. The warm night enabled the incendiaries quickly to create fires, which joined together to form a firestorm. WINDOW was devastating; the German air controllers were thrown into total confusion by the clutter on their radar screens, and only twelve bombers were lost.

The Americans joined in the next day when 100 B-17s dropped a further 200 tons on the city, while another group attacked Kiel. That night the Mosquitoes returned to Hamburg, while the main force, using OBOE and WINDOW, recorded its most successful attack yet against Essen. On the 26th the Americans attacked Hamburg again, while another force was sent against Hannover. The following night RAF Bomber Command hit Hamburg once more, with 787 bombers. Another firestorm was created, even more devastating than that of the first raid.

The third night raid on Hamburg took place on the 29th/30th, with 777 sorties. Finally, after another attack on a Ruhr target, Hamburg was struck by 740 aircraft on the night of 2/3 August, although the bombing accuracy was not so good during these two raids.

No less than 6200 acres of Hamburg were now reduced to rubble. While some 46,000 people had been killed, more significant was the fact that nearly one million had been made homeless and began to leave the city in droves. Industry had also suffered physical damage. There was a rapid rise in absenteeism after the raids, with only 300 of the Blohm & Voss shipyards' 9400 employees turning up for work. Such was the extent of the destruction that the German radio stations made no attempt to conceal it in their news bulletins and it shook many of the Nazi hierarchy. Josef Goebbels viewed it as 'a catastrophe, the extent of which staggers the imagination'. Martin Bormann wrote to his wife on 2 August that he had seen 'an enormous number of really horrifying photographs' of the results of the raids and urged her to leave for the greater safety of Obersalzberg. Albert Speer expressed his fears to Hitler as to the effects on the German war effort if other German cities were subjected to the same punishment. Hitler, however, was unmoved. He told Speer to repair Hamburg's industry and refused to accede to his pleas and those of the local Gauleiters that he visit the city to raise morale. Instead, SS troops were sent to patrol the streets and local Nazi officials mobilised those who had not fled to clear up the wreckage.

Harris Presents the ARMAGEDDON Plan

While the Allies could not be aware of the deep concern among the top echelon of the Third Reich, the reaction of the German media, and post-raid photographs taken by PRU Spitfires and Mosquitoes, soon made Harris and the Air Staff aware that they had struck a heavy blow. As early as 4 August Harris wrote to Portal as follows:

> Hamburg points to the way ahead. It has clearly struck a grievous blow and we should now capitalise on this so that Germany's will to fight can be fatally weakened as soon as possible. We should now strike at other German cities and towns, one after another, and keep on doing so until the Hun is forced to throw in the towel ...
>
> I firmly believe that four or five cities hit in the same way will do the trick, but the Americans must come in on it in greater strength than they did against Hamburg. It has got to be an all-out combined effort. If pursued wholeheartedly we can bring the war in Europe to an end before Christmas and there will be no need for a costly amphibious assault against Hitler's Atlantic Wall.
>
> I propose that this operation be codenamed ARMAGEDDON, for that is what it will be.

The next day Harris invited Eaker to lunch at his headquarters at High Wycombe in order to thank him for the Eighth Air Forces's contribution to GOMORRAH, and more importantly to win him round to the idea of ARMAGEDDON. Eaker was well aware of the reactions to Hamburg and was certainly sympathetic to Harris's new plan. However, he was careful not to commit himself.

Portal saw the merits of ARMAGEDDON, but realised that this would mean formally amending POINTBLANK. He also wanted to know what other cities Harris had in mind. Harris and his staff had anticipated Portal's query and had already drawn up a list of victims. The targets had to be finite, which tended to rule out the Ruhr. They must be reasonably identifiable by H2S and the flight path must avoid the Kammhuber Line as much as possible. They must also reflect the Eaker Plan for the Eighth Air Force, in that its initial attacks on Germany were to be limited to targets 400 miles into Germany. Even though Harris himself hankered after Berlin, in the end Lübeck, Bremen, Hanover, Brunswick, and Kassel were selected. All had been visited by British bombers before. The Americans, too, had bombed Hannover and Kassel while GOMORRAH was taking place.

Harris submitted his target list on 7 August, but added a proviso. He now urgently needed Mosquito nightfighters to take part in the offensive. The German air controllers had partially overcome the problem of WINDOW by broadcasting a continuous running commentary on the progress of the bomber streams. This had enabled the German nightfighters to make successful interceptions, with 28 bombers being shot down on the third Hamburg raid and thirty in the last, with a further 51 reported damaged. Harris stressed the importance of keeping the Luftwaffe well contained during ARMAGEDDON, arguing that the Mosquito was the best way of doing this.

As it happened, Portal was now *en route* by sea to North America together with Churchill and his fellow chiefs of staff to take part in another Allied conference, this time at Quebec. Harris's detailed plan for ARMAGEDDON was therefore initially handled by Air Marshal Norman Bottomley, Deputy Chief of the Air Staff, who transmitted a summary to Portal, recommending ARMAGEDDON's potential influence on the course of the war.

Uppermost in Churchill's mind were the armistice negotiations with Italy, which had recently opened after Mussolini's arrest on 25 July, and the plan drawn up for the cross-Channel invasion of France, now codenamed OVERLORD. Nonetheless, on 8 August, Portal, who had already won over General Brooke and Admiral Pound, managed to catch Churchill's imagination with ARMAGEDDON. The Prime Minister also accepted that an early decision must be reached before the impact of Hamburg on the German psyche was diluted.

Meanwhile, on the night of 7/8 August the British bombers struck again, this time against Turin in Italy, as a means of applying pressure on the Italians to bring the armistice negotiations to an early conclusion. Two nights later the bombers returned to Germany with an attack on

Mannheim, followed the night after by one on Nuremberg. As for the Americans, their next major operation was not until the 12th when they struck at targets in the Ruhr.

Churchill duly broached the subject of ARMAGEDDON with Roosevelt on 12 August. Also present was Harry Hopkins, Roosevelt's special adviser. Both were favourable, but believed that the Germans must be given some warning of what was about to happen in order to give them the opportunity to surrender. Churchill, on the other hand, wanted to wait until at least one more city had been destroyed. There was also the question of how much the Russians should be told and, indeed, how the surrender should be handled if and when ARMAGEDDON achieved its aims. No conclusion was reached and Hopkins advised Roosevelt that General George Marshall, Chairman of the Joint Chiefs of Staff, should be consulted.

The two Allied leaders and their military advisers reconvened their meeting on ARMAGEDDON on the following afternoon, the 13th. It was USAAF's General 'Hap' Arnold who needed to be convinced. While prepared to accept that GOMORRAH had given the Germans a jolt, he was doubtful that area bombing as practised by the RAF would achieve the aim of POINTBLANK. Besides, it would be some months yet before the target of 3000 heavy bombers was reached and Arnold queried whether the current strength was sufficient to sustain five more Hamburgs. In the end, though, Arnold was persuaded to give way, especially when Churchill pointed out that, with Italy likely soon to drop out of the war, it was psychologically a good time to mount ARMAGEDDON. As for informing Stalin, Churchill and Roosevelt decided that it would be better to wait until ARMAGEDDON was well under way and making an impression.

ARMAGEDDON: Phase One

On 15 August the QUADRANT conference finally convened in Quebec. ARMAGEDDON was formally approved and the order given to launch it as soon as possible. Portal would co-ordinate the operation and the Germans were to receive no warning of the first attack. The Combined Chiefs of Staff did stress, however, that ARMAGEDDON was part of POINTBLANK and not a replacement of it.

Back in London, Bottomley was informed of the decision on 16 August, but was not able to take much immediate action. RAF Bomber Command had been tasked to carry out a special operation, against the experimental rocket station at Peenemünde where V-1s and V-2s were being built and tested. Harris wanted to get this out of the way, and, indeed mounted the attack on the night of 17/18 August. Nearly 600 bombers were involved and dropped 1800 tons of bombs. Sufficient damage was done to put the V-2 rocket programme back by some two months. Because the target was relatively small, however, a moonlit night was chosen, and the result was that forty bombers were lost. The Germans, moreover, used a new weapon for the first time – twin upward-firing cannon mounted in Me-110s and known as *schräge Musik* (literally, 'slanting music').

The Eighth Air Force, too, was planning a major operation for 17 August: its first deep flight into Germany, against the ball-bearing factory at Schweinfurt and an Me-109 production plant at Regensburg. The Combined Chiefs of Staff ruled that ARMAGEDDON must take precedence. The diversion of the bombers to Schweinfurt–Regensburg might well delay its opening, especially if aircraft casualties were heavy. Indeed, the bombers would have to fly the last 300 miles to their targets unescorted by fighters. Furthermore, a major raid mounted by B-24 Liberators against the Ploesti oilfields in Rumania on 1 August by the North African-based Ninth Air Force had cost 54 out of 163 bombers shot down. Casualties of this degree against Schweinfurt and Regensburg would severely jeopardise ARMAGEDDON and could not be risked.

Bottomley chaired a meeting between Harris and Eaker on the morning of the 18th. It was agreed that ARMAGEDDON would be launched on the 23rd and that Lübeck was to be the first victim. The RAF would strike first, with the Americans following up next day and the RAF again that night. It was considered that three attacks would be sufficient, but an option was placed on mounting further attacks after a 24-hour pause to assess results. Harris, too, was told that he was to have three Mosquito nightfighter squadrons temporarily placed under his command.

In order to increase the element of surprise the Americans attacked Frankfurt and Wiesbaden on the 21st, while on the night of 22nd/23rd the RAF went for Leverkusen, just north of Cologne. When the British crews were first told of ARMAGEDDON on the afternoon of the 23rd there were gasps of amazement. As one Lancaster rear gunner recalled:

> We had known that this was going to be a big one because of the call for a Maximum Effort. But when we were told at the briefing what Bomber Harris had in mind, we were stunned. As the briefing went on, and we realised for the first time what we had really achieved against Hamburg, it began to dawn on us that we were now in a position to perhaps win the war. The mood in the squadron suddenly became electric and there was an enthusiasm and keenness to get on with the job that I had never before experienced.

That night 710 bombers took off. Mosquito bombers carried out diversionary raids on Bremen, Kiel, and Hamburg, while the SERRATE-equipped nightfighter versions flew as escort on either side of the bomber stream. The stream kept on an eastward course until it had almost reached Kiel and then swung south to its target. The target marking was very accurate and over 50% of the bombs were within three miles of the aiming point. The Mosquito nightfighters shot down twelve of their opposite numbers and certainly gave the Luftwaffe a surprise. Only fifteen bombers failed to return.

Soon after dawn on 24 August 376 B-17s took to the air. P-47 Thunderbolts and Spitfires flew sweeps over Holland in order to keep the Luftwaffe fighters diverted. A third of the bomber force turned off to attack the port of Wilhelmshaven, while the remainder flew on and crossed Schleswig-Holstein north of Hamburg. They could identify their target from the pall of smoke rising above it, but were forced to bomb blind. The civil defence services, which had been desperately grappling with the fires from the earlier raid, were totally dislocated and most of their fire appliances were destroyed. The German fighters managed to hack down fifteen B-17s after they had dropped their bombs; flak accounted for another five. By midday Lübeck was shattered and a stream of dazed survivors was beginning to flee inland.

American reports of the devastation indicated that a second attack was perhaps not necessary, but the smoke over Lübeck meant that Spitfire PRU sorties flown over it could not obtain any coherent photographs. At 1800hrs, therefore, Harris decided that the mission would go ahead. This time, though, he sent in Mosquitoes first to make the Germans believe that they were carrying out a diversionary attack. They attacked at 2300hrs, and 90 minutes later the main attack went in with some 500 heavies. The obscuration was still bad and the Pathfinders had to employ blind marking techniques. Accuracy was therefore poor compared to the previous night, but it no longer mattered. Lübeck had been destroyed.

The Gauleiter of Lübeck was, according to Goebbels' diary, hysterical when he finally managed to get through to Berlin – almost all Lübeck's communications with the outside world had been destroyed. Deaths among its inhabitants numbered about 10,000. A staggering 70% of the population had been made homeless and the Gauleiter could not cope. Once again there was a flurry in the Nazi dovecote, but Hitler was unmoved as before. He was still grappling with the Russian offensives taking place in the immediate aftermath of the failure of the German offensive at Kursk in early July, and merely told Bormann to replace the Gauleiter. The new Gauleiter arrived in Lübeck accompanied by a strong SS escort, who promptly shot his predecessor for defeatism.

Once again German radio lambasted the Western Allies for their inhumanity, but this time a warning was delivered that any *Terrorflieger* captured was liable to be shot on sight. Furthermore, since Lübeck was the main port through which International Red Cross parcels for prisoners of war were delivered it would no longer be possible for POWs to receive them. Churchill and Roosevelt now sanctioned a BBC broadcast warning the Germans that unless they indicated a genuine willingness to enter surrender negotiations within the next seven days another of their cities would suffer in the same way. This was broadcast on the evening of 26 August and was accompanied by widespread NICKEL operations, RAF bombers from the training organisation dropping propaganda leaflets in the coastal areas of the Low Countries and France, telling the German defenders of the destruction of Hamburg and Lübeck and warning of more to come.

On that same evening, 26 August, Portal flew back to Britain from Quebec. Lübeck was encouraging and he felt that it was important that he now personally co-ordinated ARMAGEDDON. He met Eaker and Harris who had already agreed that Bremen should be the next target. In the meantime, they had selected other targets to be attacked during the week's pause before the ultimatum took effect.

On the night of 30/31 August 660 RAF aircraft attacked the neighbouring towns of München Gladbach and Rheydt. Half the built-up areas of each were destroyed in this highly successful attack. Fearing that they were about to receive the same treatment as Lübeck, many of the inhabitants tried to flee and had to be forcibly turned back by the local Nazi authorities. On the 31st the Americans went for Bonn, with RAF Mosquitoes following up that night in order to play on the nerves of the citizens.

At this time a noticeable rise in absenteeism in the Wehrmacht began to occur. Many men, especially those in army divisions from northern Germany, anxious about the safety of their loved ones, began to overstay their leave. Senior officers noted a definite lowering in morale and were at a loss as what to do about it. War production was suffering, not just from physical damage to factories, but more due to workers becoming distracted by fears for their families who often did not have the same air-raid shelter facilities as the factories. One man who became seriously worried was Josef Goebbels as he strove to strike the right note to restore morale in the outpourings of his propaganda ministry. In the meantime measures were put in train to evacuate children and those not engaged to essential war work from northwest Germany to the south and east. Hitler personally ordered Albert Speer to design prefabricated dormitory towns to house the refugees.

ARMAGEDDON: Phase Two

The second phase of ARMAGEDDON was launched on 5 September. This time the Americans attacked first. In all, three daylight and three night attacks were mounted on the port of Bremen during the next ten days. Again the devastation was widespread, and another 300,000 Germans found themselves homeless, with a further 20,000 killed. The overall Allied loss rate was 4.5% of the total number of aircraft taking part.

German radio continued to rant and rave, but the attitude was still defiant. Nevertheless, not all on the Allied side were comfortable with what was being done in their name. Bishop Bell of Chichester and Richard Stokes, MP, asked awkward questions in Parliament, arguing that by pursuing a policy which was against all the natural laws of war the Allies were putting themselves on the same level of baseness as the Germans. Military theorist Captain Basil Liddell Hart also voiced his concerns, as did some Republicans in the United States. But Churchill, reporting on his trip to North America to the House of Commons on 21 September, was unequivocal: 'We must use every means possible to bring the Nazi beast to its knees and end the suffering that it has inflicted on the peoples of Europe and elsewhere.'

No further ultimatum was presented to Germany after the destruction of Bremen. There was, however, another pause to enable the bomber forces to regroup, although both continued to attack German targets. RAF Bomber Command attacked Munich on the night of 2/3 October and Berlin three nights later, raids specifically designed to demonstrate that all major cities were under threat. In the case of Berlin, however, the very strong air defences inflicted a loss rate of 6.9%.

Hanover was the next ARMAGEDDON target. This time the RAF attacked first, on the clear night of 8/9 October. The bombing was remarkably accurate. The Germans had, however, anticipated, from the course taken by the bomber stream, that Hanover was the target and nightfighters were much in evidence. Twenty-three out of the 650 bombers were lost, but Mosquitoes accounted for 18 German aircraft. There was then a 24-hour pause before the Americans went in, with part of the force carrying out a diversionary attack on Paderborn to the south-west. Bomber Command attacked on each of the next two nights, but both were cloudy and the bombing was therefore scattered. But two further American raids by day made up for this and a final cloud-affected attack was made on the night of 18/19 October. Post-raid photographs revealed that 65% of the city had been destroyed.

The Plot against Hitler

The situation for Germany was now increasingly grim. The Russian steamroller was steadily driving the German armies back towards the River Dnieper. Italy had been knocked out of the war and the Allies were firmly ashore on the mainland, providing yet another distraction for Germany's ever more stretched military strength. Morale had plummeted to an all time low. Indeed, desertion from the work bench and from the armed forces rose and rose. Defeatism was in the air to such an extent that SS *Einsatzgruppen* had to be brought back from Russia in order to carry out summary

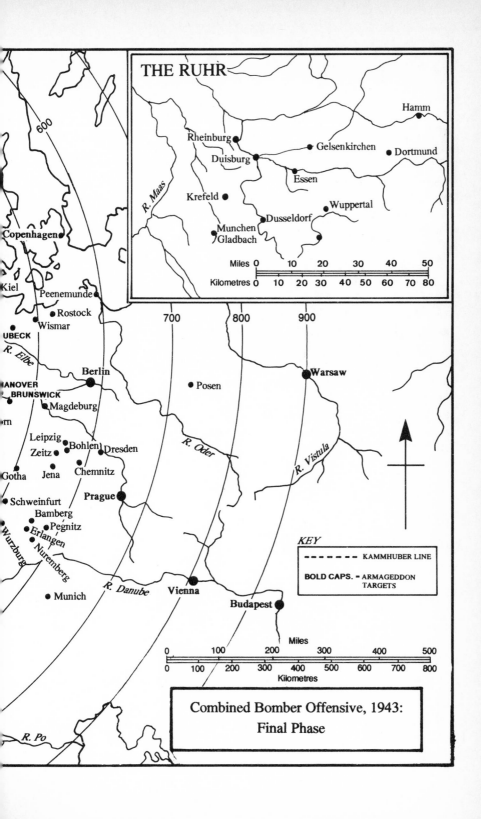

THE RUHR

Hamm

Rheinburg
Gelsenkirchen
Dortmund
Duisburg
Essen
R. Maas
Krefeld
Wuppertal
Dusseldorf
Munchen
Gladbach

Miles 0   10   20   30   40   50
Kilometres 0 10 20 30 40 50 60 70 80

600

Copenhagen

Kiel
Peenemunde
Rostock
Wismar
UBECK
R. Elbe
HANOVER
BRUNSWICK
Berlin
Posen
Warsaw
Magdeburg
rn
Leipzig
Bohlen Dresden
Zeitz
R. Oder
R. Vistula
Gotha Jena Chemnitz
Schweinfurt
Prague
Bamberg
Pegnitz
Erlangen
Wurzburg
Nuremberg
R. Danube Vienna
Munich
Budapest

700   800   900

KEY

– – – – – – – KAMMHUBER LINE

BOLD CAPS. = ARMAGEDDON
                        TARGETS

Miles
0   100   200   300   400   500
0   100   200   300   400   500   600   700   800
Kilometres

Combined Bomber Offensive, 1943:
Final Phase

R. Po

executions, the bodies of those they killed sometimes strung up on lamp posts as a warning.

Yet Hitler remained unmoved by the growing devastation and suffering of the German people. It was now that the various Resistance Groups within Germany, whose determination to rid the country of Hitler had been stiffened by the disaster at Stalingrad earlier in the year, decided that they must act quickly to prevent the country sliding into total chaos.

The inner circle of the Resistance, which included such figures as Admiral Wilhelm Canaris, Count Helmuth von Moltke, Field Marshal Erich von Witzleben and General Friedrich Fromm, sent emissaries to win over key commanders, notably Gerd von Rundstedt (C-in-C West), Erwin Rommel and the army group commanders on the Eastern Front. Until now the bulk of the Prussian military hierarchy had refused to have anything to do with the plotters. Field Marshal Erich von Manstein, commanding Army Group South on the Eastern Front, had exclaimed 'Prussian Field Marshals do not mutiny'. But now they were only too aware that Germany's eventual defeat was inevitable, and they had no option but to side with the plotters. All concurred that terms should be agreed with the Western Allies prior to any negotiations with Moscow.

While the staffs drew up plans for seizing key points and arresting hard-core Nazi elements such as the Gestapo and SS, Canaris, as head of the Abwehr, organised trusted agents to contact the Allies in neutral Lisbon and Switzerland. First contacts were made in mid-October, but both Roosevelt and Churchill were adamant that Hitler must be deposed and a non-Nazi government installed in his place before they were prepared to treat with Germany. Until this happened and terms for an armistice were agreed, the bombing would continue.

During the last part of October there were further raids against the Ruhr and elsewhere. Then on the night of 3/4 November the attack on Kassel began. The pattern was very much as before; ten days later the town was little more than a heap of rubble. This put added pressure of the plotters to act quickly. They had, however, now recruited a new and key figure to their ranks.

Since GOMORRAH Albert Speer, Minister for War Production and Armaments, had grown ever more disillusioned with Hitler, and realised that he was prepared to sacrifice the whole German nation on the altar of his now insane belief in ultimate victory. At the same time, Speer's conscience was deeply troubled by the fact that he, as a Reich minister, had played his part in bringing Germany to its present situation. Discreet enquiries led him to the door of General Fromm and his chief of staff, the battle-scarred Colonel Claus von Stauffenberg.

The three met on 10 November, at the height of the attacks on Kassel. It was von Stauffenberg who proposed the use of a briefcase bomb, and Speer revealed that he had been summoned to the Wolf's Lair for 17 November in order to go through plans for the refugee dormitory towns with Hitler. And so it happened that on that day Hitler, Göring, Goebbels and Bormann, together with members of the staff of OKW, met their end. But Speer had to sacrifice his own life to ensure the success of the venture.

Final Attack and German Surrender

Thereafter events moved quickly. Fromm's troops rapidly secured government buildings and radio stations in Berlin. The same happened in Paris and Rome. A new German government duly took power, with von Witzleben as its figurehead. Its first step was to publicly order the cessation of all offensive operations on land, at sea, and in the air. There were, however, incidents of bloodshed, as some of Hitler's more fanatical followers tried to resist the inevitable.

The von Witzleben government initially tried to negotiate with the Western powers alone, but Roosevelt and Churchill insisted that they had to deal with Stalin as well. As it happened, the Big Three were scheduled to meet at Tehran at the end of November. Stalin agreed that the conference should be brought forward and it was convened on 24 November. The Allies issued their surrender terms. All German forces in occupied territory were to stand fast until Allied forces could be deployed to supervise their disarmament and withdrawals. Greater Germany, including pre-war annexations, was to be occupied by the Allies and all war industries dismantled. Berlin was warned that until they accepted the terms, the bombing would continue.

There was some initial prevarication, but one attack on the fifth ARMAGEDDON target, Brunswick, was sufficient for German emissaries, both military and civilian, in order to avoid any echoes of the 1918 'stab in the back', to sign the initial terms in Lisbon on 14 December 1943. Thus ARMAGEDDON vindicated the air theorists, although its success had been more through its timing than its bludgeoning ferocity.

THE REALITY

This narrative follows history as it happened up until the end of GOMORRAH (see p.191). In truth neither RAF Bomber Command, nor, for that matter, Portal or Churchill really appreciated just how much the destruction of Hamburg jolted the Germans. Harris had set his heart on Berlin as his ultimate objective for POINTBLANK, and hoped that the Americans would join in. But the Schweinfurt–Regensburg raid of 17 August severely dented Eighth Air Force's confidence and forced it to withdraw to the fringes. This was exacerbated by the second attempt on Schweinfurt on 14 October. Consequently, for ARMAGEDDON to be feasible the first Schweinfurt–Regensburg raid had to be cancelled.

In my scenario, 'Hap' Arnold's initial reservations about ARMAGEDDON are designed to represent opposition from U.S. airmen that would have initially existed, especially given the fact that one of their foremost theorists of the time, Major Alexander Seversky, had already condemned the 'unplanned vandalism' of area bombing.

The technical aids employed by RAF Bomber Command are as they were in the latter half of 1943, apart from the SERRATE Mosquito nightfighter. It was true that Hanover did not show up well on H2S.

The last part of the chapter is almost total fiction. Suffice to say that Speer, according to his own testimony, did consider assassinating Hitler, albeit not until 1945.

BIBLIOGRAPHY

Freeman, Roger A., *The Mighty Eighth War Diary* (London, 1990)

Messenger, Charles, *Bomber Harris and the Strategic Bombing Offensive. 1939–1945* (London, 1984)

Middlebrook, Martin & Everitt, Chris, *The Bomber Command War Diaries: An Operational Reference Book. 1939–45* (London, 1985)

Speer, Albert, *Inside the Third Reich* (London and New York, 1970)

CHAPTER 10

Bloody Normandy
The German Controversy
MAJOR TIM KILVERT-JONES

The Looming Threat

The threat of an Anglo-Saxon invasion in the west had become a very real concern to the Führer and his principal staff by November 1943. For over two years their attention and the Schwerpunkt of the Axis alliance had been directed to the East against the Communist and Slav threat to the Greater Reich. The Russian Front was now consuming the finest units of the Wehrmacht and Waffen SS at an appalling rate. In the Mediterranean and in the air over Europe the Secondary European Fronts had already been opened. The air war alone was absorbing 900,000 Germans simply manning the ground-based defences which consisted of observation posts, radar stations and the gun batteries, all struggling to keep at bay the Allied Air Forces bombing commercial, industrial and military targets across the Reich. However, in late 1943 the Führer all too briefly turned his thoughts to North West Europe. Adolf Hitler once again displayed that astute vision and cunning reasoning which had been implicit in his early campaign victories; on 3 November 1943, he signed his Führer Directive Number 51:

> Everything indicates that the enemy will launch an offensive against the Western Front of Europe, at the latest in the spring, perhaps even earlier. I can no longer take responsibility for further weakening the West, in favour of other theatres of war. I have therefore decided to reinforce its defences, particularly those places from which the long-range bombardment of England will begin. For it is here that the enemy must and will attack, and it is here – unless all indications are misleading – that the decisive battle against the landing forces will be fought.

Enter Rommel

Erwin Rommel was to be appointed as Inspector of Defences in the West, following a brief and fruitless attempt to rationalise the campaign in Italy after the fall of Tunis and the invasion of Sicily. By the end of November he had gathered about him an inspection team of gifted specialists who would work with him and the Staff of Army Group B to study coastal defences. The sector covered by Army Group B included the Netherlands seaboard, Belgium including the Scheldt estuary and the coast of France north of the Loire. This was an area already fortified against seaborne invasion in the eyes of the Führer and his people, thanks to the excellent propaganda of Reichsminister Goebbels and the frequently pressed labour of the Todt Organisation.

In reality the much vaunted 2400 miles of the Atlantic Wall consisted of little more than light static outposts connected by routine patrols, with the exception of fortified ports and estuaries, such as Calais, Le Havre and Cherbourg. To Rommel, the state of the defences was a shocking testament to years of neglect, sloth and a naive belief that the united nations would repeat the errors of Dieppe in some larger and more costly direct assault on a major harbour area.

Soon, as a result of Rommel's inspections and his final critical report to Field Marshal von Rundstedt (Commander-in-Chief West and Army Group D) and subsequent presentation to the Führer of his findings, a major operational debate was to open. The debate involved Hitler and all his key commanders in the West, and drew comment from innumerable field and staff officers alike. It would revolve around how to defeat an invasion of continental Europe and how best to utilise limited combat assets, particularly the armoured and mechanised panzer grenadier divisions stationed in the West.

Erwin Rommel's forthright conclusions were based on his own experiences fighting the Western Alliance in North-Africa. He had seen at first hand the impact of the enemy's air superiority, their apparently endless material reserves and that skilful command capability displayed by Eighth Army under Bernard Montgomery. He had also seen the Americans mature rapidly after their blood-letting at Kasserine. If the British Commonwealth and the United States were allowed to gain a beachhead in the West the war would be lost.

In the absence of any effective air or naval combat power the defeat of an invasion would clearly rest on the Navy, Luftwaffe, Army and Waffen SS units spread thinly along the coastline of North-West Europe. Well behind the often unsophisticated coastal defences were the more important mobile reserves consisting of panzer and panzergrenadier divisions; these would form the counter-attack forces capable of conducting offensive operations. They would shatter any coastal bridgehead and then push the remnants of the Allied armies back into the sea.

Rommel's conclusions to the Führer highlighted the need to destroy any

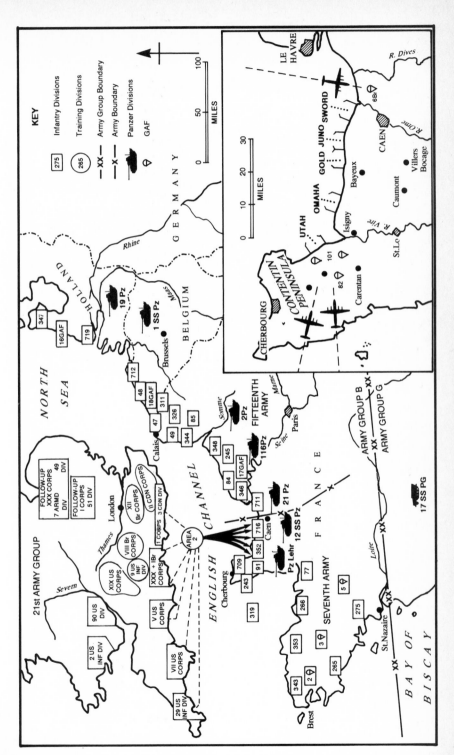

The Assault on 6 June 1944

invasion on the beaches. Should an enemy toehold be formed he would then have to destroy it with swift and timely armoured counter-attacks. His concept of operations had been guided by his own combat experiences and those learned in the East. The lessons of Dieppe and Anzio were also clear to the Field Marshal – clearly any invasion had to be stopped on the beaches. A German success in the west would enable Hitler to impose such an effective blow on the united nations that the full resources of the Reich could then be directed to the East. However, Rommel realised that any enemy toehold on the European coastline could be consolidated with Allied combat power at a rate far exceeding his own build-up capability, particularly if the united nations used their air power to interdict the selected combat area.

This single deduction led to Rommel's conclusion that the vital armoured reserves held under command of OB(W) and OKW must be delegated to him and moved from their depth concentration areas forward to tactical assembly areas behind the most threatened coastal zones in the Seventh and Fifteenth Army Sectors. The first 24 hours of the invasion would be decisive; therefore he could not afford a delay in the deployment of those divisions.

With the assistance of his naval staff, his meteorologists and his own Chief of Engineers General Meise, Rommel was able to conclude that there were three principal areas threatened by an invasion. The most obvious, and for many the most likely area under threat was the Pas de Calais. An invasion in this coastal sector would give the united nations the shortest possible sea crossing, the greatest opportunity for deep and prolonged air cover and the quickest route into the heart of Germany. Rommel, however, was also concerned about the Cotentin Peninsula, Normandy and the Baie de le Seine northwards to the Straits of Dover. His military appreciation identified these areas as being suitable for landings, but they were less ideal for the enemy's use of air power, their potential rate of build-up and ultimately their drive on Germany. Normandy particularly required considerable work if Rommel was to create an effective barrier. This would be done by developing three defensive belts.

The first line of defence would be on the beaches; this initial belt would consist of up to 200 million mines, and a range of improvised but highly effective wooden and steel barriers designed to destroy any assault craft in the water. The open beaches would be turned into well planned killing areas covered by machine gun, anti-tank and artillery fire controlled and adjusted by skilfully sited command and observation posts. Every beach and the strongpoints established along its length would be reinforced with concrete emplacements and wire obstacles. In depth would be a further belt of fortifications designed to impose attrition and delay on any enemy penetration inland. Such a delay would give the panzer arm time to deploy from their forward tactical assembly areas into battle to smash any toehold; and of German superiority in armour there was no doubt. The Tiger and Panther Regiments of the armoured divisions were the jewel in the Heer's armoured crown: these would in turn be supported by the Mark IVs of the other panzer divisions.

Rommel now had to obtain the necessary resources, including the numerous defensive materials of war and of course the combat troops and armour so crucial to make his concept of victory on the beaches possible. There was one other resource of which he was desperately in need: Military Intelligence.

The Intelligence Campaign

Unbeknown to the Abwehr and the German chain of command the Allies were already winning their first victory in the struggle to liberate Europe by the blinding of German Military Intelligence and misleading the directors of the German war machine. The counter-intelligence plan was based on information from Allied espionage networks, resistance groups on the continent, and all forms of tactical reconnaissance.

To ensure that the OVERLORD planners could achieve both surprise and victory a deception plan was conceived under the overall codename BODYGUARD, prepared under the direction of the Combined Chiefs of Staff. BODYGUARD was designed to mislead German Intelligence into believing that Allied land operations in 1944 would begin in the spring with a combined British, American and Russian attack on Norway followed by a move into Sweden and subsequently Denmark and North Germany. Additional objectives of the deception plan were to create the impression that the main Allied effort in 1944 would be in the Balkans; that if the Allies were to invade France at all in 1944 it could not be before July; and that if and when the invasion of France did come, it would be directed against the Pas de Calais area. The BODYGUARD team would also have to encourage the belief that landings on the coast of Normandy were only a diversion designed to draw the Fifteenth Army from the Pas de Calais.

There was no single overall plan for BODYGUARD – it was decided rather to develop separate plans for specific geographical areas. FOR-TITUDE was the codename given to the deception plans to convince Hitler that a massive attack would take place on the Pas de Calais as well as an Allied landing in Norway. FORTITUDE NORTH was an outstanding success, concerned with the fictitious invasion of Norway, the bringing of Sweden into the war on the side of the Allies, and the subsequent invasion of North Germany through Denmark. A German force of over 200,000 men remained in Norway awaiting the invasion that would never come. FOR-TITUDE SOUTH was to persuade the Germans that the Allies would invade the Pas de Calais. The main element was the fictitious 1st United

States Army Group (FUSAG) commanded by General George Patton. General Dwight Eisenhower, the Supreme Allied Commander, was determined to keep the threat to the Pas de Calais alive for as long as possible so that the Germans would be unable to reinforce Normandy from their Fifteenth Army in the Pas de Calais area. In the event, FUSAG fooled the German High Command well into July – far longer than had been expected. Thousands of Germans and considerable reserves of armour remained immobile in the north-east when they might have upset the scales in Normandy.

The Great German Controversy

In the months leading up to the invasion Rommel would say with frustration, 'I know nothing for certain about the enemy'. Thus blinded, Rommel needed sufficient combat resources to cover all his enemy's most likely courses of action. To that end the control and location of the mobile panzer reserves would be critical to the successful outcome of the forthcoming battle.

Within Field Marshal Gerd von Rundstedt's Western Command was General Geyr von Schweppenburg's Panzer Group West. Geyr was responsible for training all Rundstedt's panzer units and from his headquarters in Paris he also retained an element of operational control over a total of three grenadier and panzer divisions in theatre. His responsibilities within the commands of Rommel, Rundstedt and Hitler created an additional structure in an already over complicated, confused and rigidly centralised chain of command.

Indeed, the presence of Geyr was to prove a thorn in Rommel's side. They fundamentally disagreed over the use of the armoured reserves. Given the considerable geographical area covered by Army Group B's Seventh and Fifteenth Armies the options open to the invasion forces now gathering in Britain appeared quite considerable. However, Rommel appreciated that with the seaborne invasion would come an overwhelming air fleet delivering both airborne forces and firepower to the front. Any invasion would also be supported by the guns of the combined navies massing in the ports and estuaries in Southern England. He had no illusions as to the impact of such firepower. Unless the panzers were sited close to the likely invasion sectors they would not be able to move with the freedom necessary in a hostile air environment. It would thus be critical to the successful defence of the coast that some panzer forces were in place and under his direct command so that they could react decisively and if necessarily independently in the first critical hours of any invasion.

For Geyr and his close doctrinal ally Heinz Guderian, Inspector General of Panzer Forces, this was heresy. The panzer arm must be used once the enemy's main effort had been identified in a concentrated and decisive blow. This could not be achieved if the considerable power of the eleven armoured divisions within Rundstedt's command were sited forward on the coast unable to move with speed on the limited lateral routes available from the Cotentin to the Pas de Calais. It would be far better to hold the armour back concentrated around Paris, and then allow the enemy to commit himself. Once committed, Panzer Group West could manoeuvre all available divisions into depth assembly areas and strike a blow which would cut off any bridgehead from its lines of communications.

Such a considerable divergence of doctrine inevitably led to heated debate. Rundstedt's and Hitler's views were initially governed by their own knowledge and experience of the Blitzkrieg in 1939–1940 and the great armoured clashes on the Eastern Front. With the power of the panzers spread thinly behind the coast, Geyr argued that they would be isolated by battlefield interdiction and suffer early attrition simply because they would be within range of the tactical bomber and fighter resources of the Allied air fleets.

The fundamental issue was that Geyr was prepared to accept the enemy forming a bridgehead against which he wished to mass the panzers and deliver a decisive blow. On the other hand, Rommel was prepared to accept the piecemeal deployment of panzer regiments and grenadier battalions in the immediate invasion phase before a bridgehead had been secured in order to achieve shock action and overwhelm an invasion force at its weakest moment, in the chaos of disembarkation. This destruction of the invasion would be achieved by inflicting casualties and commencing the attrition of the assault forces at sea by artillery and mine warfare. The process would continue in the shallows as the assault craft tried to weave their way through the beach obstacles. When the infantry finally debouched onto the sands of Northern France they would find the beaches a lethal trap: mines underfoot and track and the open expanse raked by machine guns, mortars and cannon. If a breach in the Atlantic Wall then occurred the armoured reserves would be committed to support the belt of strongpoints sited in depth, first pinning and then crushing any penetration before it could be exploited. Likewise any airborne forces dropped in depth or to the flanks of the invasion could be similarly isolated and crushed by swift and overwhelming armoured action.

Strengthening the Defences

Rommel's confidence and drive had a dramatic effect on his Army Group. From early January 1944, he visited formation headquarters and combat units along the threatened coast, galvanising and inspiring even the most lethargic troops. The 'Rommel doctrine' was clearly understood by all – the

defeat of any invasion must take place on the beach, and any local penetration must be destroyed immediately by localised counter-attacks.

For some commanders Rommel's activities proved a disruption to their
routine and comfortable lives. Manpower was in short supply. The Todt
Organisation and French labour resources were all now directed to execute
the new works fortifying the coast. British Intelligence could only watch in
horror as new emplacements were detected and reported by a range of
sources.

The debate over the panzer reserve could only be resolved by Hitler, the
Supreme Commander; yet here was a man who viewed his Army Commanders with obsessive suspicion and Rommel in particular as an officer
now flawed by doubt in his Führer. Throughout the winter and spring of
1944 Hitler was to receive a series of visitors all lobbying for their concept of
either a centralised reserve based on Panzer Group West, or a decentralised
and delegated force deployed forward under the control of Army Group B.
Guderian describes how he attempted to win Hitler over to the concept of
an armoured 'Front Reserve', to which the response was a long explanation
of the fortification programme in the west and an endorsement of Rommel's
policy.

So Rommel was now winning the doctrinal argument, at the cost of the
support of some of his most able armoured commanders. Nor did he have as
yet the necessary command authority over those panzers in OB(W). This
would bring him into conflict with Rundstedt himself. Their argument over
the deployment of 2nd Panzer Division astride the Somme at Abbeville was
typical of the often acrimonious relationships developing in Western
Command. What Rundstedt needed was a unified army in the west, a single
and accepted doctrine, a loyal chain of command and the resources to meet
the massive combat power of the united nations. As the spring of 1944 gave
way to early summer he now lacked not only these essentials but also the
strategic intelligence so vital to a successful defence of the Atlantic Wall.

Rommel alternated between enthusiastic confidence in his concept and
the ability of his Army Group, to bouts of abject defeatism. Such swings of
temperament were noted even by Hitler who in May backed a decision by
OKW to deny Rommel's request for control of Panzer Lehr and 12th SS
Panzer Division, located between 75 and 110 miles behind the Normandy
beaches. This left Rommel in an invidious position, victim of a compromise
which met neither his, nor Geyr's, doctrined concepts. Six out of the total of
eleven armoured divisions were sited within the boundaries of Army Group
B. Three of these formations now formed a weak Panzer Group West under
Geyr and were sited between Brussels and Chartres. South of the Loire at
Niort and Saumur was 17th Panzer Grenadier Division, while the
remaining three divisions were under Rundstedt's direct command located

between Falaise and the Pas de Calais. This deployment was further complicated by Hitler's insistence that no move of the reserves, or of Panzer Group West, could be ordered without his personal approval. The vital arteries of command were now hardening; crucial hours and days could now be lost in simply getting a command decision from the Supreme Commander deeply engrossed in the Eastern Front and the threat of a forthcoming Soviet summer offensive.

Rommel meets Hitler on 2 June

On 19 May 1944, shortly after losing his argument over 12th SS and Panzer Lehr, Rommel was surprised to receive a shower of compliments from Hitler who had been briefed on the progress of defence in the west. On 28 May his personal diary reflects his contempt for Hitler's immediate court which evidently continued to hide the truth from the Führer. He resolved to go to Berchtesgarden and strike while the Supreme Commander was still looking favourably on his preparations. A working breakfast was arranged for 2 June following which Rommel would go home to Herrlingen and deliver his wife's birthday present. With Rundstedt's agreement and the Army Group under the control of the Chief of Staff Hans Speidel, Rommel departed from France confident that a deteriorating weather pattern would guarantee little enemy activity for the next few days.

Rommel had memorised a statistical summary of mines laid since January, fortifications constructed and earthworks built. He would again brief the Führer on his concept of operations and outline how he intended to fight the defensive battle. He would weave into his brief the need for additional troops sited close to the assault beaches to avoid the threat posed by the enemy's control of the air. His demands would be for immediate command and control of 2 additional panzer divisions – preferably Panzer Lehr currently in the area of Le Mans, Chartres and Orléans and Fritz Witt's 12th SS Panzer Division 'Hitler Jugend' in their assembly area around Lisieux south of the River Seine. In slower time he would need a flakkorps and a rocket brigade to support his combat formations with air defence and close support rocket artillery.

As he was approaching Berchtesgarden in the warm early dawn of 2 June he remembered his visit to 21st Panzer Division a few weeks earlier. The visit had been arranged because one of General Edgar Feuchtinger's battalion commanders had designed and built up an assault gun battalion based on a number of old Hotchkiss chassis discovered at their works near Paris. Major Becker had also built a number of rocket launchers which had been demonstrated to Rommel on the coast. Major Hans von Luck had also been at the demonstration and he had taken the opportunity of chatting with his brilliant ex-reconnaissance commander. The life of von Luck and many others would now depend upon the outcome of his discussions in those peaceful Bavarian mountains.

After refreshing himself and changing his now crushed uniform Rommel was escorted into a rather dark room illuminated by the light of a single window. A moment later the doors opened again and the Führer entered, followed by Linge, his servant. Rommel was immediately put at ease by the Führer's evident delight in seeing him and the tight double-handed handshake with which Hitler grasped his outstretched palm. With his loyalty to the Führer strengthened and in the absence of the Führer's corrupt courtiers, Rommel felt reassured and free to speak about the thorny problems of the Western Command. Interrupted by the occasional pene-trating question of detail, Rommel presented his briefing, conclusions and recommendations. The unnerving silence which followed was a heart-stopping moment; had he said too much, had he been over-critical – was he being pessimistic and defeatist?

Hitler then said 'Herr Field Marshal, I am aware of your difference of opinion with Commander-in-Chief West. I wished this matter to be resolved before now and I am disappointed that this has not yet happened. In the East I have Soviet armies approaching Hungary and I am told by the Abwehr that a Soviet offensive must be expected on the central front within weeks. You must understand that I cannot remove any further forces from the East ... the Army must hold on all fronts before I renew my next offensive. However, I am able and now willing to release Bayerlein's and Witt's Divisions to your Army Group. As for the rest of your requests, you must wait. Whatever happens do not allow Eisenhower to establish a bridgehead in France: destroy the Anglo-Saxons on the beaches, drown them in their own blood and show them that any attempt to breach the Atlantic Wall is a hazardous enterprise. Force Churchill to recognise that the fighting strength of Germany is unbroken. Do this for me. Do not fail me.'

Rommel left, buoyed up by his victory, but he did not go to Herrlingen. Instead he set off for Rennes, to attend the impending wargame there; that would be an ideal opportunity to discuss the use of the armoured reserve with his commanders West of the Orne.

Allied Hopes and Worries

On 7 April, Montgomery had presented the OVERLORD plan to an audience consisting of all the senior commanders involved in the operation. At this stage he believed 'Rommel is likely to hold his mobile divisions back from the coast until he is certain where our main effort is being made. He will concentrate them quickly and strike a hard blow, his static divisions will endeavour to hold on defensively to important ground and act as pivots to the counter-attacks ...'

However, even Montgomery had to adjust this assessment as the constantly updated picture showed that Rommel intended to destroy the Allied divisions 'near the coast, most of all on the beaches'. It was the location of the armoured reserves that would give the final combat indicator of Rommel's intent.

The location of 21st Panzer Division in the Caen area was the first critical identification confirmed and accepted without reservation by 21st Army Group on 21 May 1944: 'The exact area of the Division and its dispositions are not known, but on any reckoning it now lies but a short run from the Eastern beaches of the NEPTUNE area!' Feuchtinger's Division was now quite clearly ideally situated to interfere with both the 6th Airborne Division's landings astride the Orne and 3rd British and 3rd Canadian Divisions' landings on SWORD and JUNO Beaches to the north of Caen.

Moves of the Panzer Divisions

The move of the additional two panzer divisions from their reserve locations up to Normandy could not go unnoticed by Allied surveillance and intelligence organisations. When the orders to move north arrived both 12th SS Panzer and Panzer Lehr were already under the watchful eyes of local resistance groups. SS Brigadeführer Witt had only just moved 12th SS Panzer Division into the area between Dreux, Evreux, Vimoutiers and Bernay in April, and much time had been devoted to training, vehicle maintenance and the acquisition of essential combat equipments. When the orders to move forward arrived on 3 June there was a sense of cheerful determination amongst the formidable young soldiers of this as yet untried and unbloodied formation. Ahead of them lay a move of over 200 kilometres into a forward assembly area centred on the area of Villers Bocage and Flers.

For Panzer Lehr the road move from their hides east of Le Mans to the large, dense Forêt de Cerisey would prove nothing less than an administrative nightmare for the Divisional staff. To the attentive 'watchers' of German military activity in Normandy the arrival of the leading columns of two additional panzer divisions in the region came as a shock. There was no mistaking the arrival of recce parties to establish regimental and divisional headquarters, supply dumps, leaguers and billets. Yet no move in early June 1944 could take place without the attention of the Allied Air Forces. Both armoured formations suffered the consequences of that expression of confident air power. The first and most frustrating impact was one of delay, diversion and loss of cohesion as bridges were damaged and junctions strafed and bombed by medium bombers. By the time the main bodies of the divisions were approaching their new leaguers on the evening of 5 June, Panzer Lehr had already lost three Panthers and two PzKpfw IVs.

Max Wünsche's 12th Panzer Division fared little better, with four Pz IVs and two Panthers left blazing in one single devastating air attack. However, the real blow to these two formidable formations was not in the destruction of their armour but in the now regular attrition of the soft-skinned columns from the Stabskompanies and Versorgungskompanies. These staff and supply columns provided the essential life blood of the armoured formations and their early interdiction would have fateful consequences after the invasion had commenced. Yet for every air attack on Normandy two were taking place in the Pas de Calais, thereby supporting the Allied deception plan.

Decision to Go

The impending decision of 'Go' or 'No Go' weighed heavily on Eisenhower. With the most up-to-date meteorological data and decrypts the decision was made to invade. Yet the knowledge that three major armoured divisions were now in General Friedrich Dollman's Seventh Army Sector, almost certainly under Rommel's direct command, left the Allied leaders in no doubt that the establishment of a bridgehead would only be achieved after a hard and bloody battle of attrition.

For many German commanders and their staffs the wargame at Rennes was a welcome opportunity to see old friends and visit another beautiful French city. For the more ambitious the knowledge that Field Marshal Rommel would now be attending after an important visit to the Führer certainly encouraged those doubters of the value of the games to get to Rennes earlier than planned 'to show willing'. For Witt and Bayerlein and their less experienced comrade Feuchtinger the 'Flash' signal to attend the wargame arrived at midday on 5 June. Their attendance was requested because the Field Marshal wished 'to discuss the use of the in-place armoured reserves with the Commanders'.

With what appeared to be a long period of appalling weather in the Channel continuing, the key commanders in the 84th Corps sector were now moving to Rennes. At La Roche Guyon Speidel was left to conduct a private dinner with a number of personal friends – conspirators in the forthcoming bomb plot against Hitler. Meanwhile at 21st Panzer Division von Luck was informed that he would be acting Divisional Commander in the absence of Feuchtinger who was now forced to cancel his planned trip to see a lady friend in Paris. A similar act of delegated authority was taking place at Château Balleroy with a message taken by despatch rider on Bayerlein's authority to Rudolf Gerhardt in his Regimental Headquarters at Cerisey La Forêt. So in turn the control of 12th SS Panzer Division was handed briefly by Witt to SS Standartenführer Kurt Meyer. Much of the combat power in Seventh Army was now, for the most part, in the hands of seconds in command.

As the great coiled spring of military power was released under the codenames NEPTUNE and OVERLORD towards Normandy the outcome of the greatest amphibious military operation in history still hung in the balance. Eisenhower nervously penned a signal to be released if the landings failed. Indeed the presence of the leading elements and headquarters of Panzer Lehr and 12th SS Panzer in Normandy was most unnerving. Montgomery had been justified in demanding the full weight of the Eighth Air Force and RAF heavies from D-Day in case the interdiction of the enemy armour proved essential.

Assault from the Air

During the early hours of 6 June, in the east of the NEPTUNE Area, the 6th Airborne Division's operations were proceeding with the seizure of the bridges over the Orne river and its canal, while subsequent assaults at Merville and on the river Dives were of mixed success. In the west the 101st and 82nd U.S. Airborne Divisions were landing in the elbow of the Cotentin Peninsula. Their widely scattered glider and parachute drops caused confusion and chaos in the rear area of the 352nd and 709th Divisions holding the UTAH and OMAHA sectors. However, reduced to 30% of their strength through losses and disposition, the men of the 82nd and 101st struggled to secure the shoulder of General Omar Bradley's vital coastline. For the local German commanders' garbled reports of parachutists, gliders and decoys dropping across the Normandy region did much to weaken their initial response to the developing threat. If confusion was endemic in the local units and their commanders in the early hours of 6 June, that confusion was magnified up the chain of command. With many key commanders effectively isolated in Rennes, the night duty staffs across Normandy struggled to make sense of the reports being received from sentries and outposts now fighting for their lives. The most effective response came from Major von Luck in 21st Panzer Division. Realising that this was no raid but the first act of an invasion, von Luck was ordering an immediate response to the loss of the Orne bridges by 0100hrs.

In Rennes, Rommel leapt into action despatching all the commanders back to their units and formations, signalling von Rundstedt and ordering immediate counter-attacks on any enemy landings and concentrations. With telephone lines cut by bombing and resistance activity north of the Loire the secure command radio nets were already being activated, thereby giving the ULTRA decrypters a flood of raw data to work on.

Rommel received news that elements of 21st Panzer Division were already pushing north along the Orne, in accordance with his anti-paratrooper orders, to retake the vital crossings between Benouville and Ranville. Panzer Lehr and 12th SS Panzer Division were still in their hides but now at alert state Level II. Along the coast the now fully alert coastal garrisons peered into the chill pre-dawn, nervously listening. Just before dawn the presence of the invasion armada became known as the naval bombardment commenced.

The events of D-Day developed at frightening cost to invader and defender alike. East of the Orne 125th Panzer Grenadier Regiment with the Mk IVs of the IInd Battalion of 22nd Panzer Regiment under Major Vierzig drove north towards the Orne river bridge. To the west of the canal the 192nd Battalion and von Gottberg's tanks of the I Battalion were edging towards Ouistreham.

It was 0130hrs by the time the armoured columns were making their first contact. To their shock the lead MK IVs of both battalions were soon burning after successful ambushes sprung by infantrymen with PIATs, Gammon Grenades and Bren guns. The ardour of the reconstituted 21st Panzer Division was severely shaken, but von Luck determined to strike hard for the river bridge while detaching a battalion of infantry and tanks to support the garrison at Merville. As this flying column moved past the now vicious little fire-fight west of Ranville it heard, rather than saw, the arrival of first the parachutists of 5th Airborne Brigade and then the gliders landing on the Ranville DZ.

In these gliders were the anti-tank guns which General Richard Gale had intended to halt the suspected German counter-attack. Vital minutes were lost as the Germans asked for orders and tried to identify the location of the new threat. The Mk IVs were soon to prove no match for the hastily deployed 6-and 17-pounder guns which were firing from well concealed positions amongst the tall corn. The Panzergrenadiers were shocked by the violence of these ambushes, thus allowing the depleted paras the opportunity to exploit surprise even though they were as yet outnumbered and out-gunned.

But the airborne troops knew that they could not retain a defensive outpost on the river bridge; but they could pull back, and using the German defences (including the well sited captured 20mm cannon) reinforce the canal bridge until relieved. As von Luck's men swept towards the bridge they were caught in a lethal cross-fire of small arms and PIATs from north and south of the road. The bridge commander withdrew, firing an improvised mine which caused only minimal damage to the bridge but killed a number of panzergrenadiers using the bridge as cover. In the confusion and with a new battle raging around Ranville on the road to Merville von Luck decided to wait for first light. Situation reports were sent, but little support was promised in return as the coastal defences north of Caen were engaged by the fleet now lying offshore.

Assault from the Sea

At UTAH Beach the landings were successful beyond belief, Bradley's initial relief being marred by the news, or lack of it, emerging at OMAHA. Unwilling to give any seaborne invasion the space to develop a bridgehead, Rommel ordered his two uncommitted panzer divisions into action. Panzer Lehr's task was twofold: 'establish a blocking position on the line Carentan–Bayeux and push battalion-strength armoured columns to the beaches at St Laurent [OMAHA].'

With Bayerlein still in transit the orders were sent by radio and decoded both at Château Balleroy unbeknown to him at Bletchley Park. A response by the Allied Air Force was now just a matter of time.

For the still incomplete staff of 12th SS Panzer Division the presence of 'Panzermeyer' at their headquarters was a great relief. As the orders were received from Rennes to drive on Bayeux and the area of Arromanches – now undergoing the attention of Force GOLD – Meyer made a quick assessment and immediately despatched the Reconnaissance Battalion north to the Caen–Bayeux Road. The tanks were also ordered to move forward to hides around Nonant before committal into action.

Battle of the Beaches

These moves would have a dramatic effect not only on the assault from the sea but also upon strategy. On JUNO (3rd Canadian Division) and GOLD (50th British Division) Beaches the landings proceeded as planned. Meanwhile 12th SS Panzer received orders at 0230hrs to move to Bayeux. The 70km journey was initially conducted in darkness but at first light was spotted by Allied aircraft. Air attacks began at 0750hrs and were soon augmented by naval gunfire. So it was a depleted and delayed spearhead which reached Bayeux at 1630hrs. Indeed it was not until last light that the division was complete. Nevertheless, by then it blocked the Caen–Bayeux road and reconnaissance elements had reached Port en Bessin and had overrun a British commando. 50th Division, therefore, could not take Bayeux as planned but instead became embroiled in a fight to save the key logistic centres of Port en Bessin and Arromanches, while endeavouring to link up with the Canadians, on their left, and deepen the bridgehead by ejecting the Germans from Bayeux. This battle would last three days, inflict 30% casualties on 12th SS Panzer and also cause severe civilian losses.

Meanwhile, on 50th Division's right at OMAHA Beach, the landing by 1st U.S. and 29th U.S. Divisions had been restricted by 352nd and 716th Infantry Divisions to only a shallow bridgehead, a near disaster which was turned into a crushing defeat when Panzer Lehr threw in a battle group. True, the Germans suffered heavy losses from naval gunfire and air attacks. But General Omar Bradley, commanding First U.S. Army, was forced to abandon OMAHA and a captured battery at Pointe du Hoc and switch his second wave to exploit the success at UTAH. The evacuation from OMAHA was reminiscent of the debacle of the Dieppe raid of August 1942, with 'Comrades dead, wounded or shocked abandoned under merciless fire from machine-guns, mortars and the tanks of Panzer Lehr'.

That night, with the bridgehead split into two, Montgomery, with Eisenhower's concurrence, decided to recast his plan. Second British Army on the left was ordered to consolidate and expand its threatened lodgement, throw back 21st Panzer, seize the vital high ground on the left flank at Breville and establish a viable logistic base. First U.S. Army was instructed to concentrate on developing UTAH, give first priority to severing the Cotentin Peninsula and to capture the port of Cherbourg. As soon as possible, for both tactical and logistic reasons, the two bridgeheads were to be linked up, concurrent with the attrition of the Germans by over-whelming firepower provided by naval gunfire and massed heavy bombers. This was Montgomery's decisive, flexible response as Allied hopes of a rapid advance into France were thwarted.

But Hitler's and Rommel's intention of destroying the invaders on the beaches was also thwarted, except for their undeniable success at OMAHA. For having committed the three immediately available panzer divisions without completely achieving his aim, Rommel was caught in a vice he could not – and probably never could – have avoided. Within the next few crucial days he would find it impossible to concentrate sufficient strength to overcome the admittedly constrained invaders. The BODYGUARD deception plans would continue to pin troops in the Pas de Calais by convincing him and the High Command that the main assault must come there. Air interdiction would severely hamper the movement of a trickle of reinforcements to Normandy. And the formations already committed there would be put through a mincing-machine of shellfire and bombing the like of which had never before been seen on a battlefield.

To make matters worse, the Luftwaffe was relegated to virtual impotence by the overwhelming Allied air power and so, together with the German Navy (whose U-boats were sunk in quantity), failed utterly, with terrible losses, to interdict the invasion fleet. Therefore, the Allied rate of build-up, despite some adverse weather and the initial problems of working across open beaches (even after one of the artificial Mulberry harbours was wrecked), kept ahead of the Germans. And moreover, the very fact that the disaster at OMAHA had forced Bradley to give absolute priority to the early capture of Cherbourg to solve the vital logistic problem was something nobody could have foreseen when the port fell earlier than expected.

But most deadly of all, the Germans were losing the most crucial battle of all – the fight for information as Allied Military Intelligence continued to blind and deceive the Germans almost completely until mid-July. The fact that Rommel was present in person to profit from the deployment he had been granted, plus the authority to act without reference to a higher command, merely dictated a different scenario to the one which might have been played if, as originally planned, he had visited his home on 5 June; or if the deployment of the panzer divisions had not been changed at the last moment.

THE REALITY

This chapter diverges from fact at the 2 June conference between Rommel and Hitler. History records that Hitler granted neither Rommel nor any other top German commander what they felt essential for the defence of France. The actual deployment on 5 June was an unsatisfactory compromise imposed by Germany's almost hopeless overall situation. For, closely run as some still believe the invasion of Normandy was, the sheer magnitude, power and support possessed by the Allies (let alone their superior Intelligence) virtually guaranteed victory, even if the attritional beachhead battle had been more severe and prolonged – as it might well have been if Hitler actually had chosen the Rommel option. Indeed, even if Rommel had been granted his way, it seems more than likely that, after the attempt on Hitler's life failed on 20 July, the subsequent course and timetable of events would not have been so very different to what they actually were; the cost of that new turn of events would inevitably have been in human lives on the tactical battlefield, not in overall strategic success.

BIBLIOGRAPHY

Ellis, L.F., *Victory in the West* (London, 1962)
Hastings, M., *Overlord* (London, 1985 and 1993)
Hinsley, F. *et al*, *British Intelligence in the Second World War*, vol 3 part II (London, 1988)
Keegan, J., *The Second World War* (London, 1989)
Lefevre, E., *Panzers in Normandy* (London, 1983)
Wilmot, C., *The Struggle for Europe* (London, 1952)

Epilogue

Quite clearly, if Hitler had adopted almost any one of the options here described, which were all available to him with the exception of that relating to the atom bomb and to the Battle of Normandy, the world would have been very different from the one in which we now live. For he might have won the war and imposed on the world a German hegemony which, until less authoritarian philosophies and government gradually evolved, would have been harsh and oppressive in the extreme.

Why then did he fail to grasp the opportunities presented in 1940 when, instead of invading England (Operation SEA LION in the form Field Marshal Göring and General Kesselring actually considered), or adopting Admiral's Raeder's Operation SPHINX, he vacillated and chose instead to concentrate on invading Russia in June 1941? Again, why did he reject the General Staff's recommendations, diverge from concentration on the capture of Moscow in August (Operation WOTAN), thus forfeiting a splendid chance to knock Russia out of the war that year? Above all, perhaps, why did he not sensibly press for Plan ORIENT by collaborating whole-heartedly with Japan, instead of paying little more than lip-service to that draft document of immense and vital intent? And why, despite an assumed grasp of advanced weapon technology, did he not give priority to improved U-boats, to jet fighters and to the atom bomb when they were within reach?

Maybe his reactions in 1943 to the threat against the soft underbelly of Europe, or the crushing attacks upon German cities (Operation ARMA-GEDDON) were of minor significance in relation to the final outcome bearing in mind that he had now, to all intents and purposes, lost the war. And perhaps it was even less important that in 1944 he compromised disastrously over a defensive strategy for France. For by then, lacking the overall strategic initiative and the strength to react effectively anywhere, he would have been better advised to adopt the penultimate option of surrender, followed by the last option he actually did take up – suicide – instead of condemning German and European culture to devastation. Nevertheless, his habitual and often perverse style of decision-making was to be detected as often in adversity as in success – reflecting the primary engagement of a brilliant but paranoiac, demagogic mind in forlorn attempts to maintain personal dominance over his peers by playing off one against another through the application of coercion and sadistic terror.

Operation SEA LION, when actually adopted in July for implementation in September, came too late because Hitler, the politician, underrated

British stubbornness, but also because his obsessive loathing of Russian communism led him to insist upon launching Operation BARBAROSSA before Britain was conquered. Operation SPHINX was likewise sidelined for this latter reason. But rejection of the General Staff's recommendation to concentrate without delay on the seizing of Moscow was as much due to a compulsive urge to subjugate the generals as to a defective, intuitive formulation of strategy. These were the flaws which from 1940 onwards threw away the chances of victory. And which, no doubt, when overlooking Plan ORIENT, influenced his mistrustful political dealings with the secretive and similarly suspicious Japanese.

As for his technological lapses? Well, let it be noted that Hitler, the war lover, in reality was only at heart a pragmatic corporal whose experience was acquired when fighting on the Western Front in World War I. Assuredly he possessed remarkable, although defective, insight into land warfare along with a phenomenal memory of army weapons performance and a penchant for the grandiose. But he was a tyro when it came to knowledge of naval warfare, warships and U-boats. So these he tended to leave to Raeder and Dönitz who, in the event, failed him by their disagreements over strategy and their lapses in keeping abreast of vital technical innovations, such as fast U-boats, centimetric radar and radio security. Likewise, Hitler was let down by the sybaritic Göring and those who allowed the Luftwaffe to slip into wholesale decline; who chose not to collaborate with the Navy (and thus lost him the Battle of the Atlantic); and who failed to convince him of the essential need to give high priority to jet fighters (temperamental and only marginally effective as they were) rather than, as he preferred, jet bombers. And as for nuclear physics and the atom bomb? Better men than Hitler never really grasped their full potential even when demonstrated in July 1945. It is hardly surprising that, unlike Churchill and Roosevelt, he was dismissive of physicists. So, fortunately, there was no call for GREENBRIER.

In a world war dominated by sea and air power, Hitler's defects as Chancellor and Supreme Commander were fatal to his own survival. Moreover, at the root of the matter there resided also the inherent weaknesses of an over-centralised, bureaucratic organisation through which so many decisions had to be channelled to a brutal, criminally minded, dictatorial politician whose paranoia intensified as the war progressed. It was the world's good fortune (including Germany's, Italy's and Japan's) that this megalomaniac side-stepped options which, if adopted, might have dragged civilisation into the slough of despond. But let it not be overlooked that it took another 45 years of Cold War to rid the world of the equally pernicious Soviet Russian Communist system which, to this day, lingers on in other nations.

Kenneth Macksey

Index